# To ra do ra !



VOL. 11

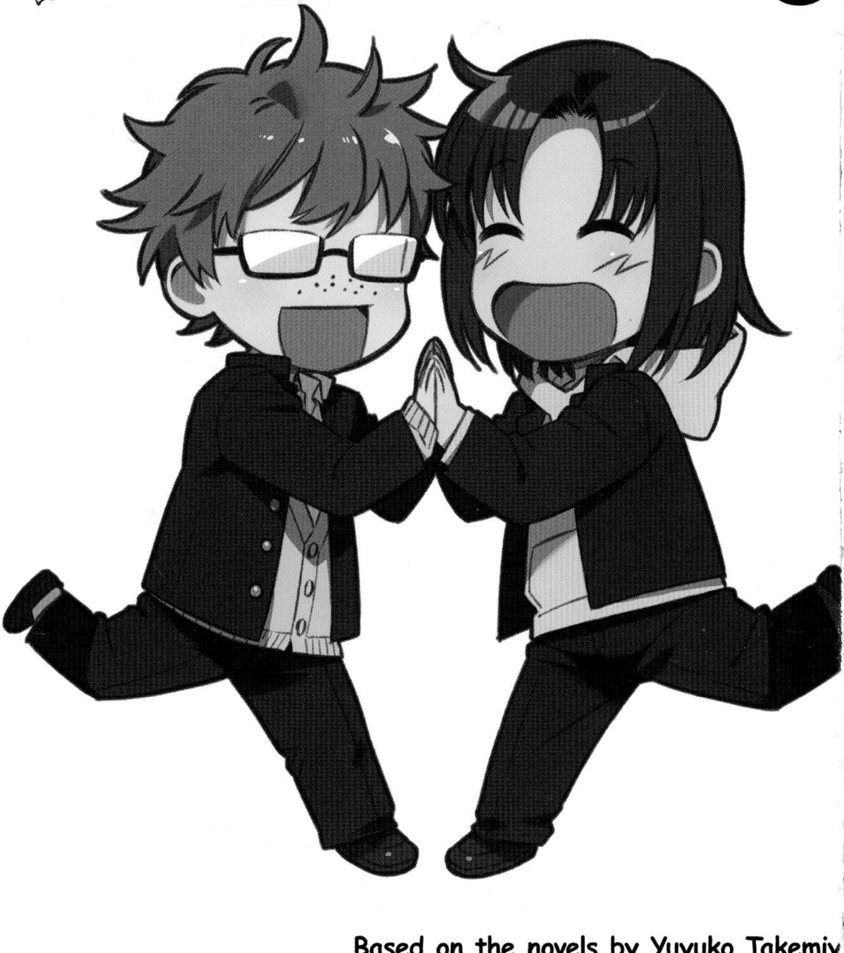

Based on the novels by Yuyuko Takemiy
Manga artwork by Zekkyo
Original character design by Yas

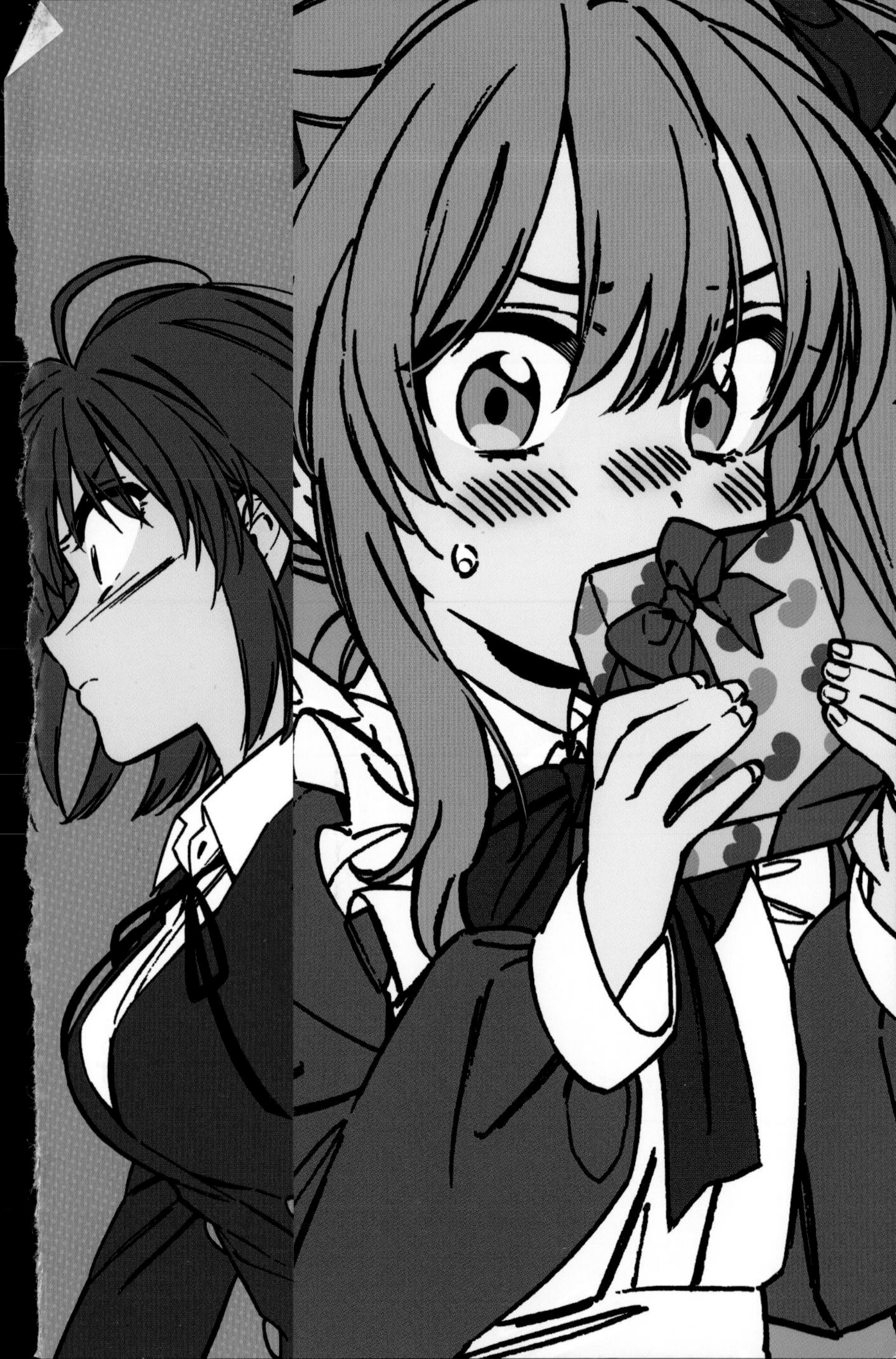

# Chapter 89
# What We Want to Do

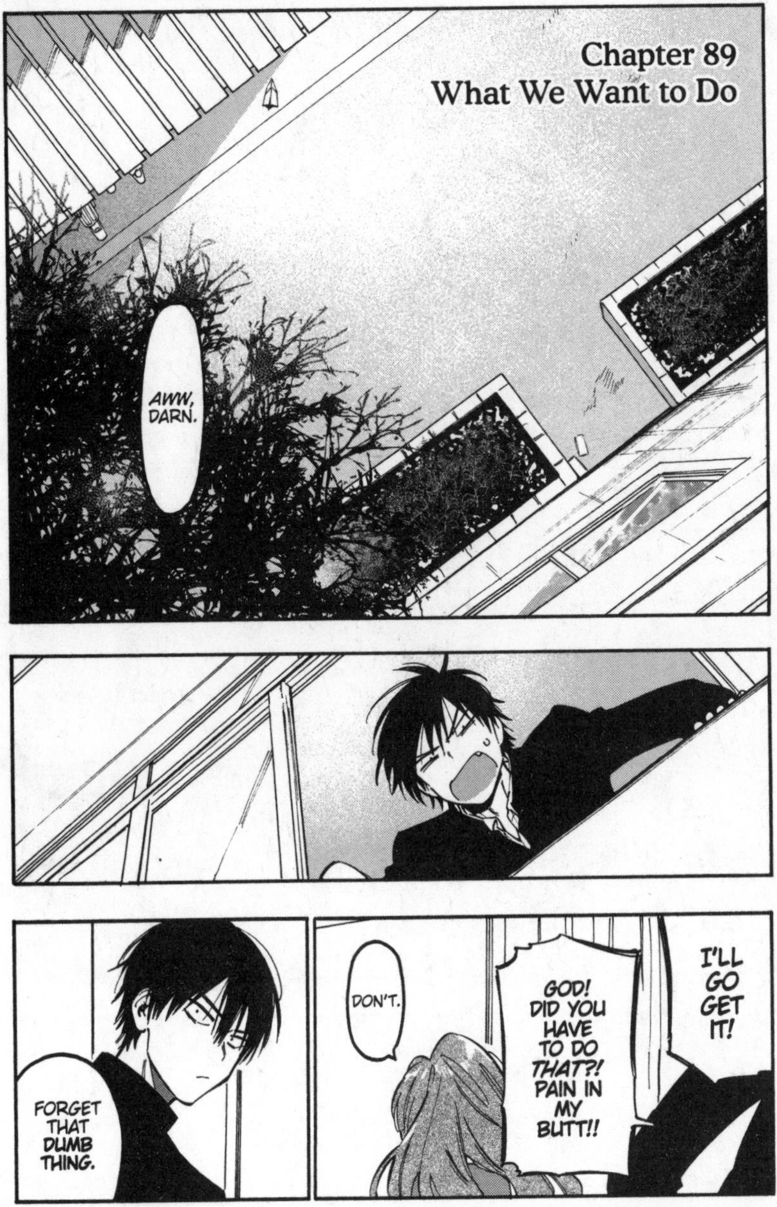

AWW, DARN.
I'LL GO GET IT!
GOD! DID YOU HAVE TO DO *THAT*?! PAIN IN MY BUTT!!
DON'T.
FORGET THAT DUMB THING.

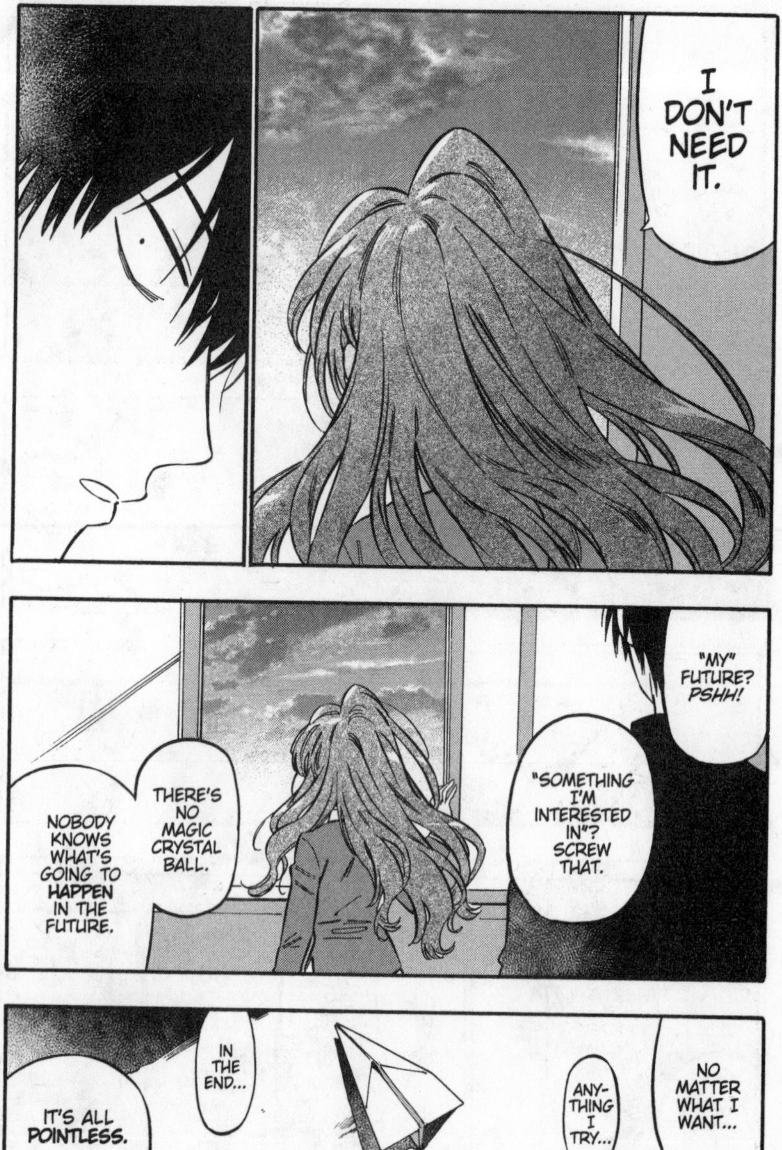
I DON'T NEED IT.
"MY" FUTURE? *PSHH!*
"SOMETHING I'M INTERESTED IN"? SCREW THAT.
THERE'S NO MAGIC CRYSTAL BALL.
NOBODY KNOWS WHAT'S GOING TO **HAPPEN** IN THE FUTURE.
NO MATTER WHAT I WANT...
ANY-THING I TRY...
IN THE END...
IT'S ALL **POINTLESS.**

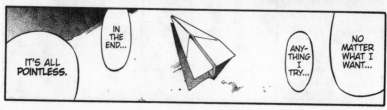

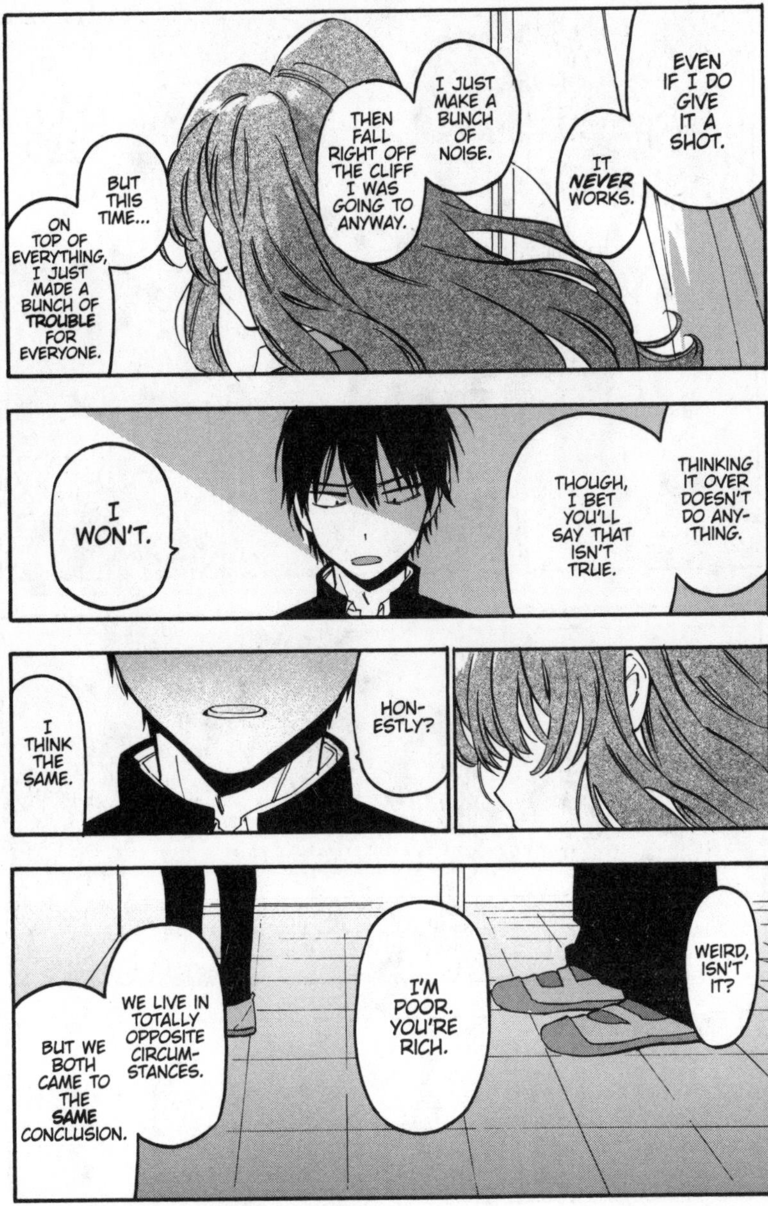

EVEN IF I DO GIVE IT A SHOT.
IT **NEVER** WORKS.
I JUST MAKE A BUNCH OF NOISE.
THEN FALL RIGHT OFF THE CLIFF I WAS GOING TO ANYWAY.
BUT THIS TIME...
ON TOP OF EVERYTHING, I JUST MADE A BUNCH OF **TROUBLE** FOR EVERYONE.
THINKING IT OVER DOESN'T DO ANYTHING.
THOUGH, I BET YOU'LL SAY THAT ISN'T TRUE.
I WON'T.
HONESTLY?
I THINK THE SAME.
WEIRD, ISN'T IT?
I'M POOR. YOU'RE RICH.
WE LIVE IN TOTALLY OPPOSITE CIRCUMSTANCES.
BUT WE BOTH CAME TO THE **SAME** CONCLUSION.

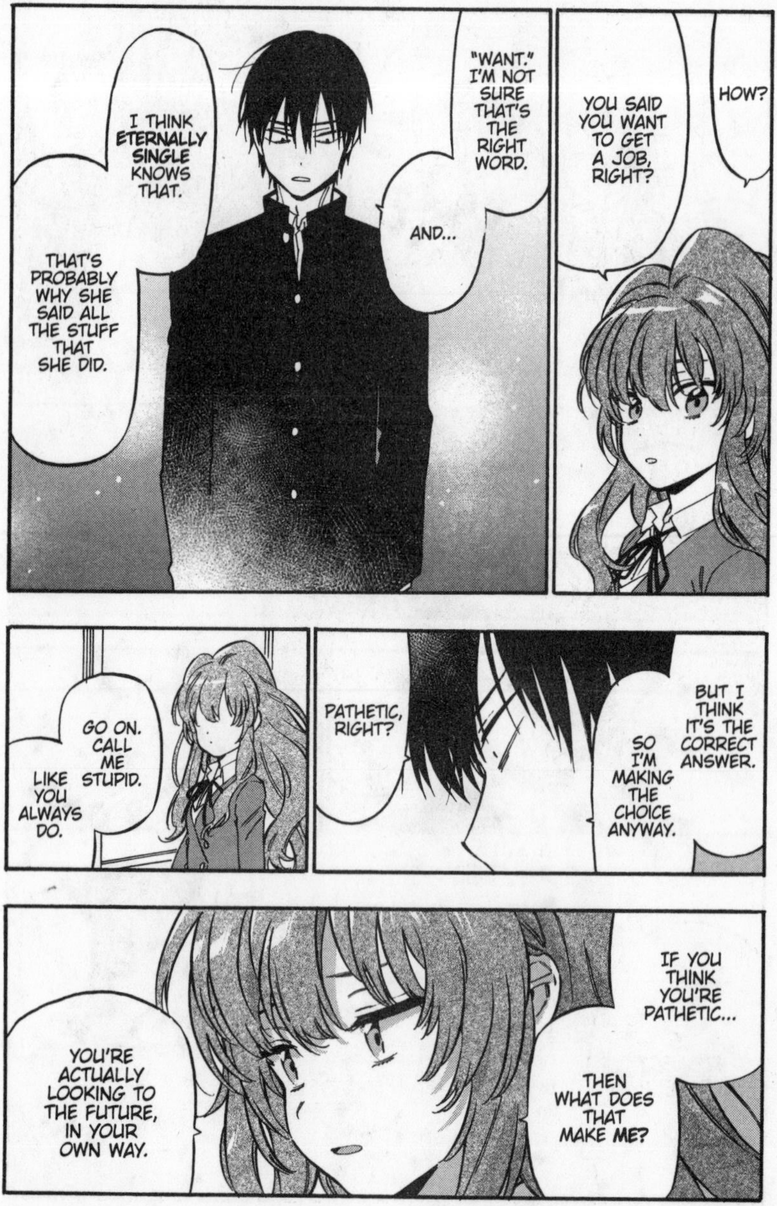
HOW?
YOU SAID YOU WANT TO GET A JOB, RIGHT?
"WANT." I'M NOT SURE THAT'S THE RIGHT WORD.
AND...
I THINK ETERNALLY SINGLE KNOWS THAT.
THAT'S PROBABLY WHY SHE SAID ALL THE STUFF THAT SHE DID.
BUT I THINK IT'S THE CORRECT ANSWER.
SO I'M MAKING THE CHOICE ANYWAY.
PATHETIC, RIGHT?
GO ON. CALL ME STUPID.
LIKE YOU ALWAYS DO.
IF YOU THINK YOU'RE PATHETIC...
THEN WHAT DOES THAT MAKE ME?
YOU'RE ACTUALLY LOOKING TO THE FUTURE, IN YOUR OWN WAY.

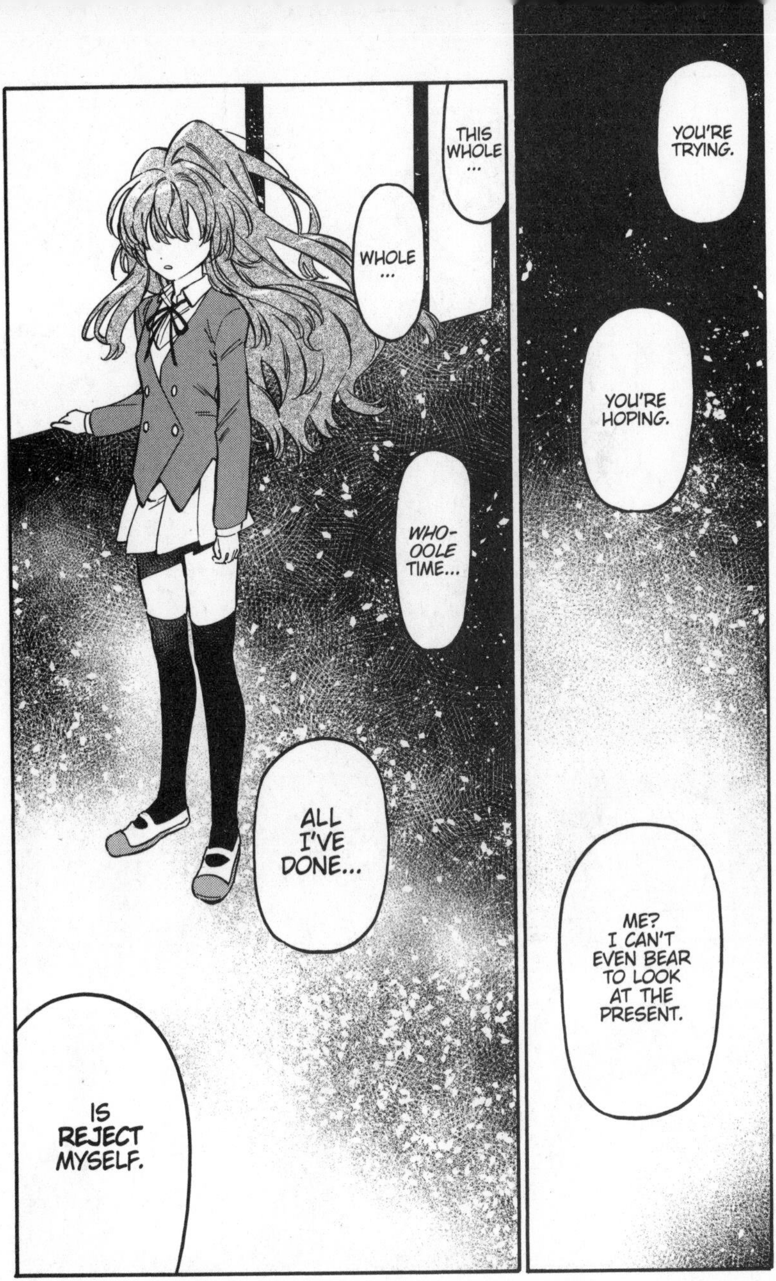
YOU'RE TRYING.
YOU'RE HOPING.
ME? I CAN'T EVEN BEAR TO LOOK AT THE PRESENT.
THIS WHOLE ...
WHOLE ...
WHO-OOLE TIME...
ALL I'VE DONE...
IS REJECT MYSELF.

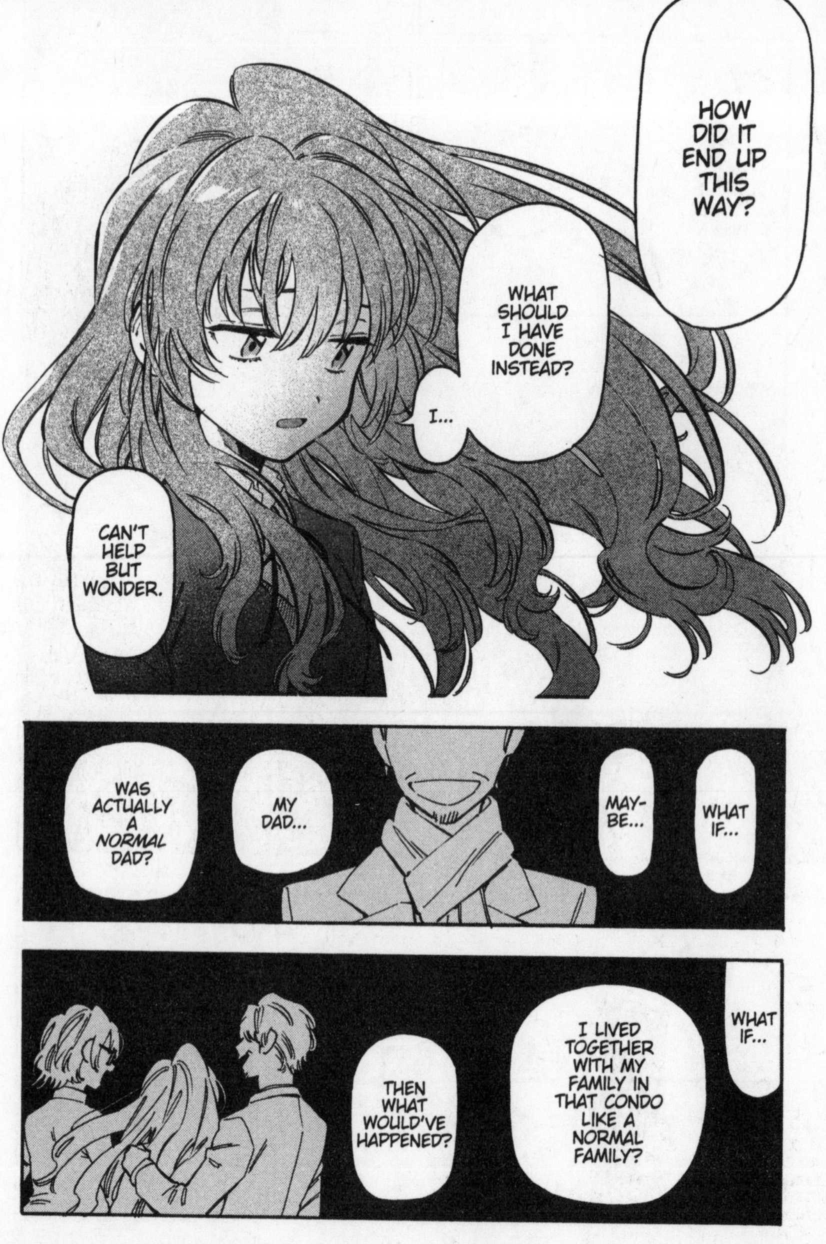
HOW DID IT END UP THIS WAY?
WHAT SHOULD I HAVE DONE INSTEAD?
I...
CAN'T HELP BUT WONDER.
WHAT IF...
MAY-BE...
MY DAD...
WAS ACTUALLY A *NORMAL* DAD?
WHAT IF...
I LIVED TOGETHER WITH MY FAMILY IN THAT CONDO LIKE A NORMAL FAMILY?
THEN WHAT WOULD'VE HAPPENED?

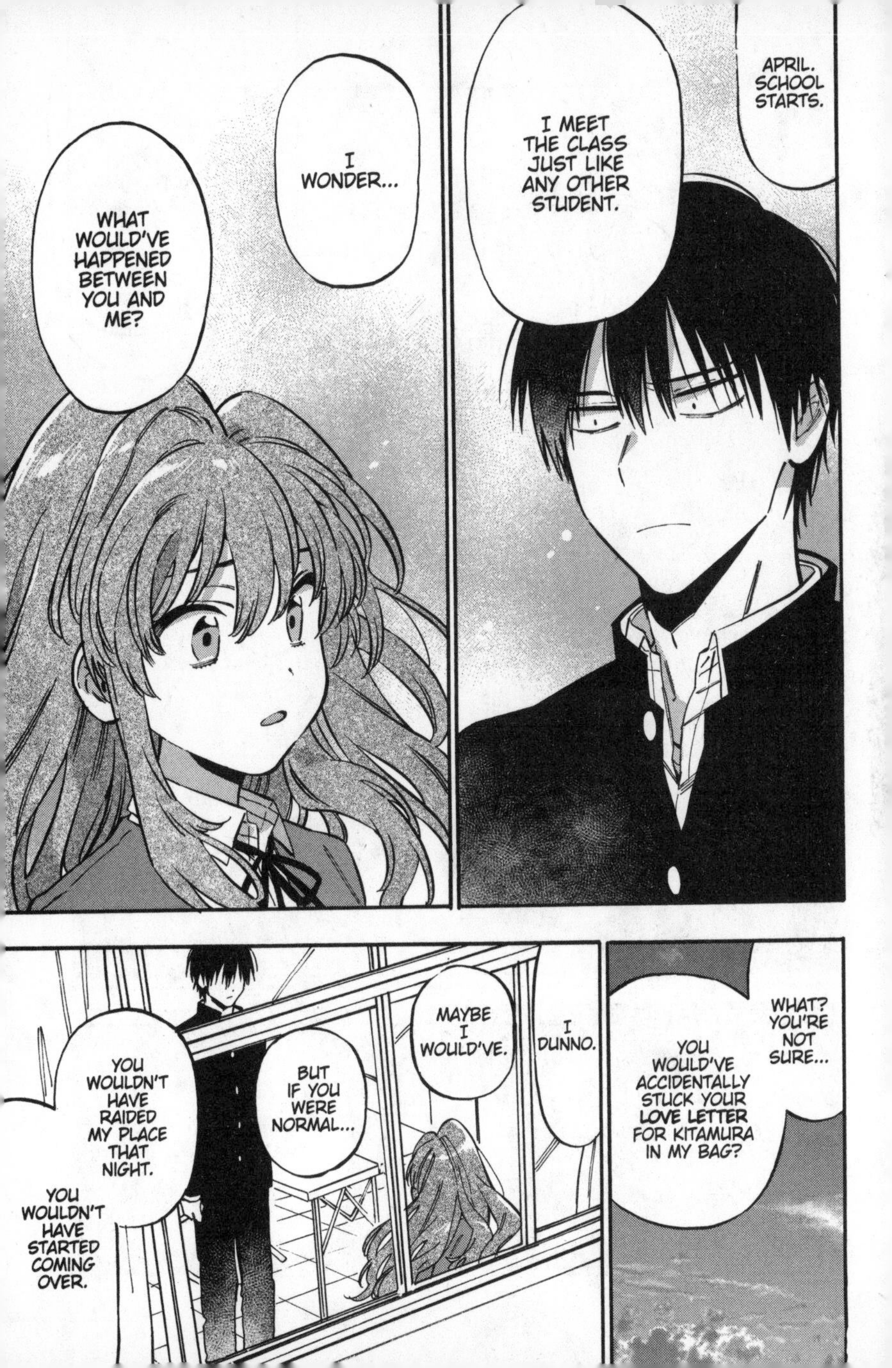
APRIL. SCHOOL STARTS.
I MEET THE CLASS JUST LIKE ANY OTHER STUDENT.
I WONDER...
WHAT WOULD'VE HAPPENED BETWEEN YOU AND ME?
WHAT? YOU'RE NOT SURE...
YOU WOULD'VE ACCIDENTALLY STUCK YOUR LOVE LETTER FOR KITAMURA IN MY BAG?
I DUNNO.
MAYBE I WOULD'VE.
BUT IF YOU WERE NORMAL...
YOU WOULDN'T HAVE RAIDED MY PLACE THAT NIGHT.
YOU WOULDN'T HAVE STARTED COMING OVER.

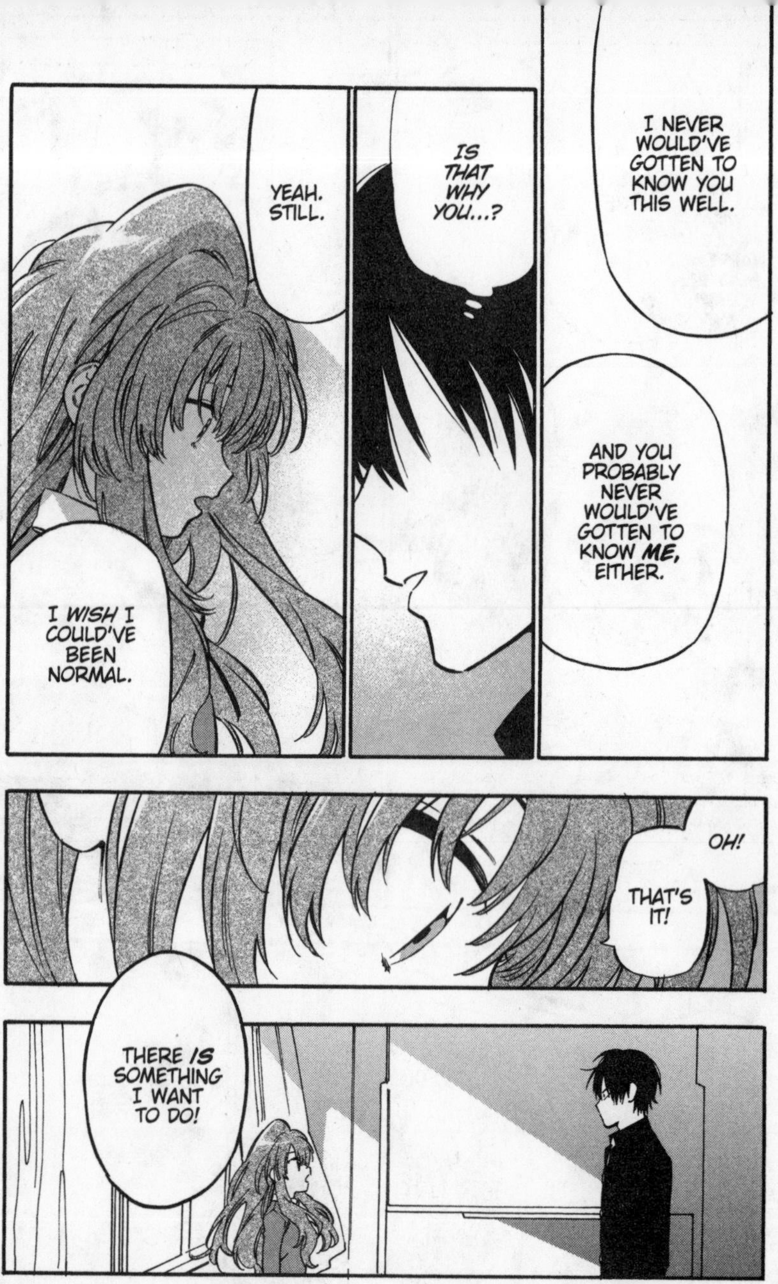
I NEVER WOULD'VE GOTTEN TO KNOW YOU THIS WELL.
AND YOU PROBABLY NEVER WOULD'VE GOTTEN TO KNOW *ME*, EITHER.
IS THAT WHY YOU...?
YEAH. STILL.
I *WISH* I COULD'VE BEEN NORMAL.
OH!
THAT'S IT!
THERE *IS* SOMETHING I WANT TO DO!

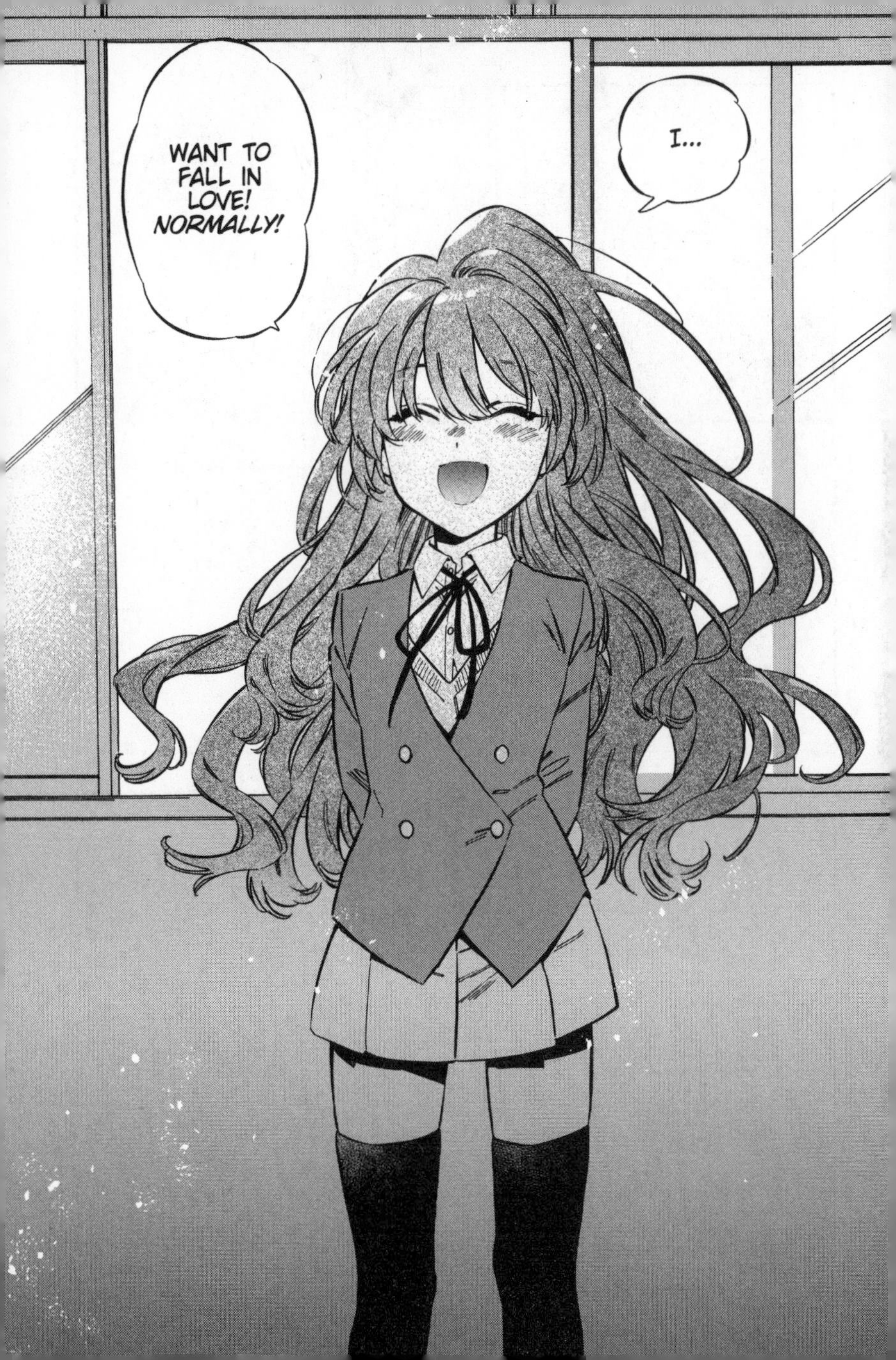
I...
WANT TO FALL IN LOVE! NORMALLY!

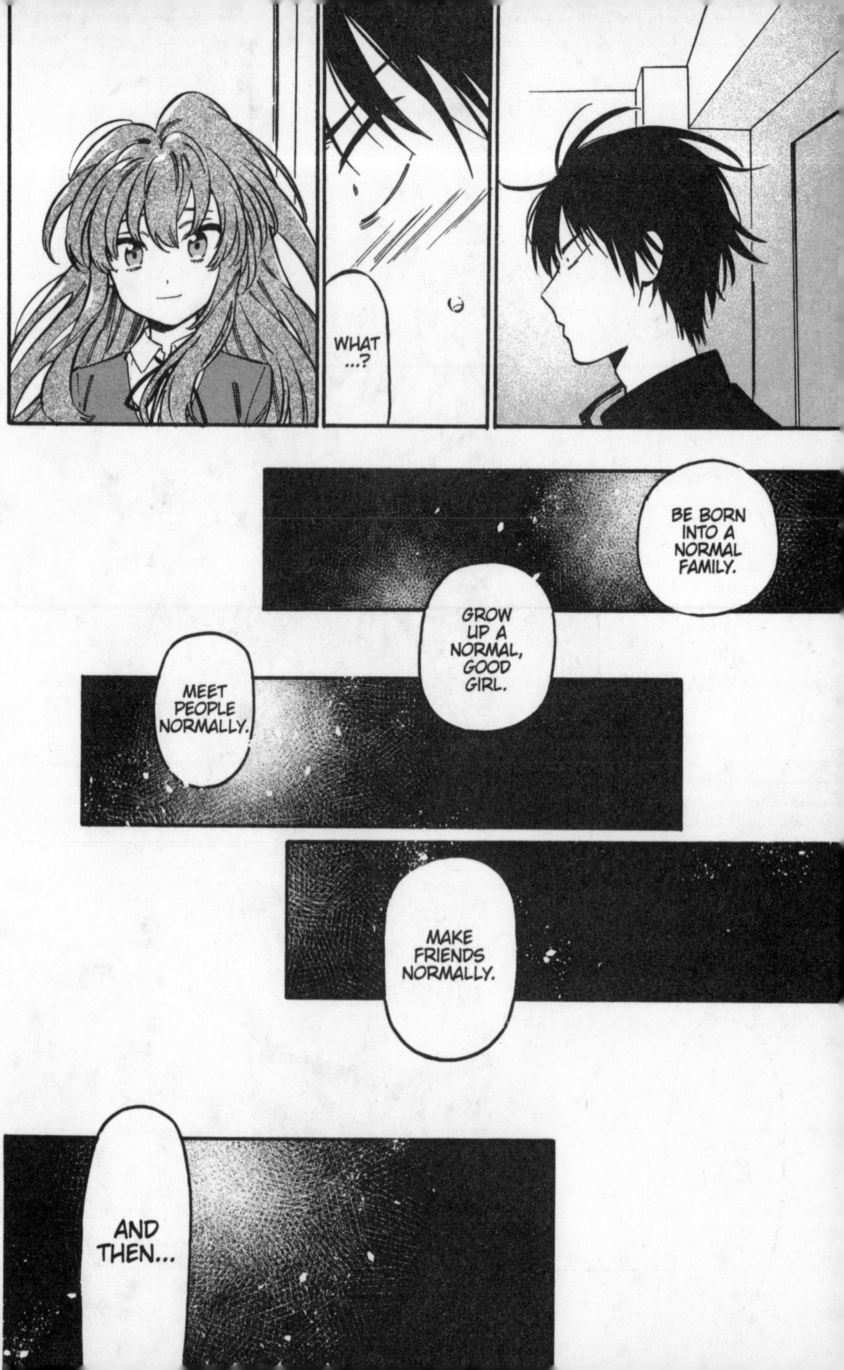
WHAT ...?
BE BORN INTO A NORMAL FAMILY.
GROW UP A NORMAL, GOOD GIRL.
MEET PEOPLE NORMALLY.
MAKE FRIENDS NORMALLY.
AND THEN...

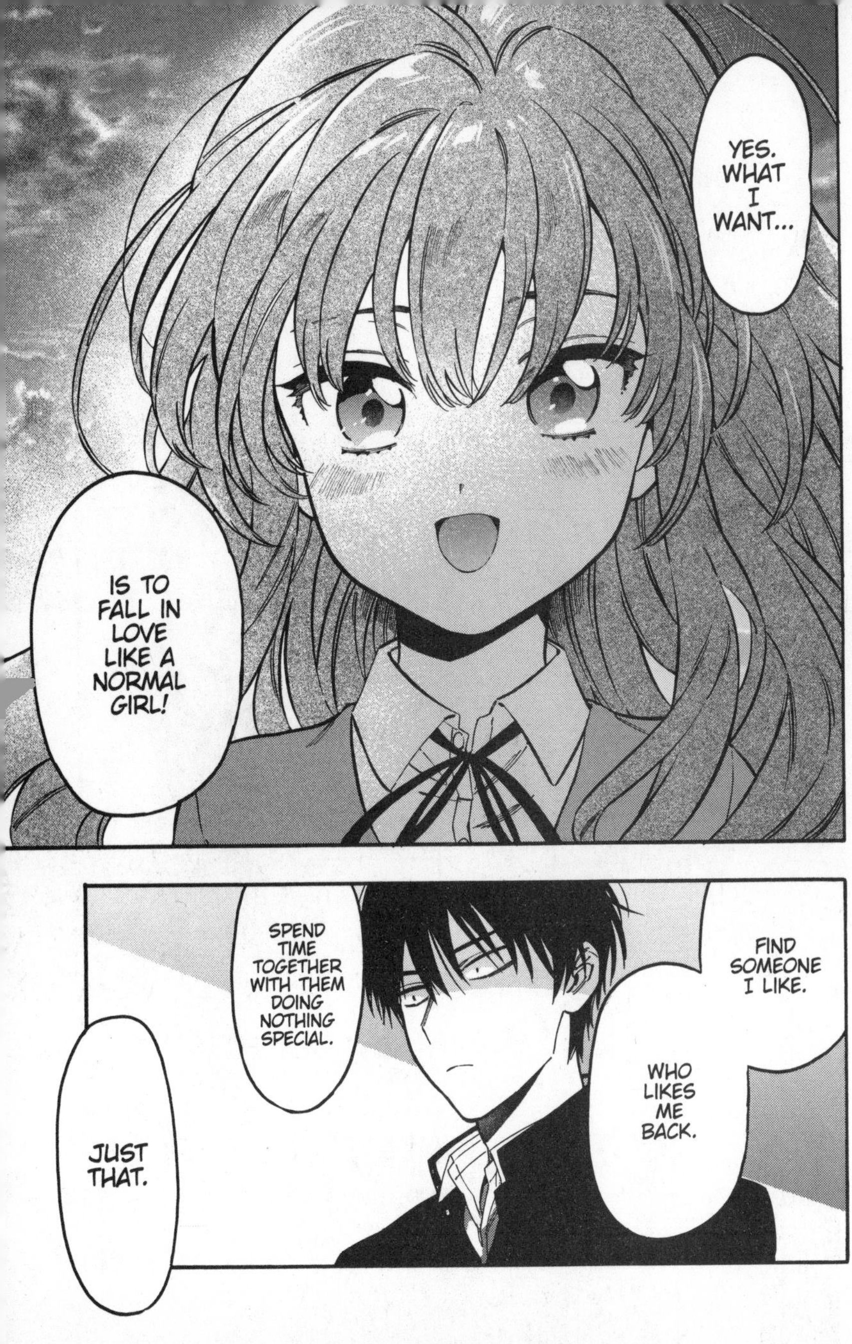
YES. WHAT I WANT...
IS TO FALL IN LOVE LIKE A NORMAL GIRL!
FIND SOMEONE I LIKE.
WHO LIKES ME BACK.
SPEND TIME TOGETHER WITH THEM DOING NOTHING SPECIAL.
JUST THAT.

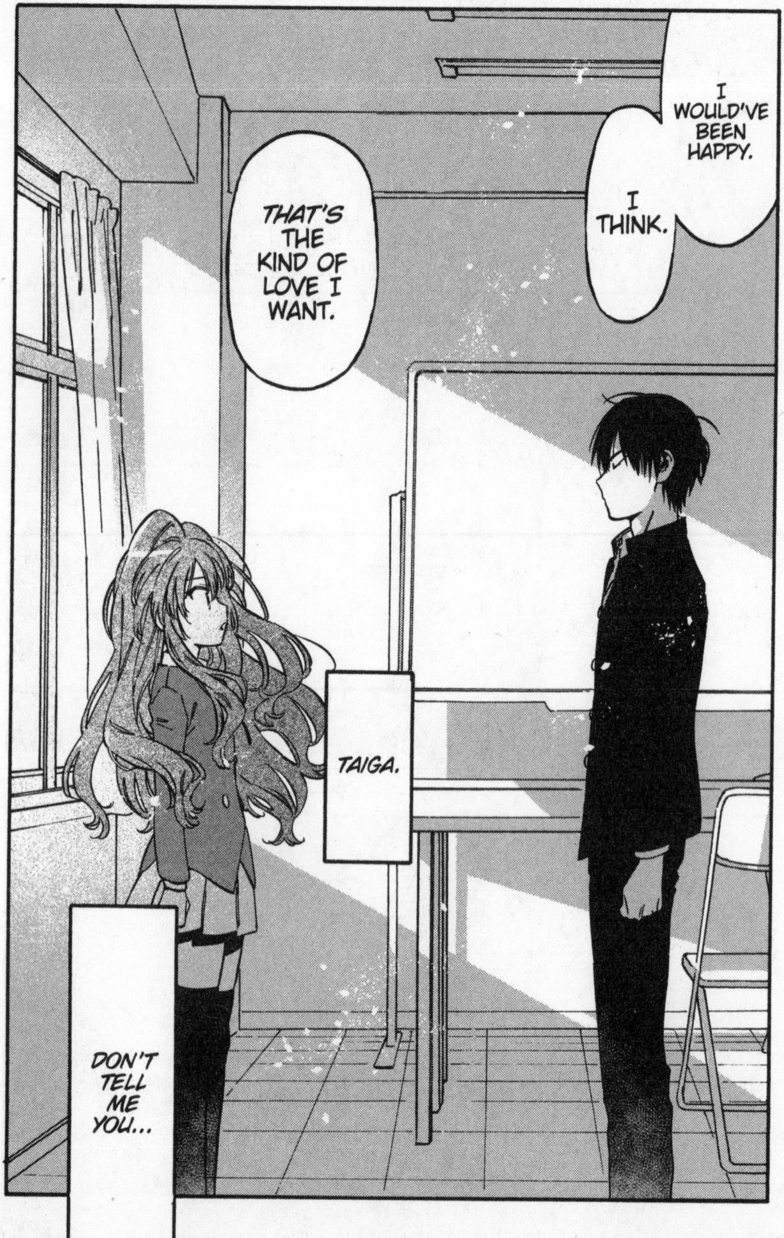
I WOULD'VE BEEN HAPPY.
I THINK.
THAT'S THE KIND OF LOVE I WANT.
TAIGA.
DON'T TELL ME YOU...

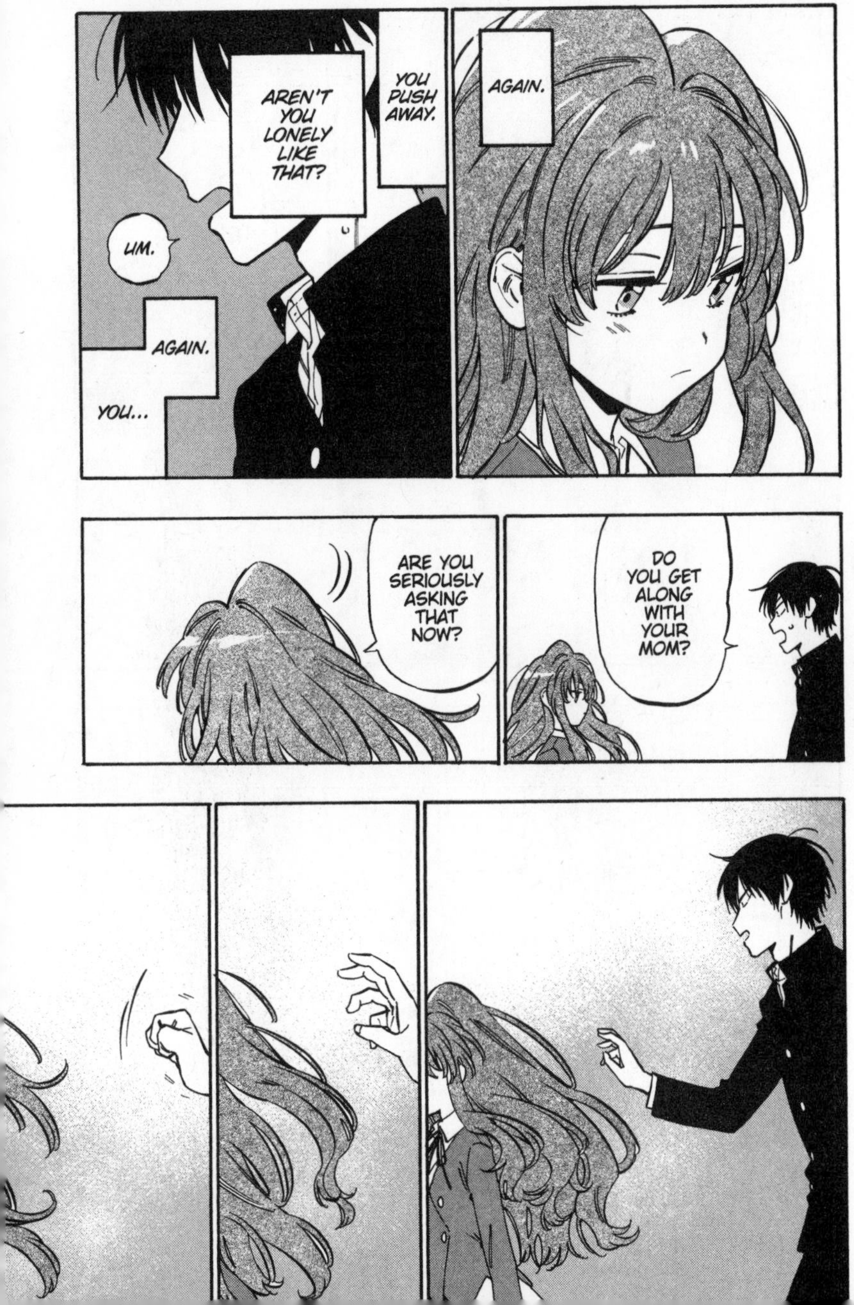
AGAIN.
YOU PUSH AWAY.
AREN'T YOU LONELY LIKE THAT?
UM.
AGAIN.
YOU...
DO YOU GET ALONG WITH YOUR MOM?
ARE YOU SERIOUSLY ASKING THAT NOW?

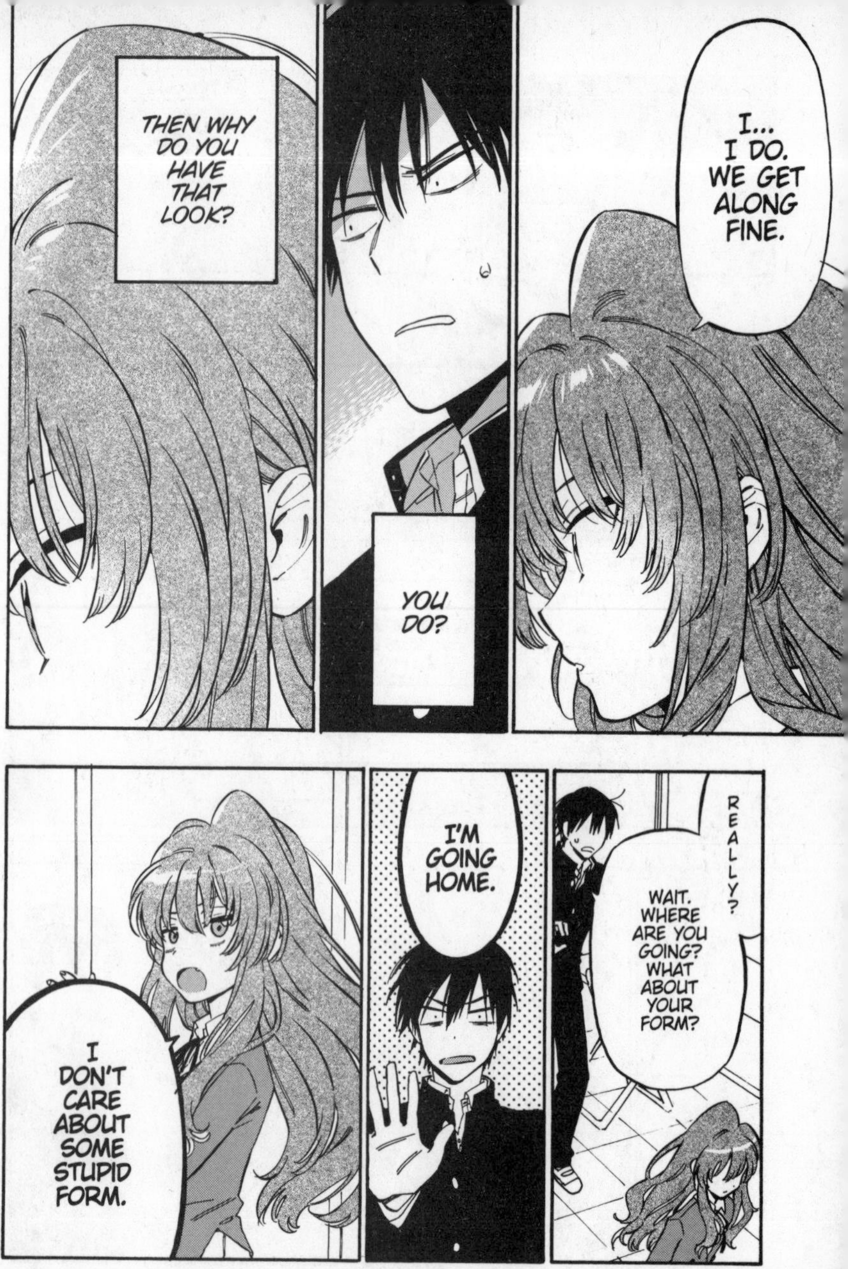
I... I DO. WE GET ALONG FINE.
YOU DO?
THEN WHY DO YOU HAVE THAT LOOK?
REALLY?
WAIT. WHERE ARE YOU GOING? WHAT ABOUT YOUR FORM?
I'M GOING HOME.
I DON'T CARE ABOUT SOME STUPID FORM.

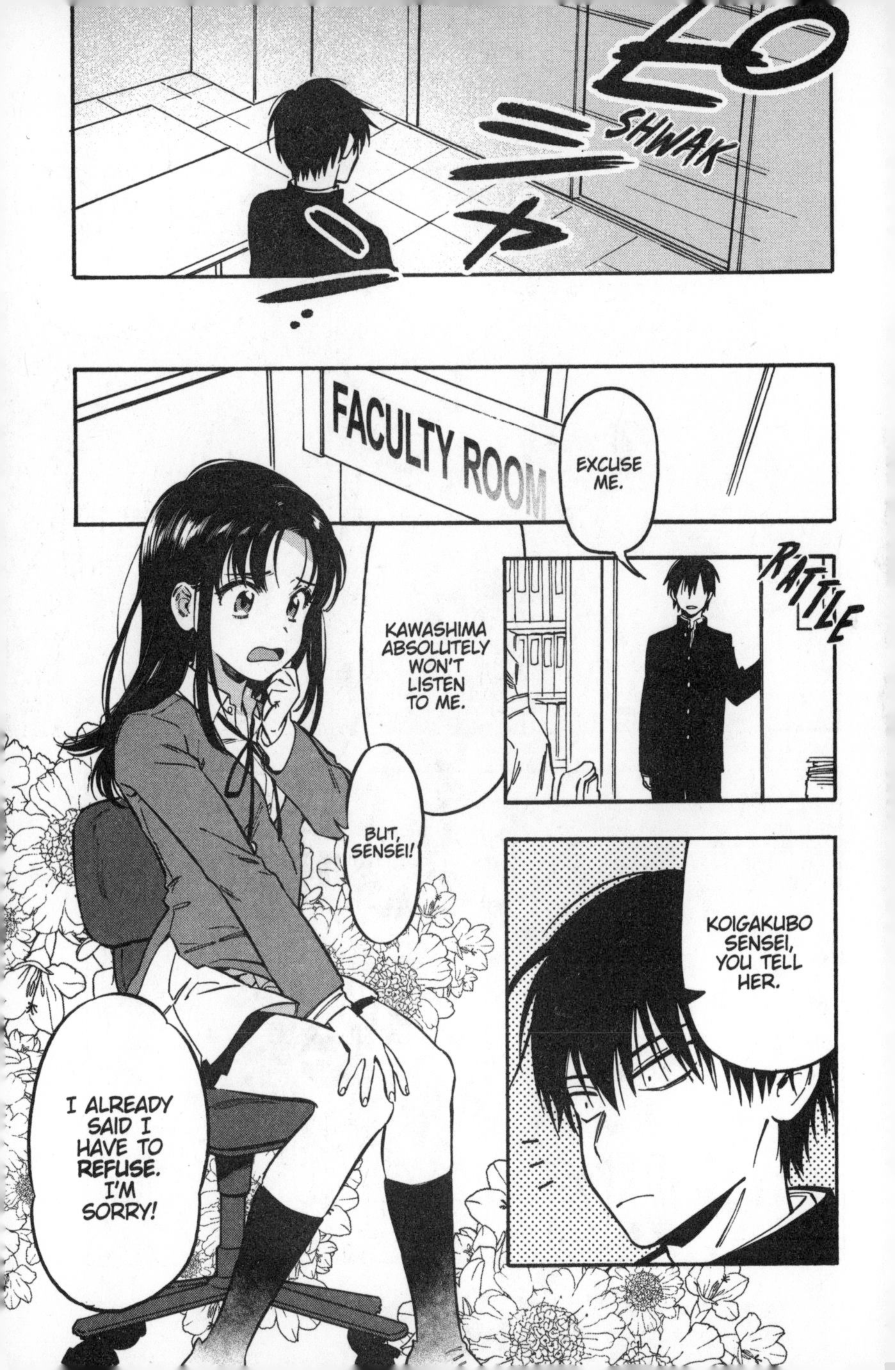
SHWAK
FACULTY ROOM
EXCUSE ME.
RATTLE
KOIGAKUBO SENSEI, YOU TELL HER.
KAWASHIMA ABSOLUTELY WON'T LISTEN TO ME.
BUT, SENSEI!
I ALREADY SAID I HAVE TO REFUSE. I'M SORRY!

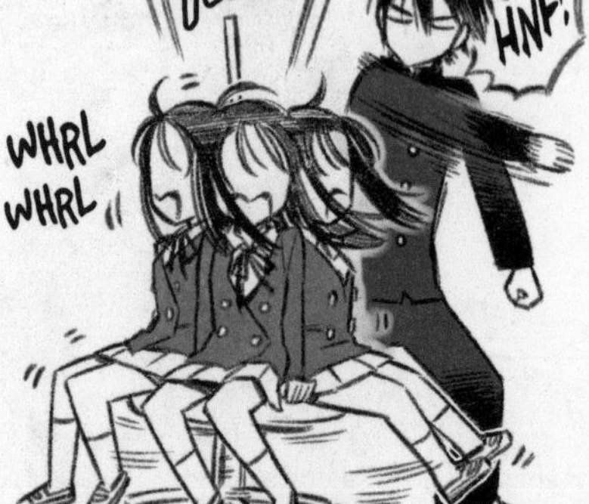
HNF!
YEEK?!
WHRL
WHRL

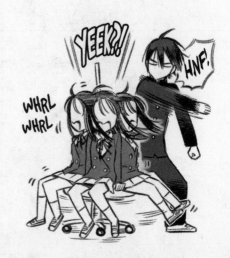

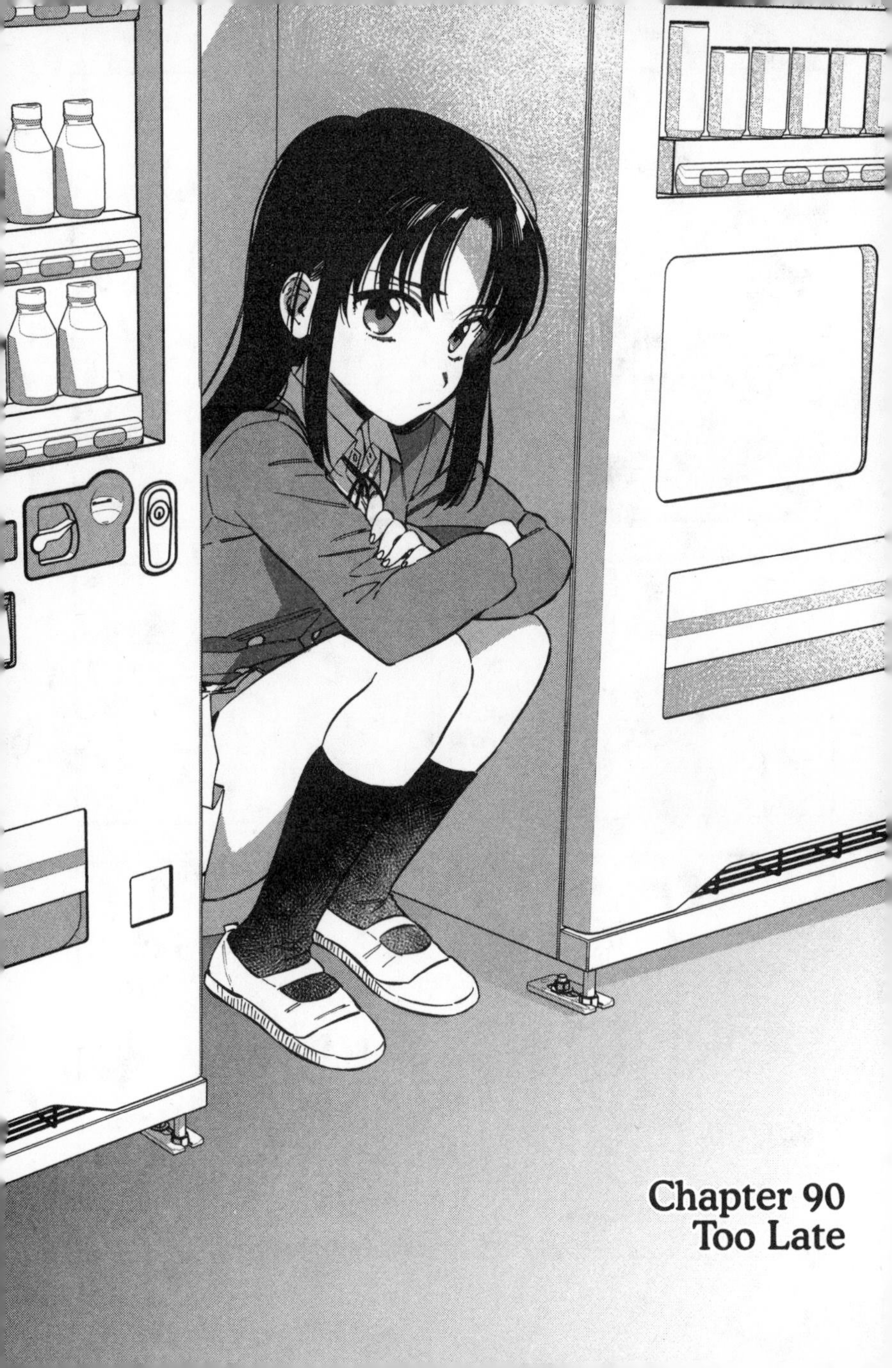

# Chapter 90
# Too Late

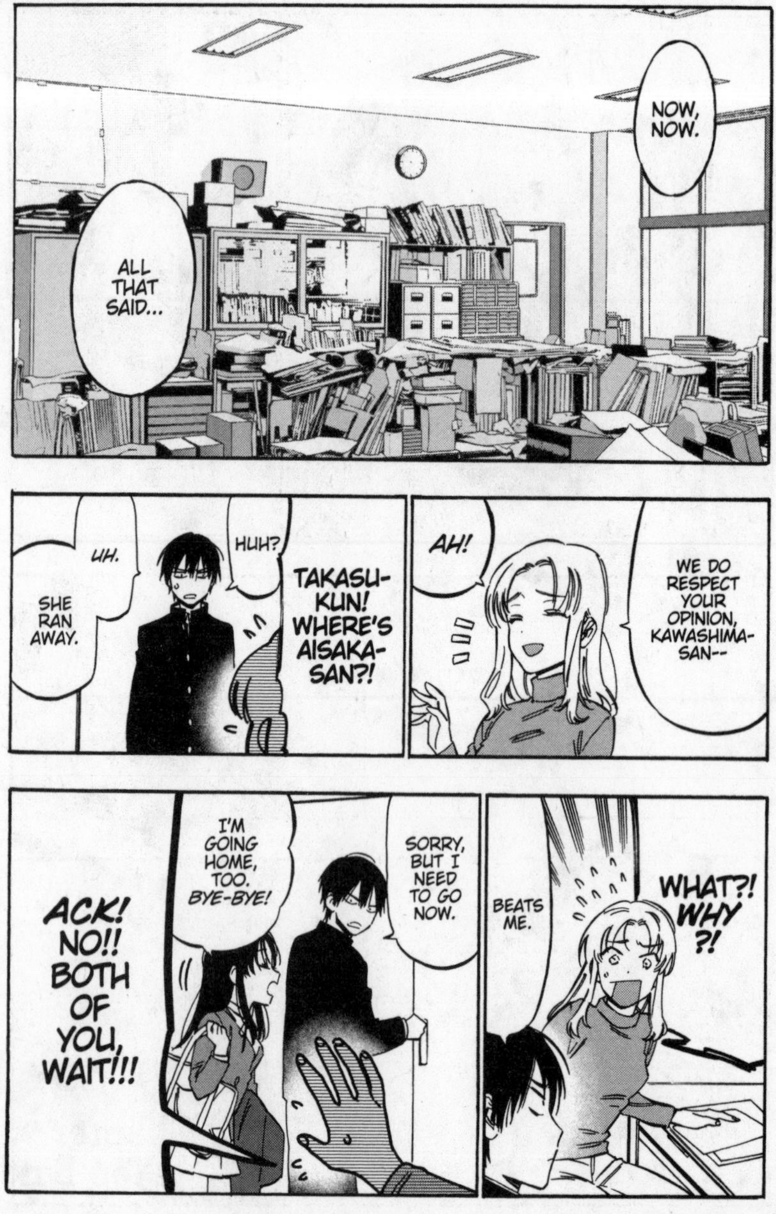
NOW, NOW.
ALL THAT SAID...
WE DO RESPECT YOUR OPINION, KAWASHIMA-SAN--
AH!
TAKASU-KUN! WHERE'S AISAKA-SAN?!
HUH?
UH.
SHE RAN AWAY.
WHAT?! WHY ?!
BEATS ME.
SORRY, BUT I NEED TO GO NOW.
I'M GOING HOME, TOO. BYE-BYE!
ACK! NO!! BOTH OF YOU, WAIT!!!

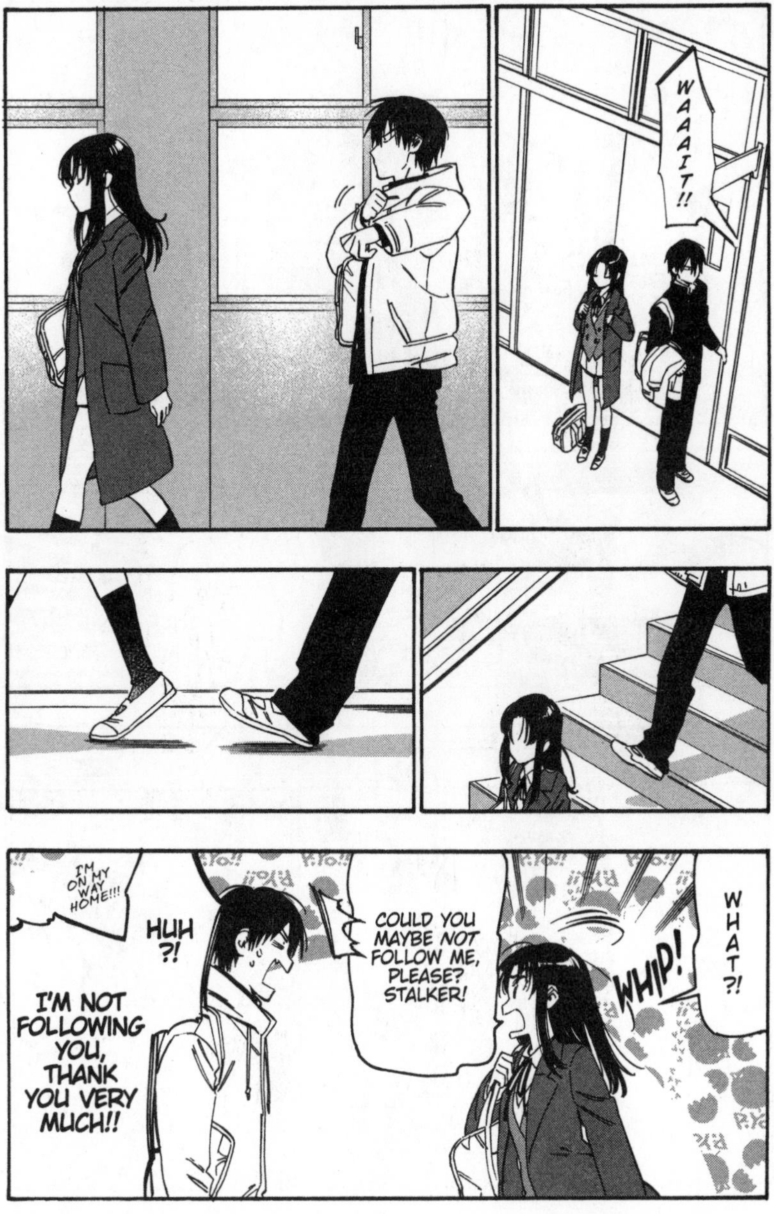
WAAAIT!!
WHAT?!
WHIP!
COULD YOU MAYBE NOT FOLLOW ME, PLEASE? STALKER!
I'M ON MY WAY HOME!!!
HUH?!
I'M NOT FOLLOWING YOU, THANK YOU VERY MUCH!!

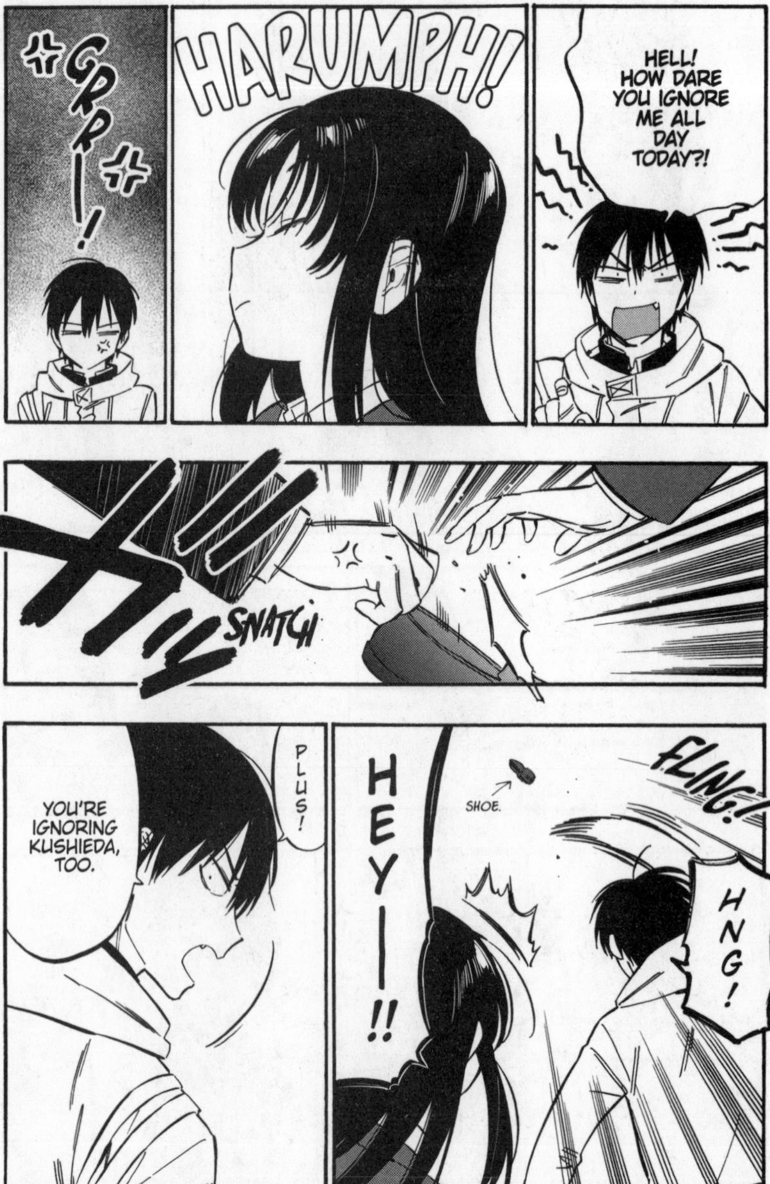
HELL! HOW DARE YOU IGNORE ME ALL DAY TODAY?!
HARUMPH!
GRR—!
SNATCH
FLING!
HNG!
SHOE.
HEY——!!
PLUS!
YOU'RE IGNORING KUSHIEDA, TOO.

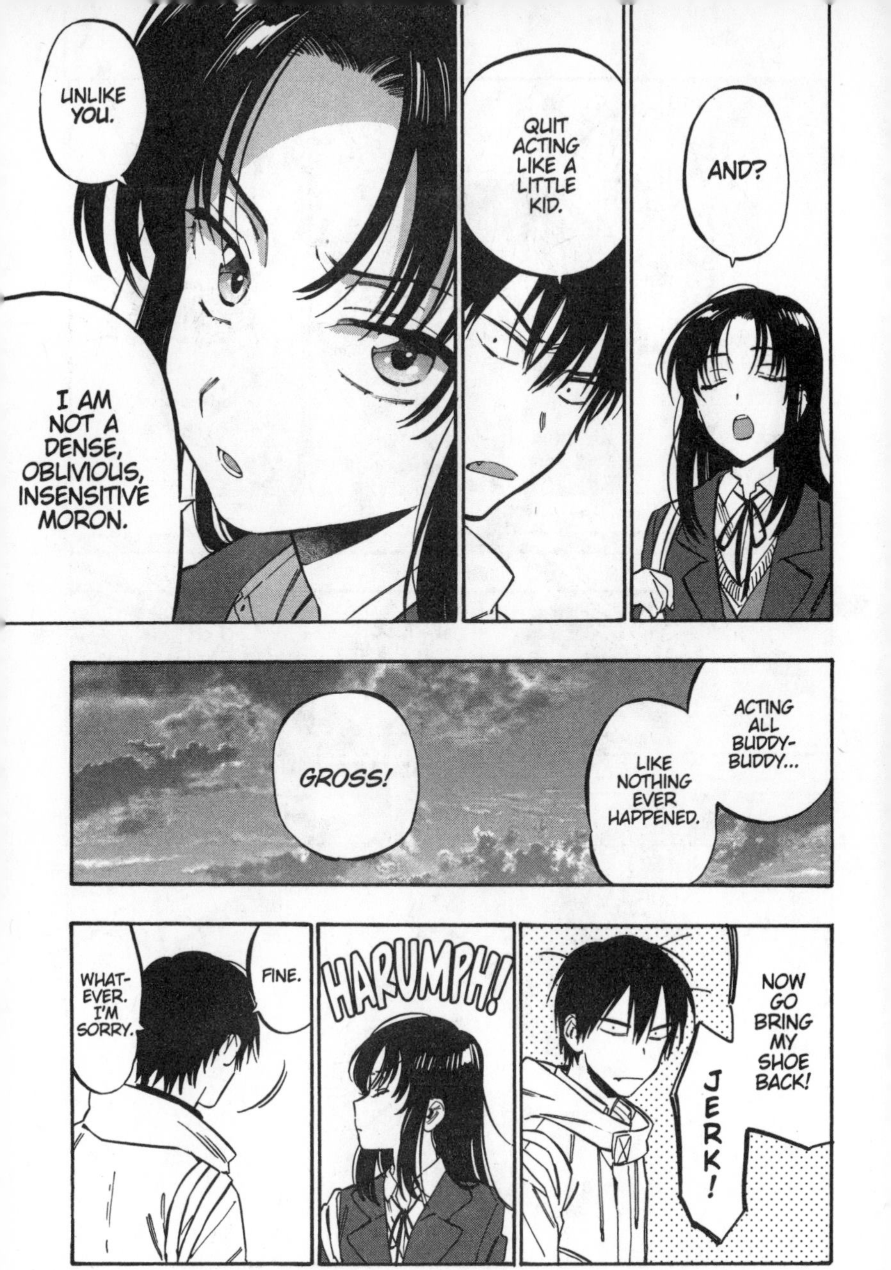
AND?
QUIT ACTING LIKE A LITTLE KID.
UNLIKE YOU.
I AM NOT A DENSE, OBLIVIOUS, INSENSITIVE MORON.
ACTING ALL BUDDY-BUDDY...
LIKE NOTHING EVER HAPPENED.
GROSS!
NOW GO BRING MY SHOE BACK!
JERK!
HARUMPH!
FINE.
WHAT-EVER. I'M SORRY.

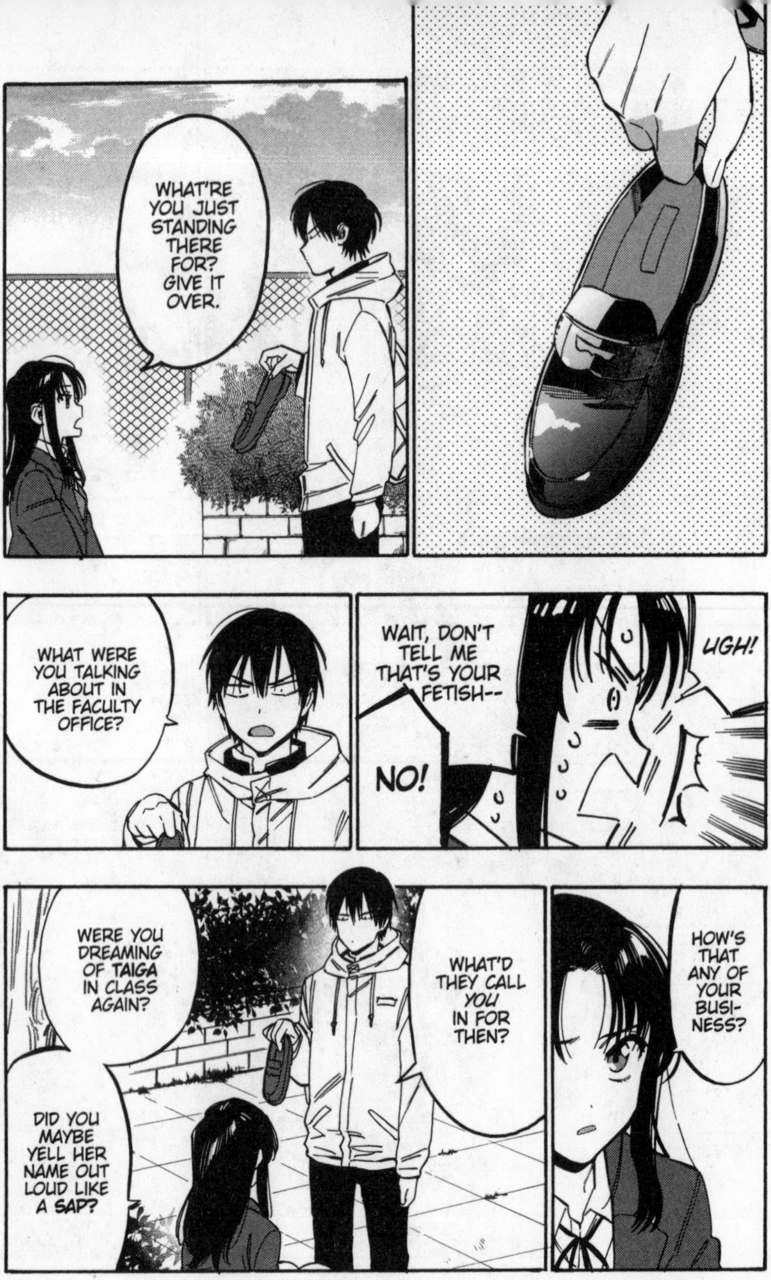

WHAT'RE YOU JUST STANDING THERE FOR? GIVE IT OVER.
UGH!
WAIT, DON'T TELL ME THAT'S YOUR FETISH--
NO!
WHAT WERE YOU TALKING ABOUT IN THE FACULTY OFFICE?
HOW'S THAT ANY OF YOUR BUSI-NESS?
WHAT'D THEY CALL *YOU* IN FOR THEN?
WERE YOU DREAMING OF **TAIGA** IN CLASS AGAIN?
DID YOU MAYBE YELL HER NAME OUT LOUD LIKE A **SAP**?

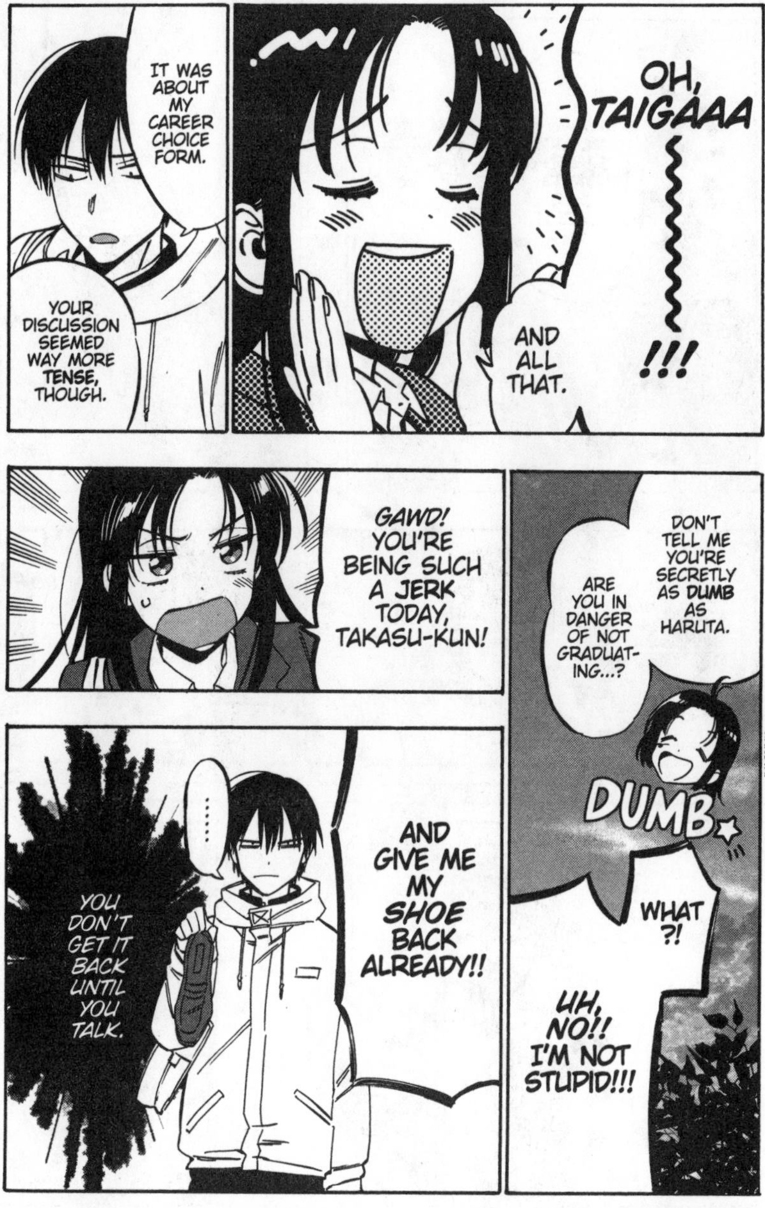

OH, TAIGAAA~!!!
AND ALL THAT.
IT WAS ABOUT MY CAREER CHOICE FORM.
YOUR DISCUSSION SEEMED WAY MORE TENSE, THOUGH.
DON'T TELL ME YOU'RE SECRETLY AS DUMB AS HARUTA.
ARE YOU IN DANGER OF NOT GRADUATING...?
HARUTA.
DUMB
WHAT?!
UH, NO!! I'M NOT STUPID!!!
GAWD! YOU'RE BEING SUCH A JERK TODAY, TAKASU-KUN!
AND GIVE ME MY SHOE BACK ALREADY!!
......
YOU DON'T GET IT BACK UNTIL YOU TALK.

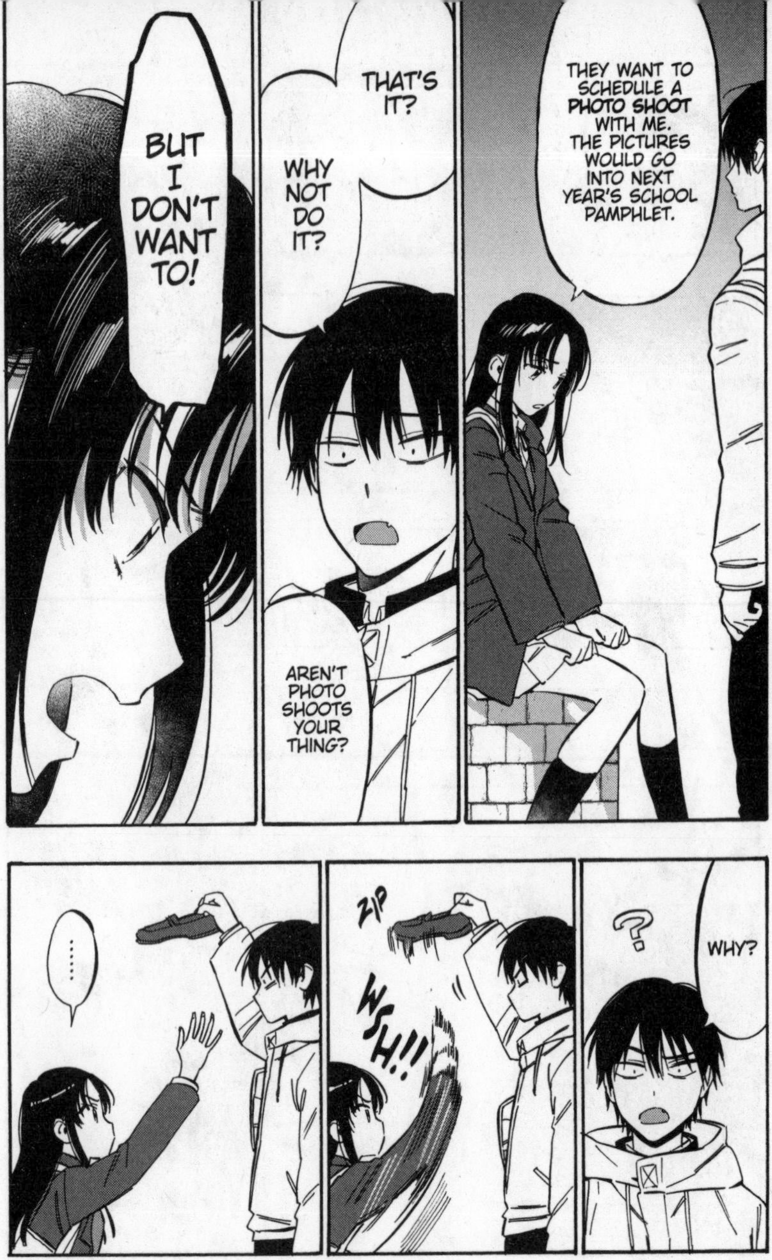
THEY WANT TO SCHEDULE A PHOTO SHOOT WITH ME. THE PICTURES WOULD GO INTO NEXT YEAR'S SCHOOL PAMPHLET.
THAT'S IT?
WHY NOT DO IT?
AREN'T PHOTO SHOOTS YOUR THING?
BUT I DON'T WANT TO!
?
WHY?
ZIP
WSH!!
......

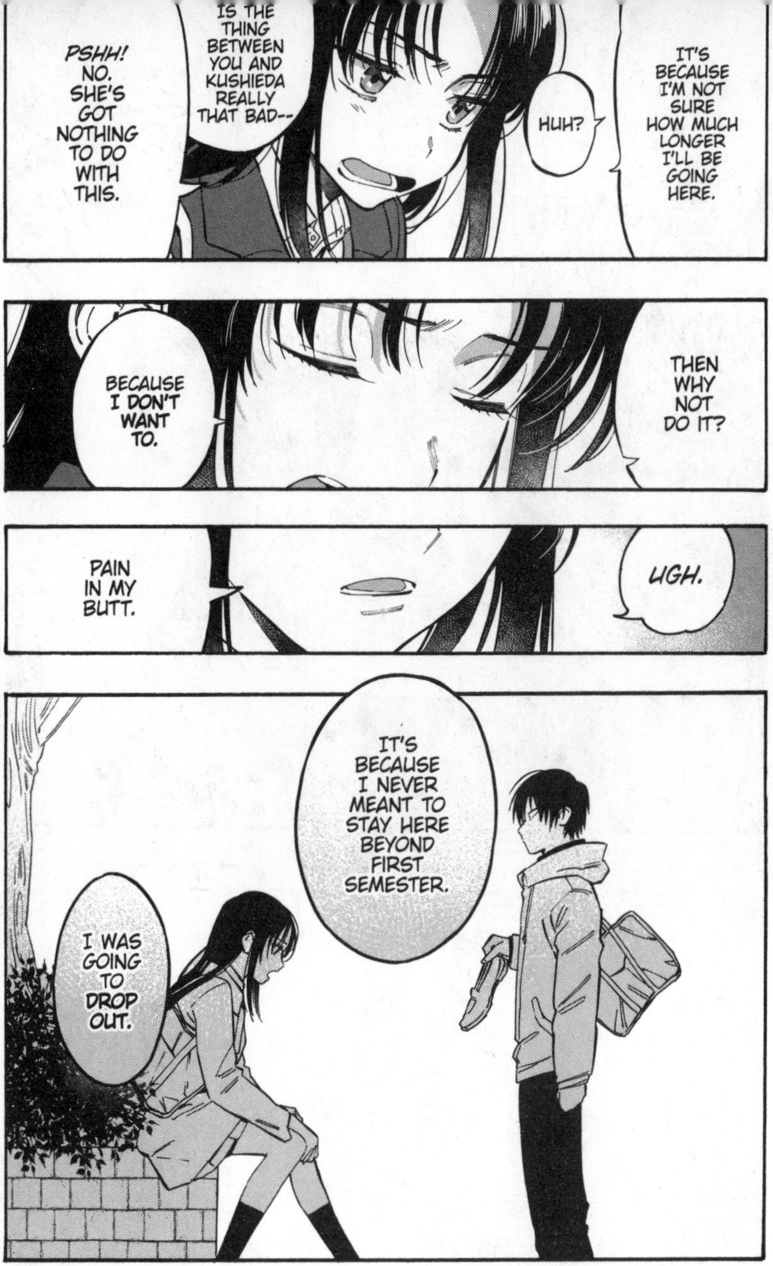
IT'S BECAUSE I'M NOT SURE HOW MUCH LONGER I'LL BE GOING HERE.
HUH?
IS THE THING BETWEEN YOU AND KUSHIEDA REALLY THAT BAD--
PSHH! NO. SHE'S GOT NOTHING TO DO WITH THIS.
THEN WHY NOT DO IT?
BECAUSE I DON'T WANT TO.
UGH.
PAIN IN MY BUTT.
IT'S BECAUSE I NEVER MEANT TO STAY HERE BEYOND FIRST SEMESTER.
I WAS GOING TO DROP OUT.

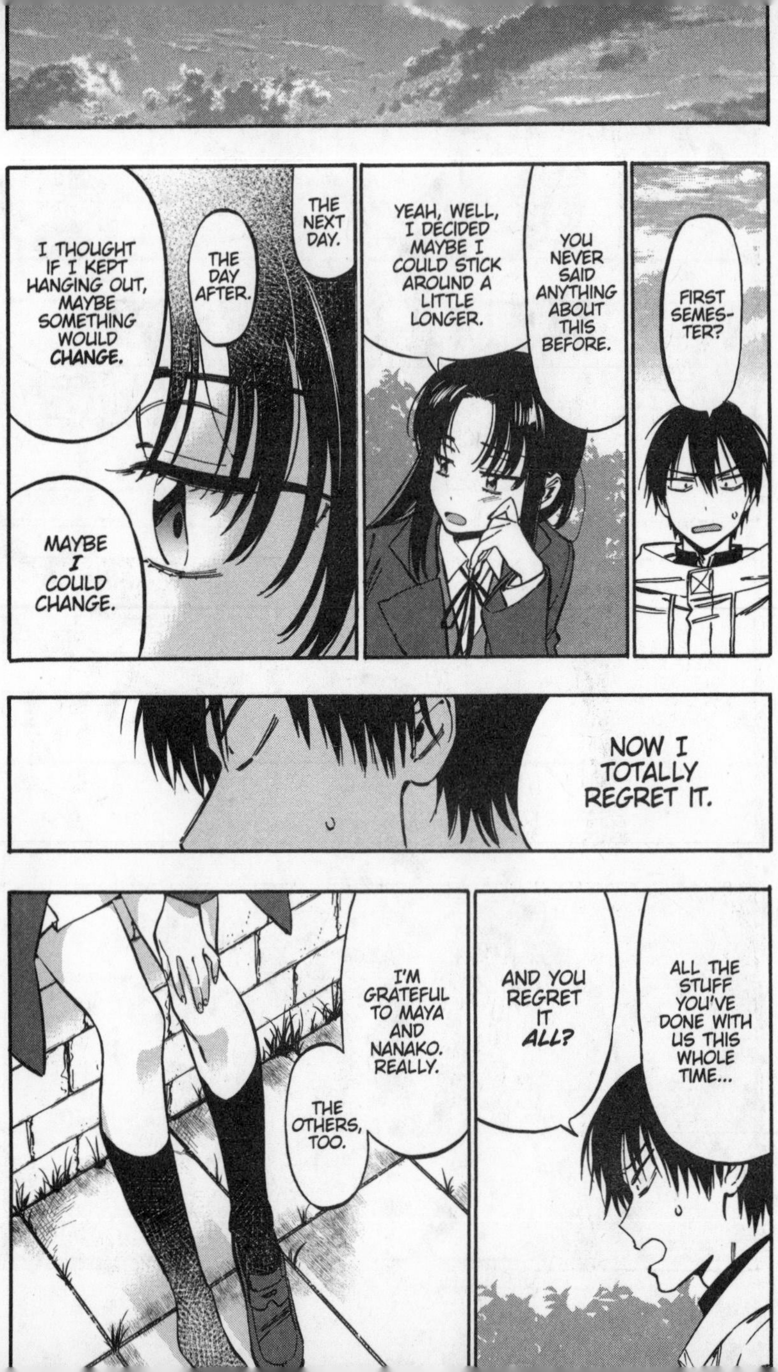
FIRST SEMESTER?
YOU NEVER SAID ANYTHING ABOUT THIS BEFORE.
YEAH, WELL, I DECIDED MAYBE I COULD STICK AROUND A LITTLE LONGER.
THE NEXT DAY.
THE DAY AFTER.
I THOUGHT IF I KEPT HANGING OUT, MAYBE SOMETHING WOULD CHANGE.
MAYBE I COULD CHANGE.
NOW I TOTALLY REGRET IT.
ALL THE STUFF YOU'VE DONE WITH US THIS WHOLE TIME...
AND YOU REGRET IT ALL?
I'M GRATEFUL TO MAYA AND NANAKO. REALLY.
THE OTHERS, TOO.

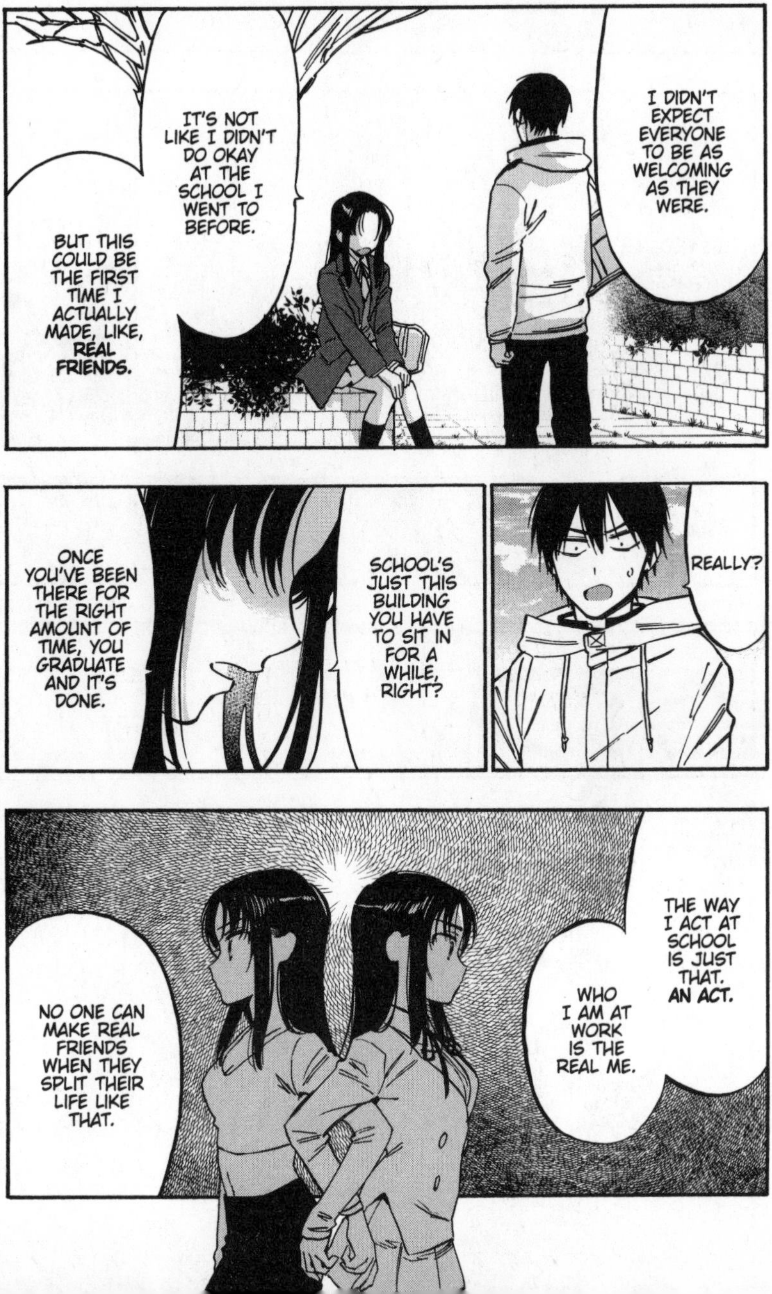
I DIDN'T EXPECT EVERYONE TO BE AS WELCOMING AS THEY WERE.
IT'S NOT LIKE I DIDN'T DO OKAY AT THE SCHOOL I WENT TO BEFORE.
BUT THIS COULD BE THE FIRST TIME I ACTUALLY MADE, LIKE, **REAL FRIENDS.**
REALLY?
SCHOOL'S JUST THIS BUILDING YOU HAVE TO SIT IN FOR A WHILE, RIGHT?
ONCE YOU'VE BEEN THERE FOR THE RIGHT AMOUNT OF TIME, YOU GRADUATE AND IT'S DONE.
THE WAY I ACT AT SCHOOL IS JUST THAT. **AN ACT.**
WHO I AM AT WORK IS THE REAL ME.
NO ONE CAN MAKE REAL FRIENDS WHEN THEY SPLIT THEIR LIFE LIKE THAT.

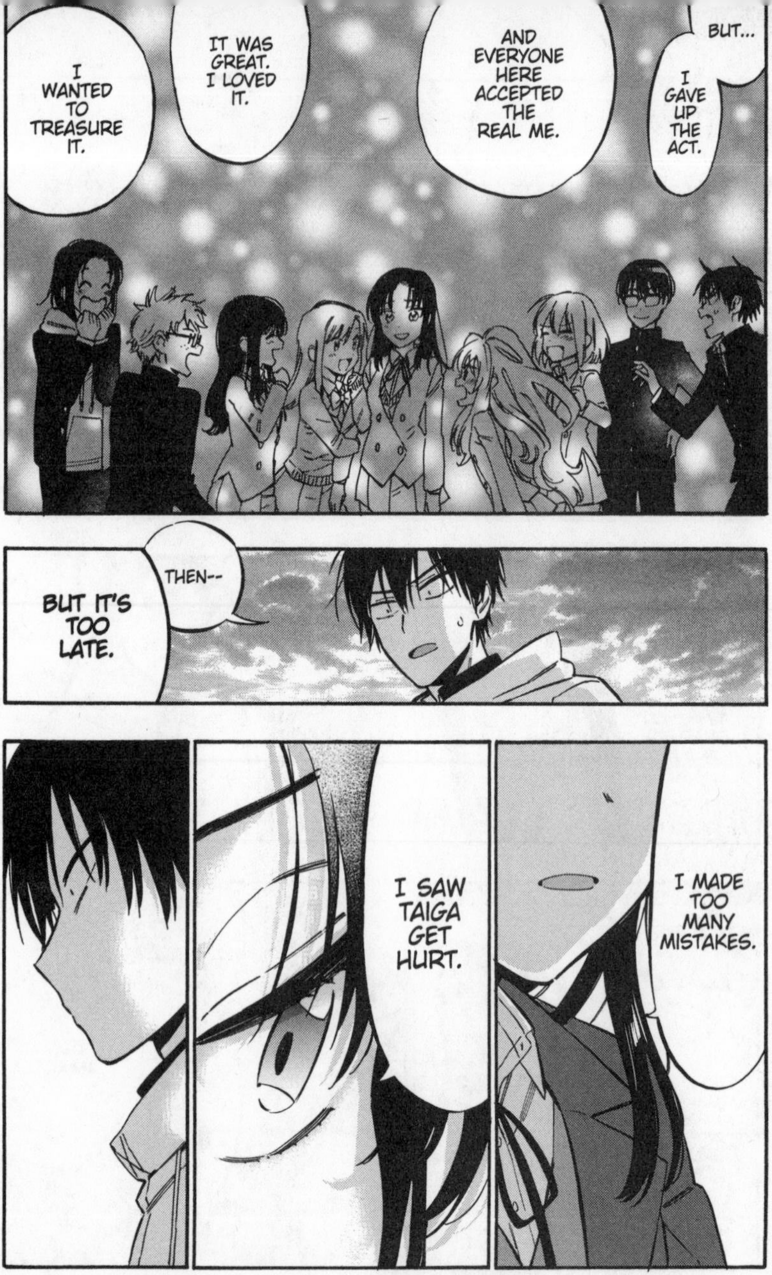
BUT... I GAVE UP THE ACT.
AND EVERYONE HERE ACCEPTED THE REAL ME.
IT WAS GREAT. I LOVED IT.
I WANTED TO TREASURE IT.
THEN--
BUT IT'S TOO LATE.
I MADE TOO MANY MISTAKES.
I SAW TAIGA GET HURT.

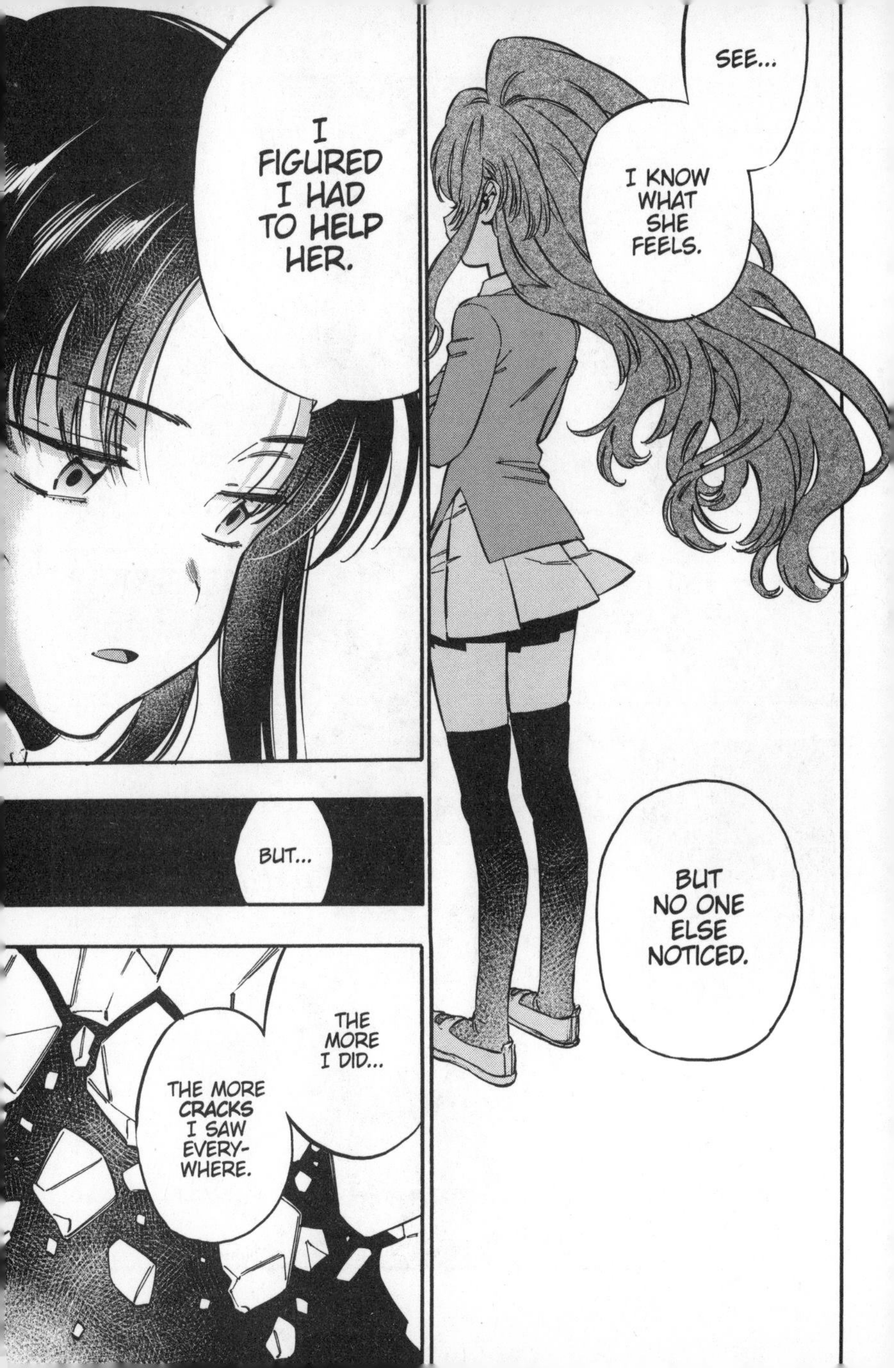
SEE...
I KNOW WHAT SHE FEELS.
BUT NO ONE ELSE NOTICED.
I FIGURED I HAD TO HELP HER.
BUT...
THE MORE I DID...
THE MORE CRACKS I SAW EVERY-WHERE.

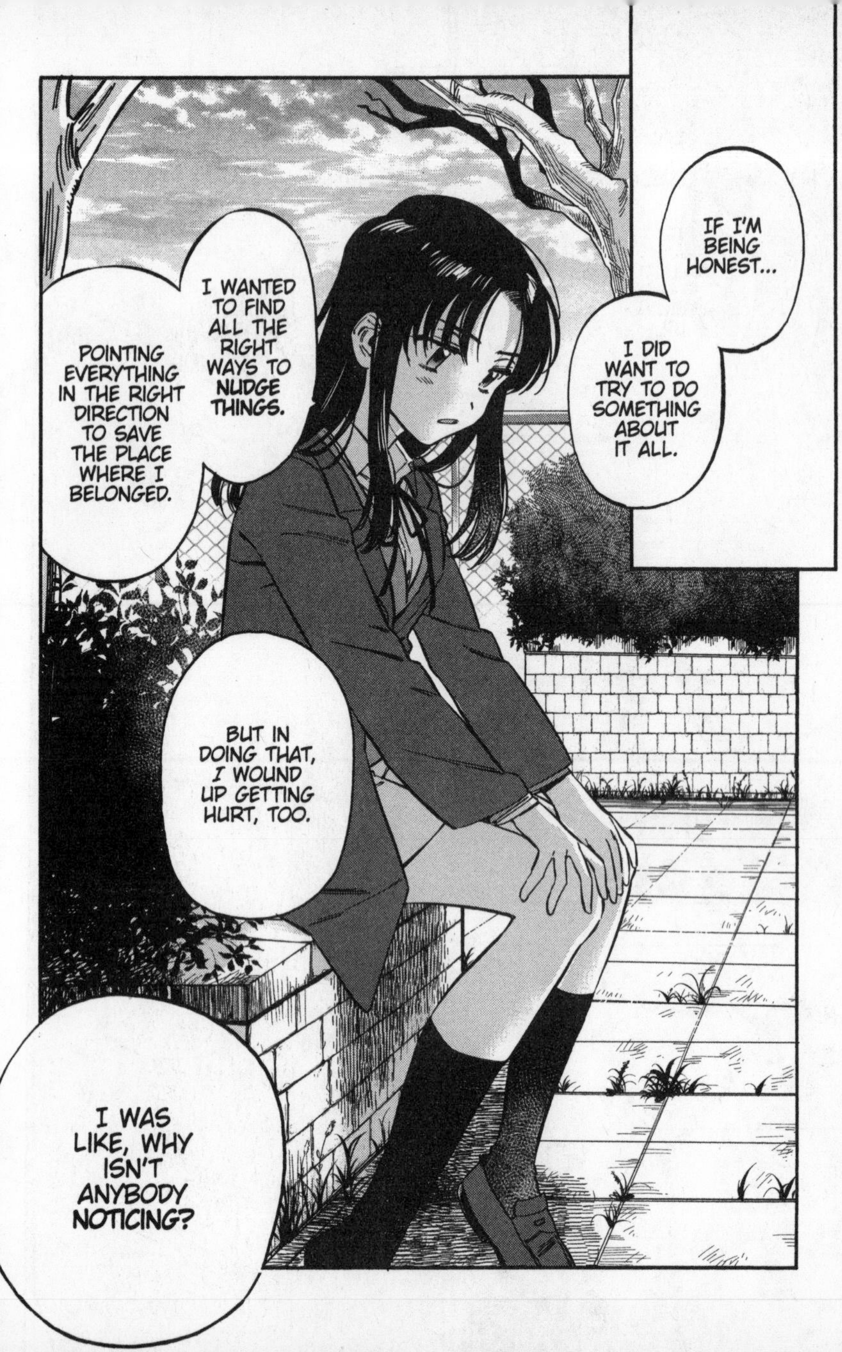
IF I'M BEING HONEST...
I DID WANT TO TRY TO DO SOMETHING ABOUT IT ALL.
I WANTED TO FIND ALL THE RIGHT WAYS TO NUDGE THINGS.
POINTING EVERYTHING IN THE RIGHT DIRECTION TO SAVE THE PLACE WHERE I BELONGED.
BUT IN DOING THAT, I WOUND UP GETTING HURT, TOO.
I WAS LIKE, WHY ISN'T ANYBODY NOTICING?

WHY WAS IT JUST ME?
WAS ANYBODY THINKING ABOUT ME AT ALL?
I STARTED PANICKING.
THANKS TO THAT, I STARTED SCREWING UP.
EVENTUALLY, I REALIZED THERE REALLY WASN'T ANYTHING I COULD DO.
I WAS JUST MAKING A PAIN IN THE BUTT OF MYSELF--
NO!!

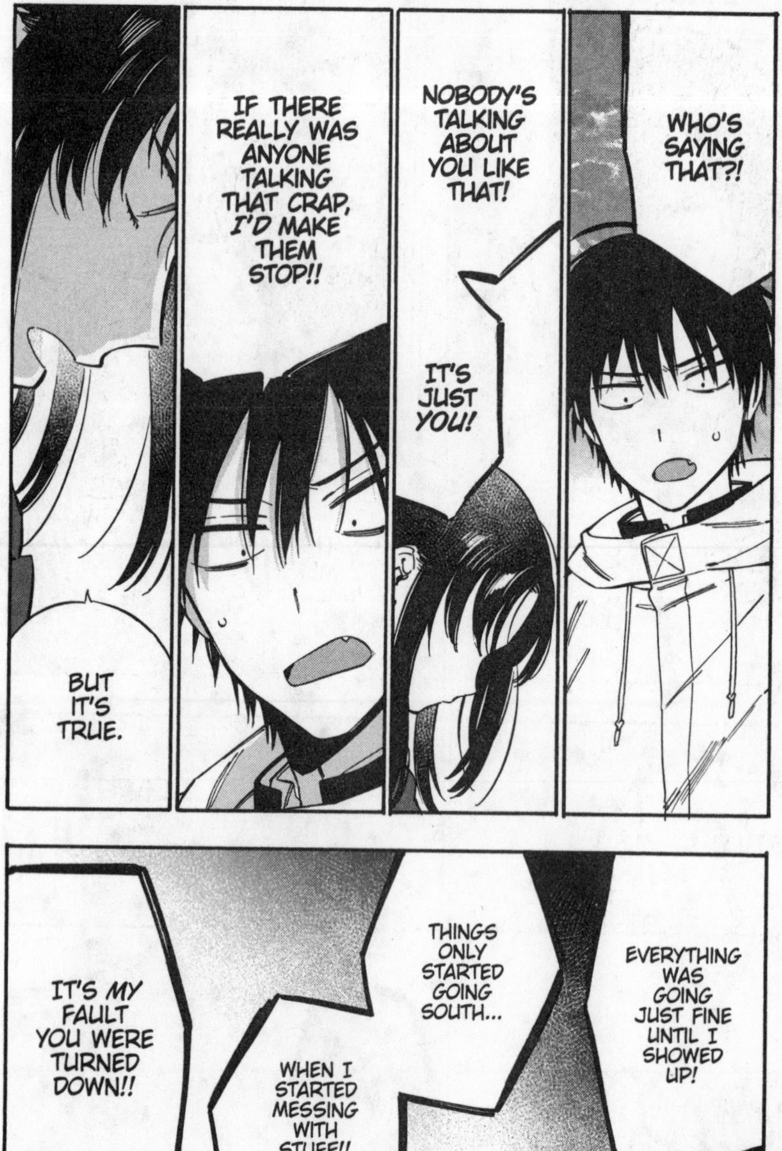
WHO'S SAYING THAT?!
NOBODY'S TALKING ABOUT YOU LIKE THAT!
IT'S JUST YOU!
IF THERE REALLY WAS ANYONE TALKING THAT CRAP, I'D MAKE THEM STOP!!
BUT IT'S TRUE.
EVERYTHING WAS GOING JUST FINE UNTIL I SHOWED UP!
THINGS ONLY STARTED GOING SOUTH...
WHEN I STARTED MESSING WITH STUFF!!
IT'S MY FAULT YOU WERE TURNED DOWN!!

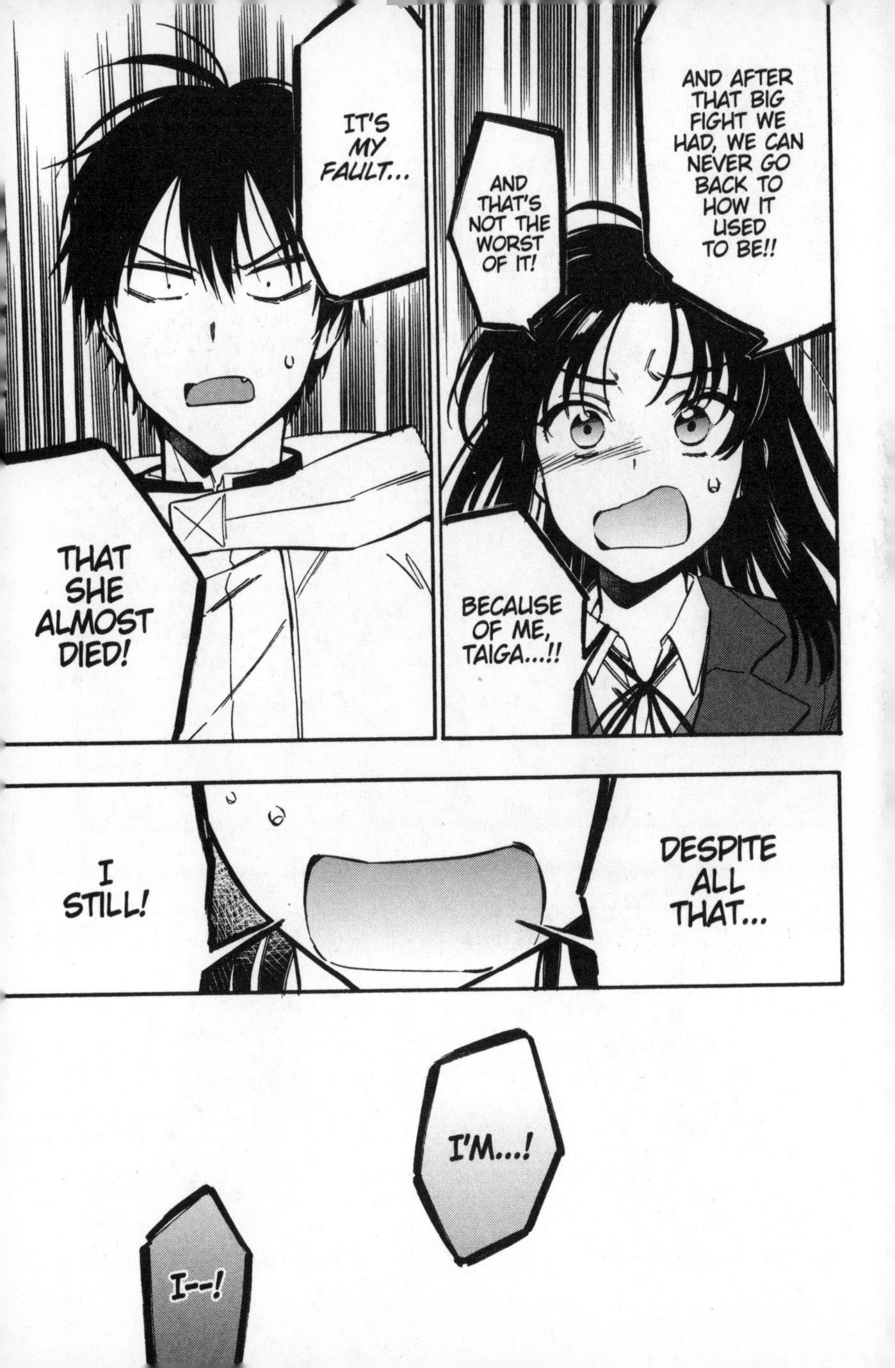
AND AFTER THAT BIG FIGHT WE HAD, WE CAN NEVER GO BACK TO HOW IT USED TO BE!!
AND THAT'S NOT THE WORST OF IT!
BECAUSE OF ME, TAIGA...!!
IT'S MY FAULT...
THAT SHE ALMOST DIED!
DESPITE ALL THAT...
I STILL!
I'M...!
I--!

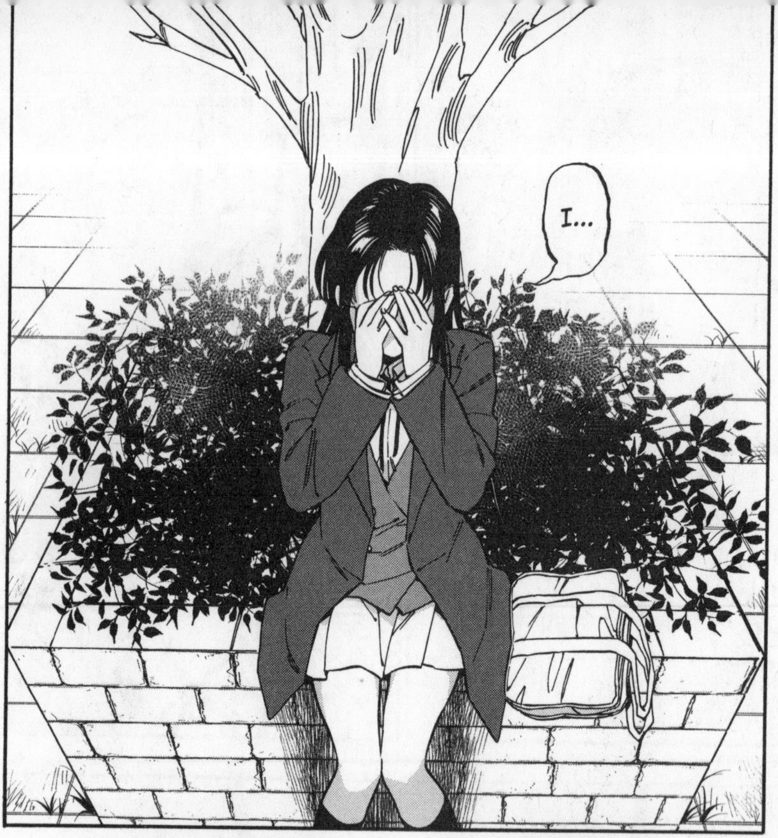
I...
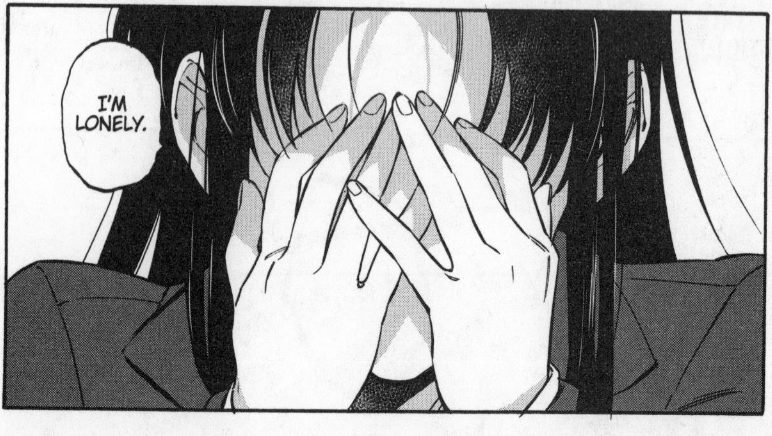
I'M LONELY.

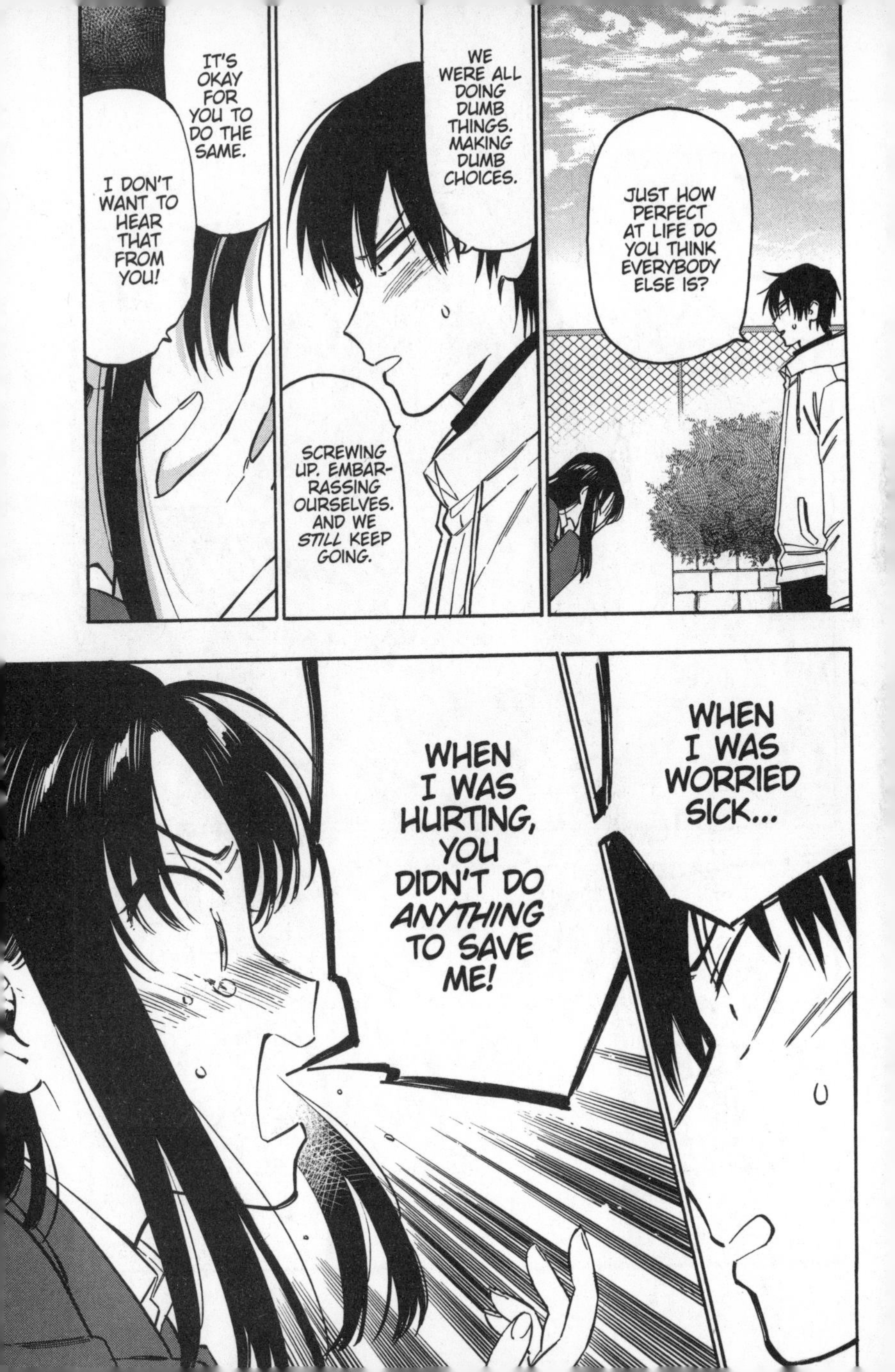
JUST HOW PERFECT AT LIFE DO YOU THINK EVERYBODY ELSE IS?
WE WERE ALL DOING DUMB THINGS. MAKING DUMB CHOICES.
SCREWING UP. EMBARRASSING OURSELVES. AND WE STILL KEEP GOING.
IT'S OKAY FOR YOU TO DO THE SAME.
I DON'T WANT TO HEAR THAT FROM YOU!
WHEN I WAS WORRIED SICK...
WHEN I WAS HURTING, YOU DIDN'T DO ANYTHING TO SAVE ME!

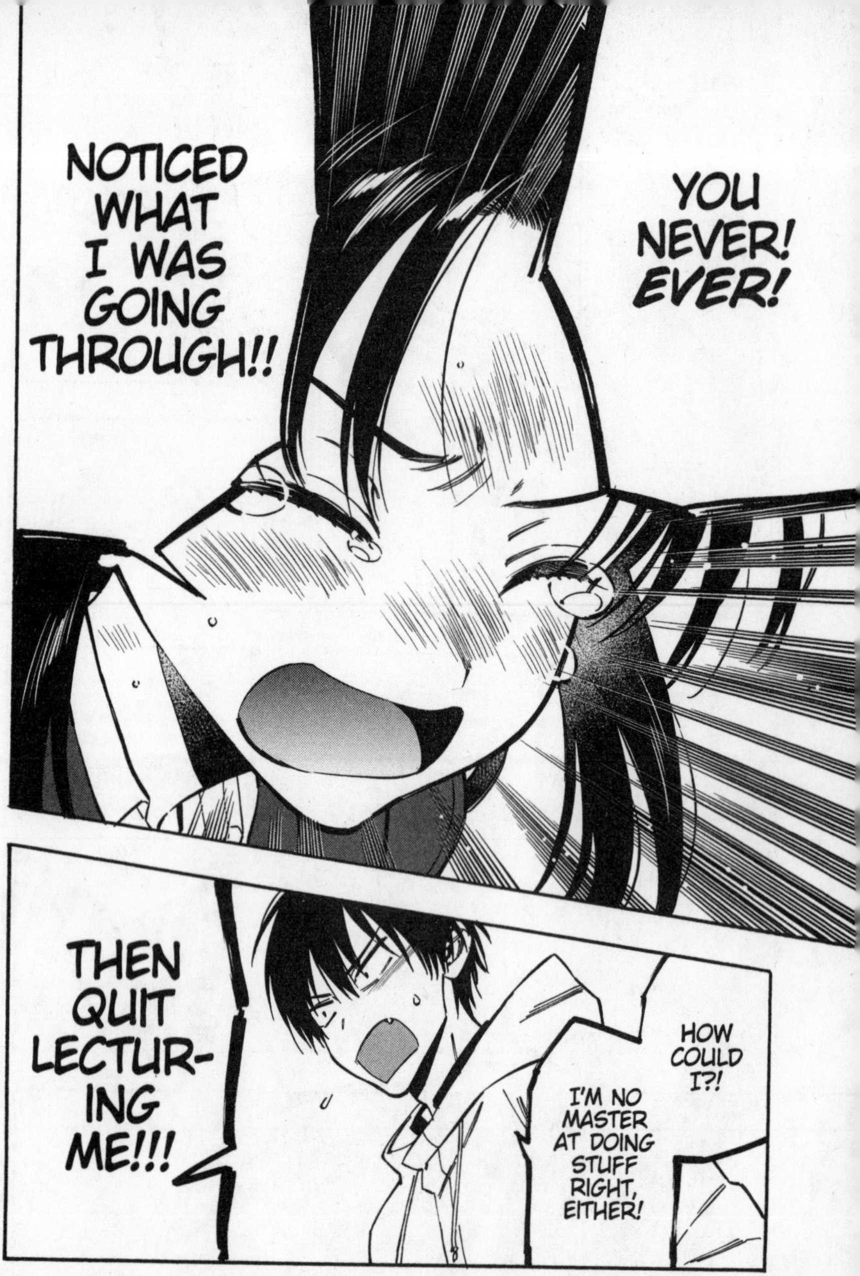
YOU NEVER! EVER!
NOTICED WHAT I WAS GOING THROUGH!!
HOW COULD I?!
I'M NO MASTER AT DOING STUFF RIGHT, EITHER!
THEN QUIT LECTUR-ING ME!!!

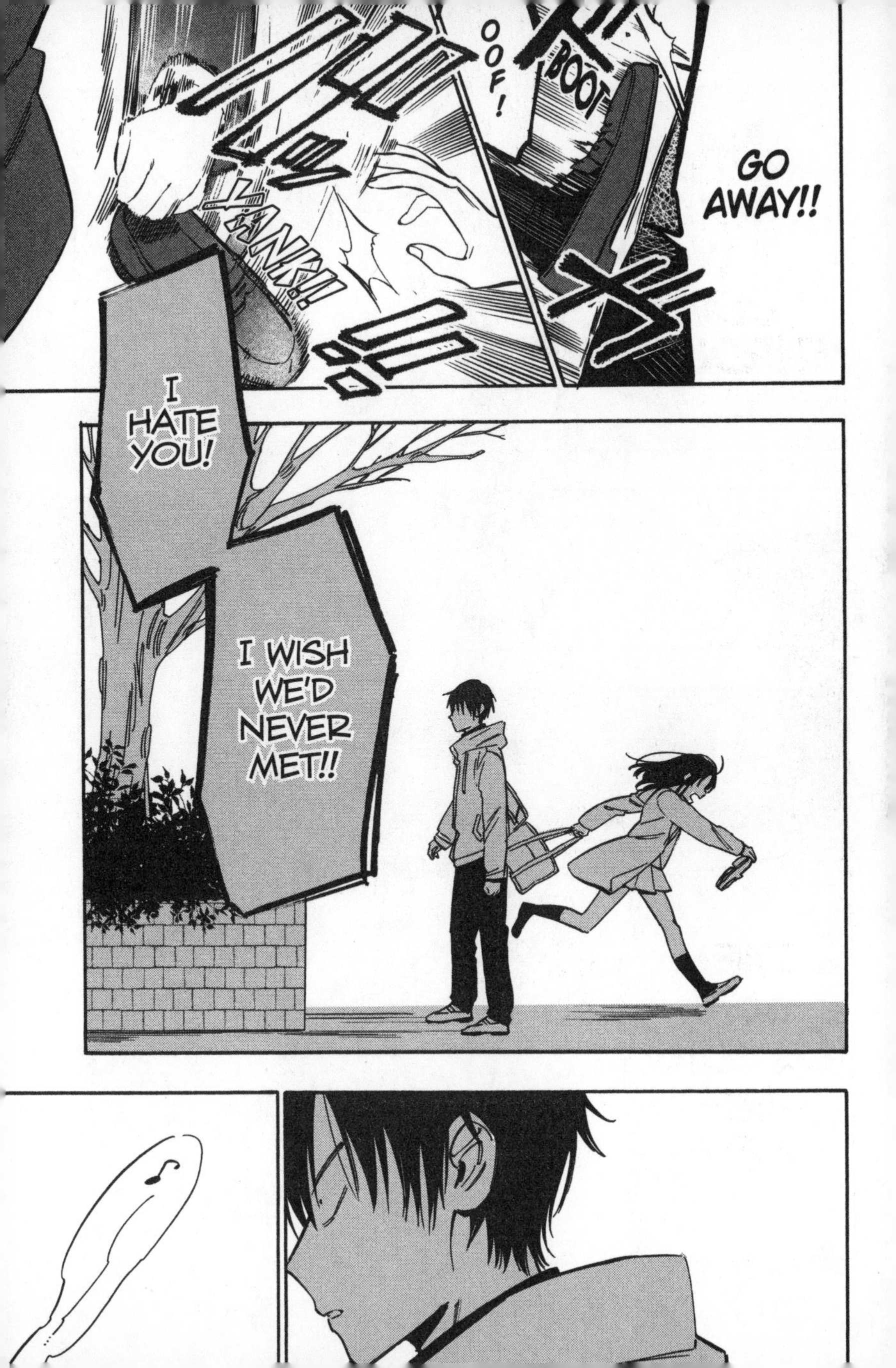
GO AWAY!!
BOOT
OOF!
YANK!!
I HATE YOU!
I WISH WE'D NEVER MET!!

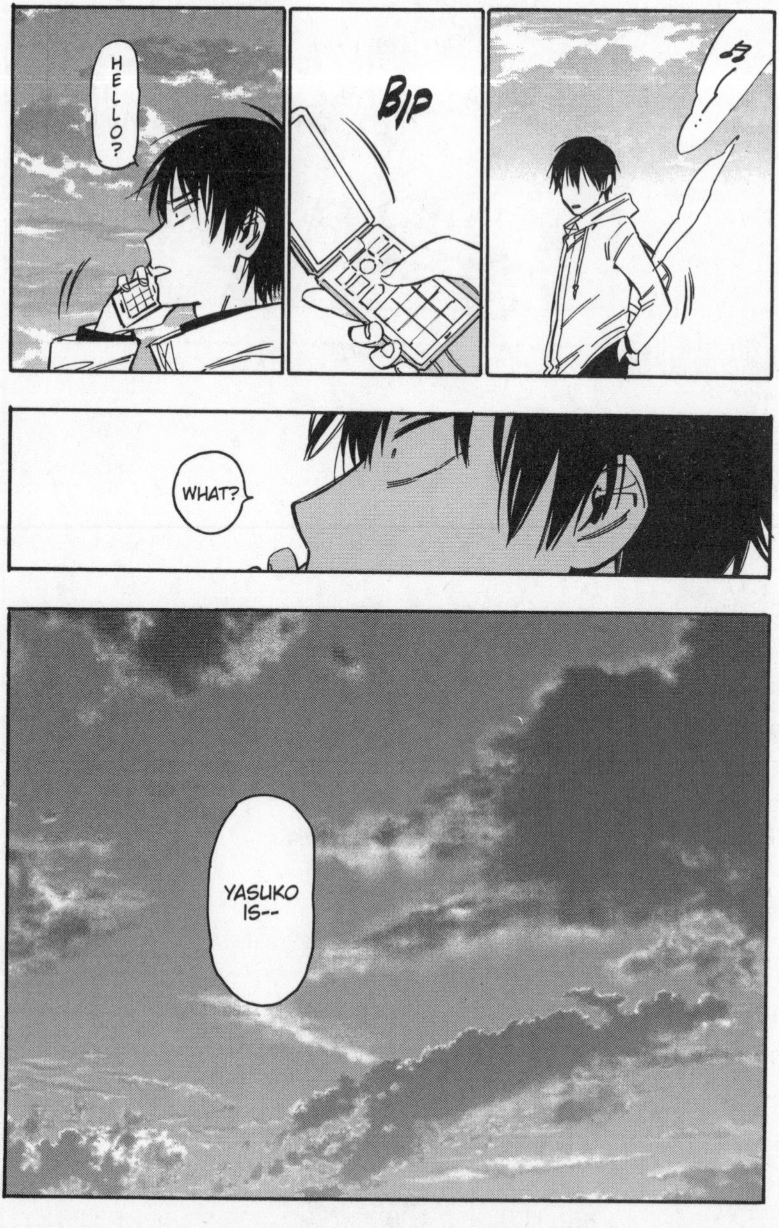
♫ —..
BIP
HELLO?
WHAT?
YASUKO IS--

Toradora!

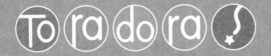

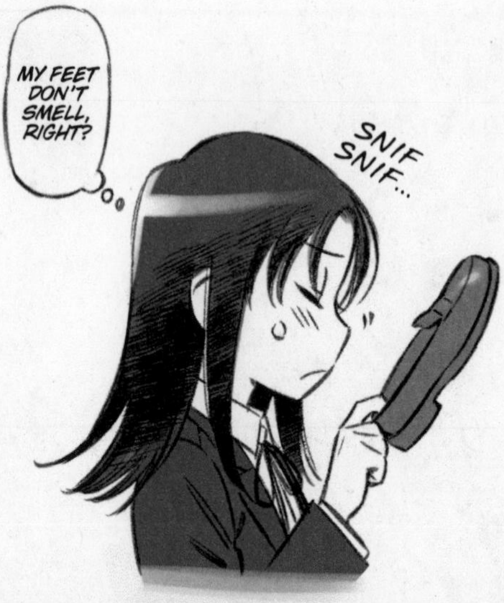
MY FEET DON'T SMELL, RIGHT?
SNIF SNIF...

# Chapter 91
# Get It Together!

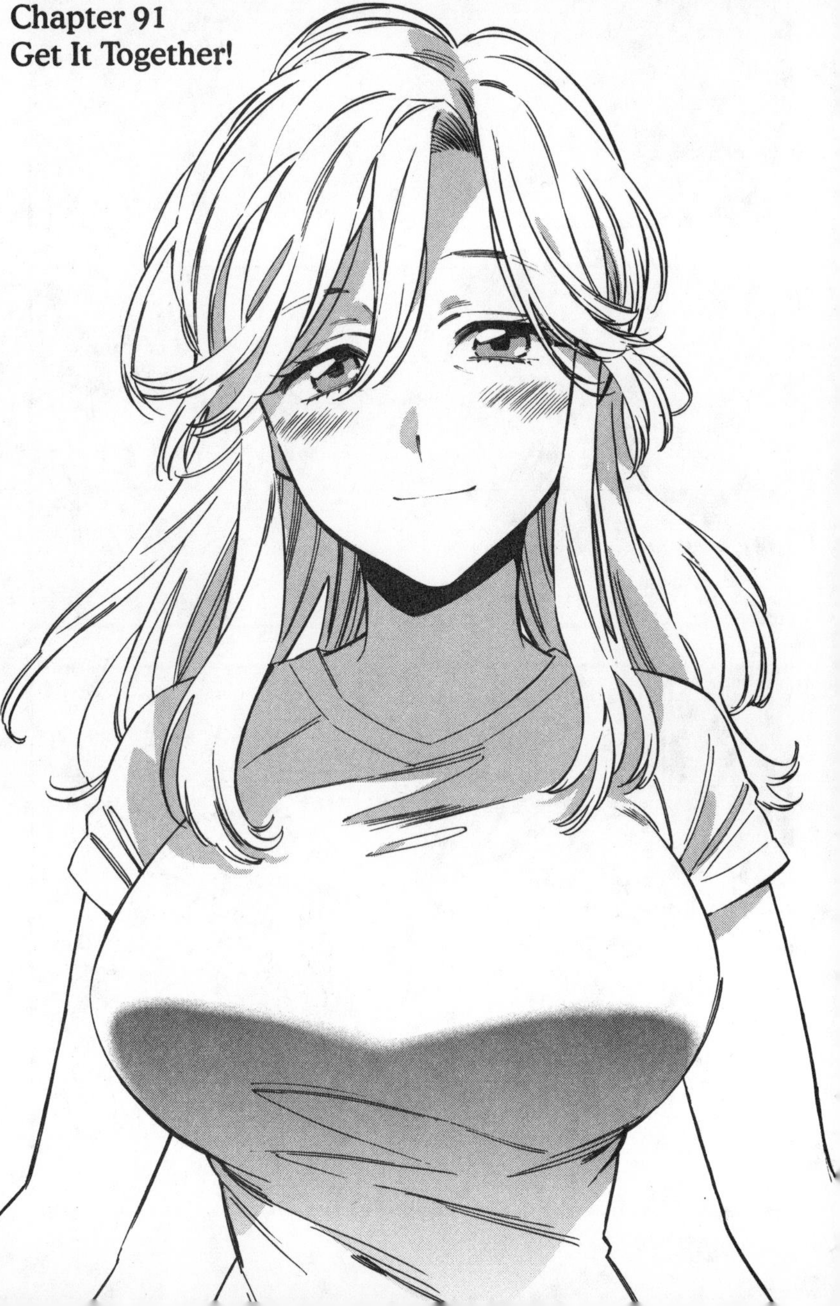

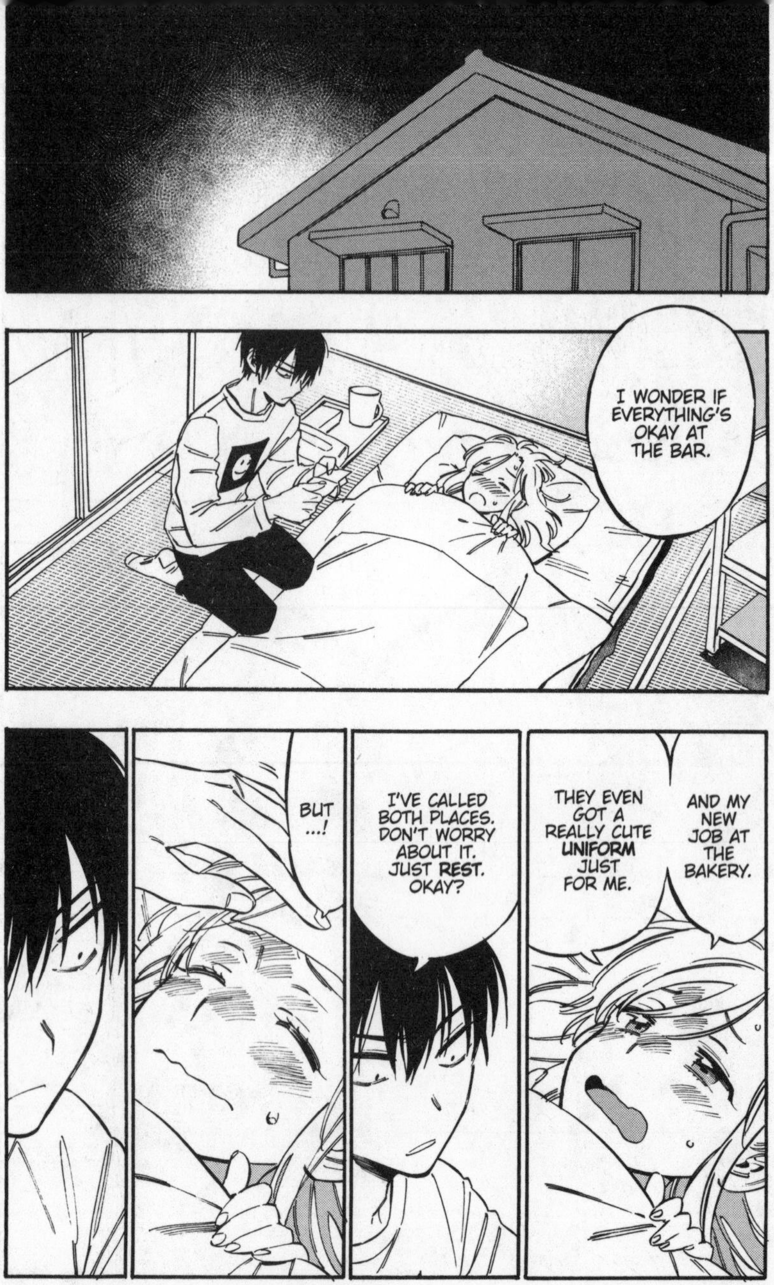
I WONDER IF EVERYTHING'S OKAY AT THE BAR.
AND MY NEW JOB AT THE BAKERY.
THEY EVEN GOT A REALLY CUTE UNIFORM JUST FOR ME.
I'VE CALLED BOTH PLACES. DON'T WORRY ABOUT IT. JUST REST. OKAY?
BUT ...!

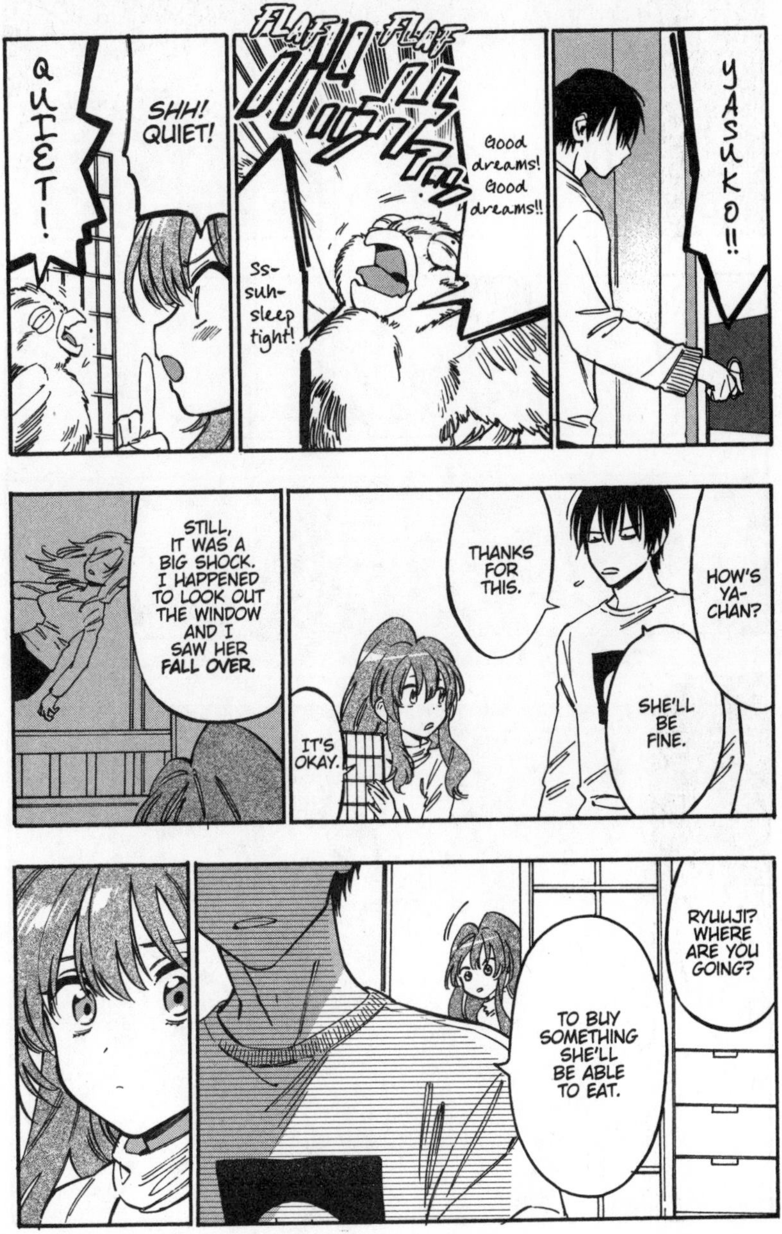
YASUKO!!
FLAP FLAP
Good dreams! Good dreams!!
Ss-suh-sleep tight!
SHH! QUIET!
QUIET!
HOW'S YA-CHAN?
SHE'LL BE FINE.
THANKS FOR THIS.
IT'S OKAY.
STILL, IT WAS A BIG SHOCK. I HAPPENED TO LOOK OUT THE WINDOW AND I SAW HER FALL OVER.
RYUUJI? WHERE ARE YOU GOING?
TO BUY SOMETHING SHE'LL BE ABLE TO EAT.

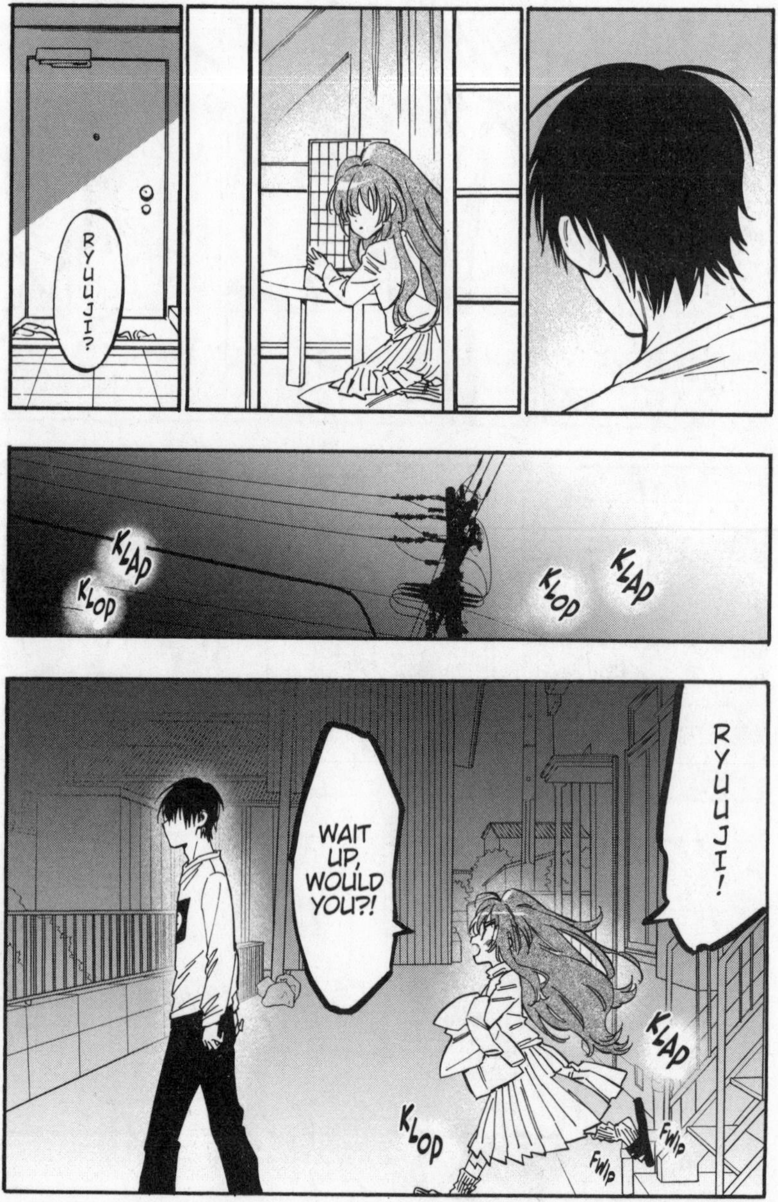
RYUUJI?
KLAP
KLOP
KLAP
KLOP
RYUUJI!
WAIT UP, WOULD YOU?!
KLAP
FWIP
FWIP
KLOP

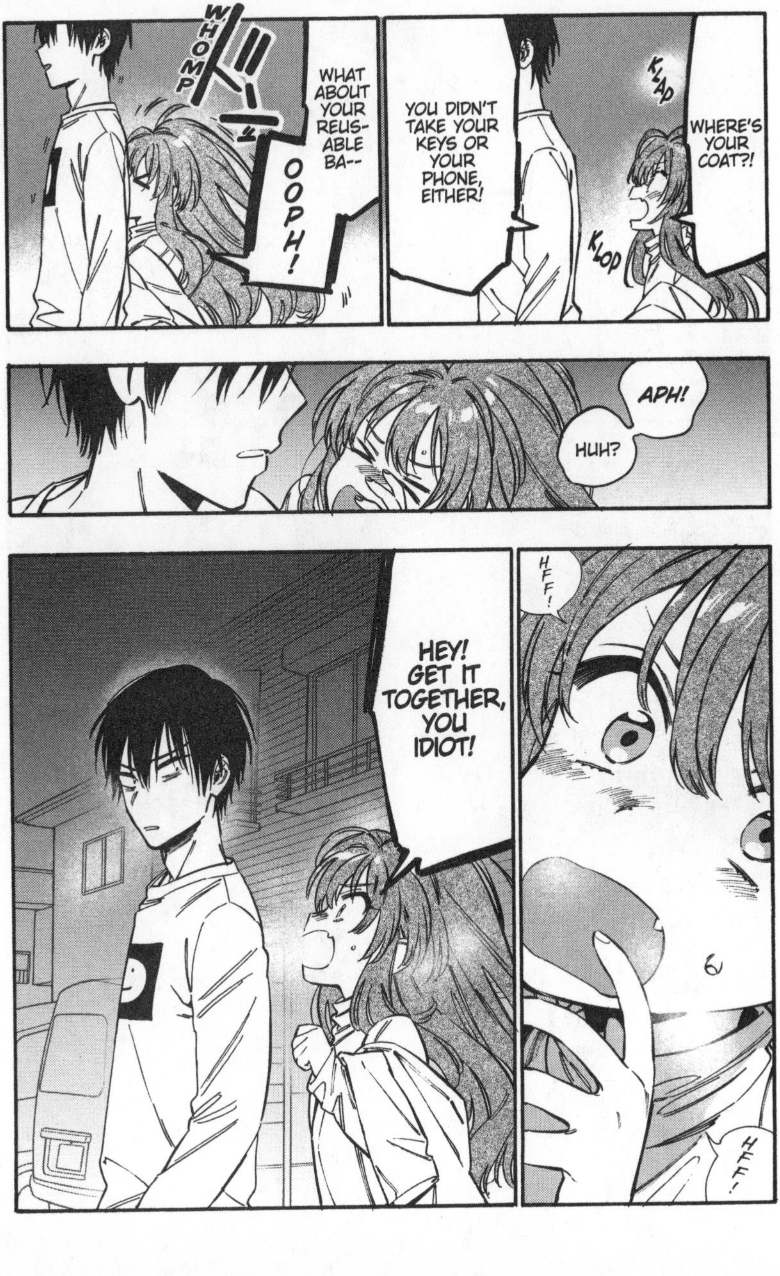
KLAP
WHERE'S YOUR COAT?!
KLOP
YOU DIDN'T TAKE YOUR KEYS OR YOUR PHONE, EITHER!
WHAT ABOUT YOUR REUSABLE BA--
WHOMP
OOPH!
APH!
HUH?
HFF!
HFF!
HEY! GET IT TOGETHER, YOU IDIOT!

GOD!

SHUN

NOW PUT THIS ON!

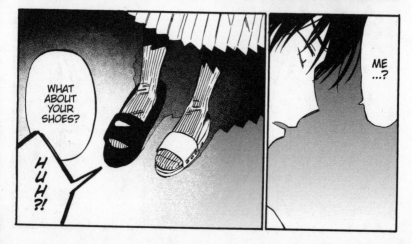

WHAT ABOUT YOUR SHOES?

HUH?!

ME...?

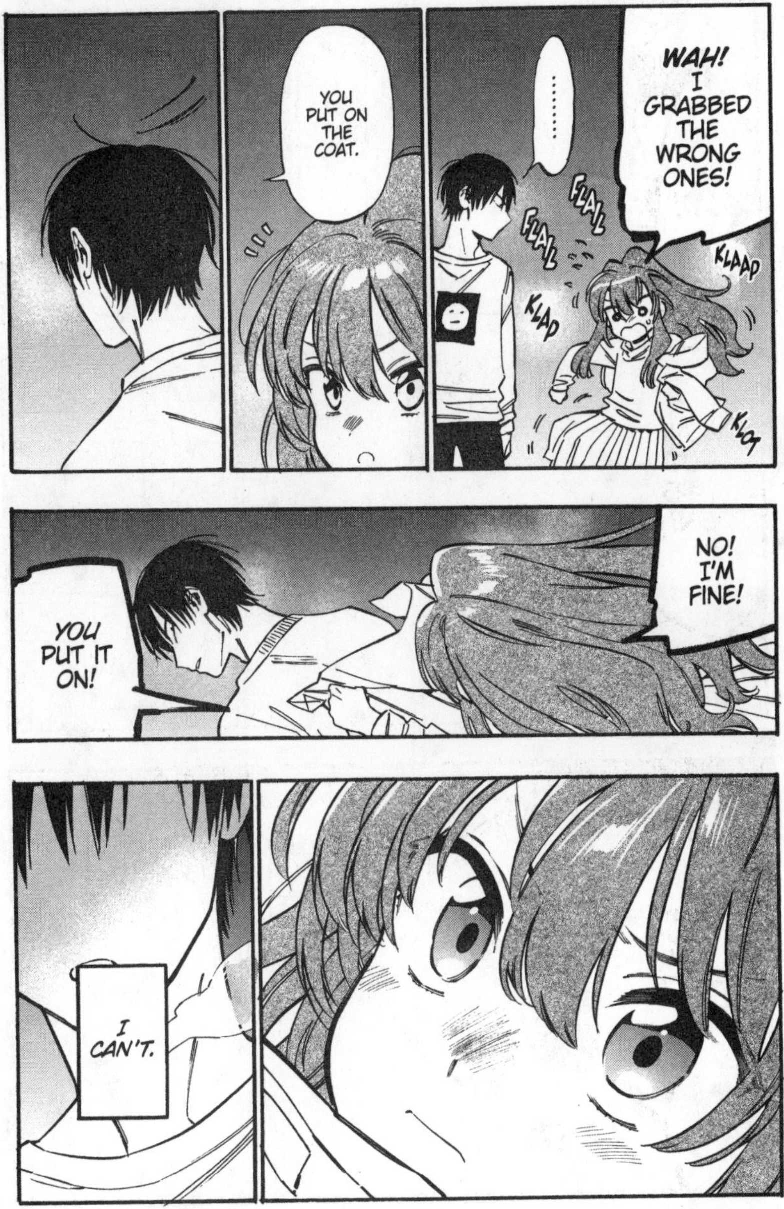
WAH! I GRABBED THE WRONG ONES!
......
FLAIL
FLAIL
KLAAP
KLAP
KLOK
YOU PUT ON THE COAT.
NO! I'M FINE!
YOU PUT IT ON!
I CAN'T.

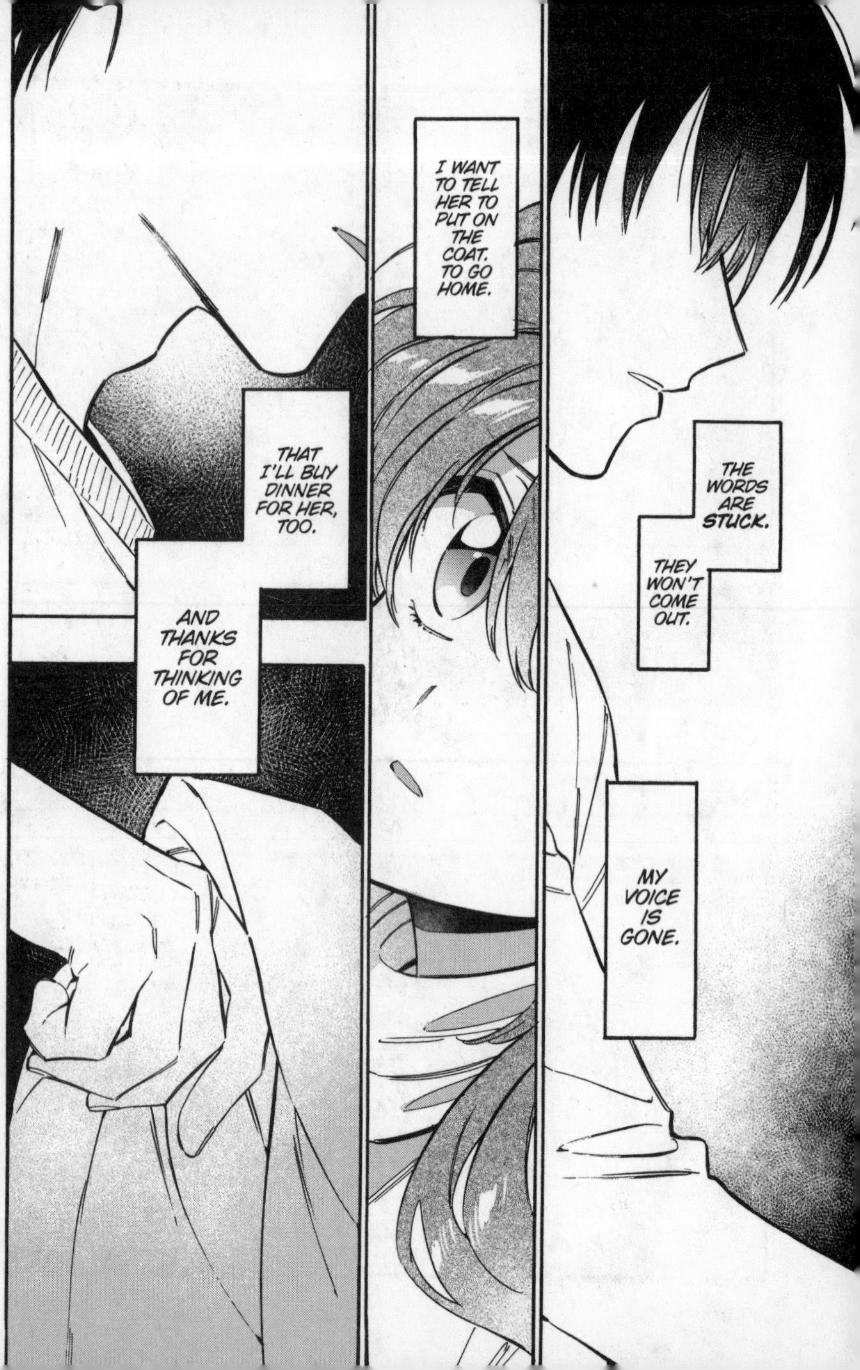
THE WORDS ARE STUCK.
THEY WON'T COME OUT.
MY VOICE IS GONE.
I WANT TO TELL HER TO PUT ON THE COAT. TO GO HOME.
THAT I'LL BUY DINNER FOR HER, TOO.
AND THANKS FOR THINKING OF ME.

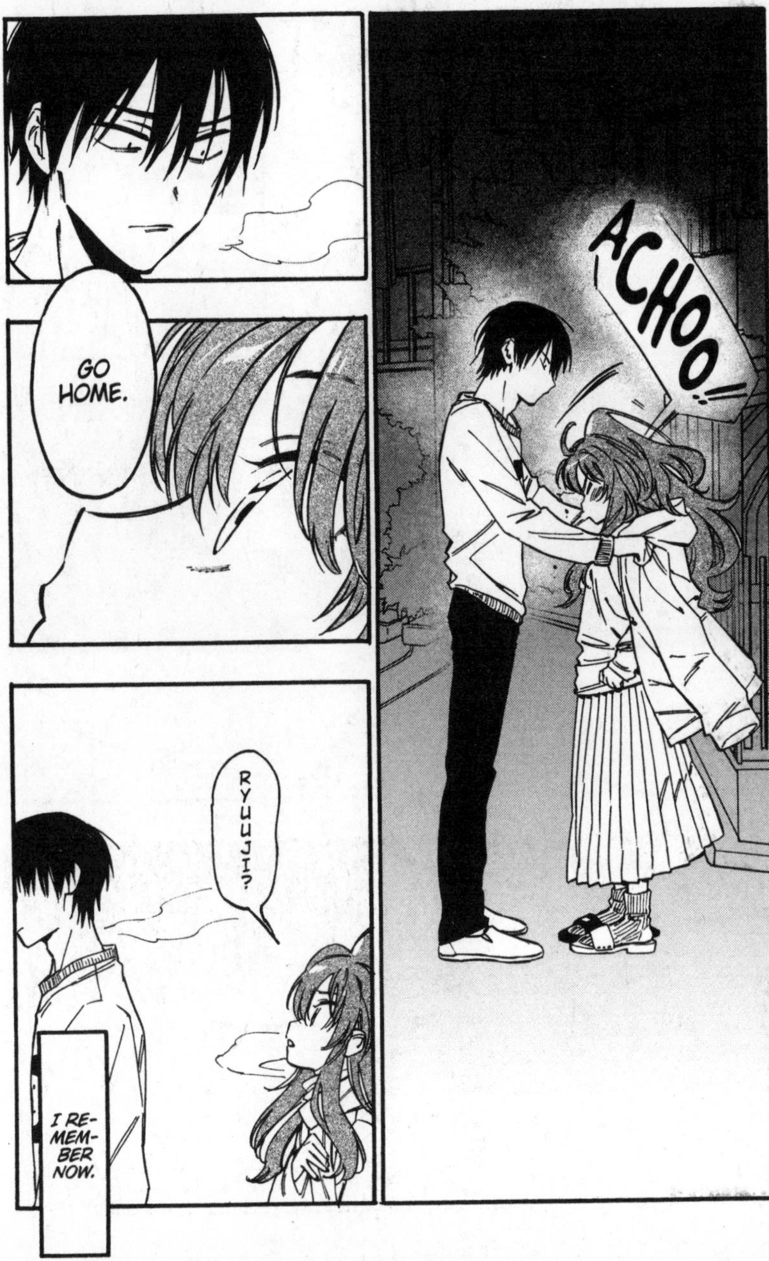
ACHOO
GO HOME.
RYUUJI?
I RE-MEM-BER NOW.

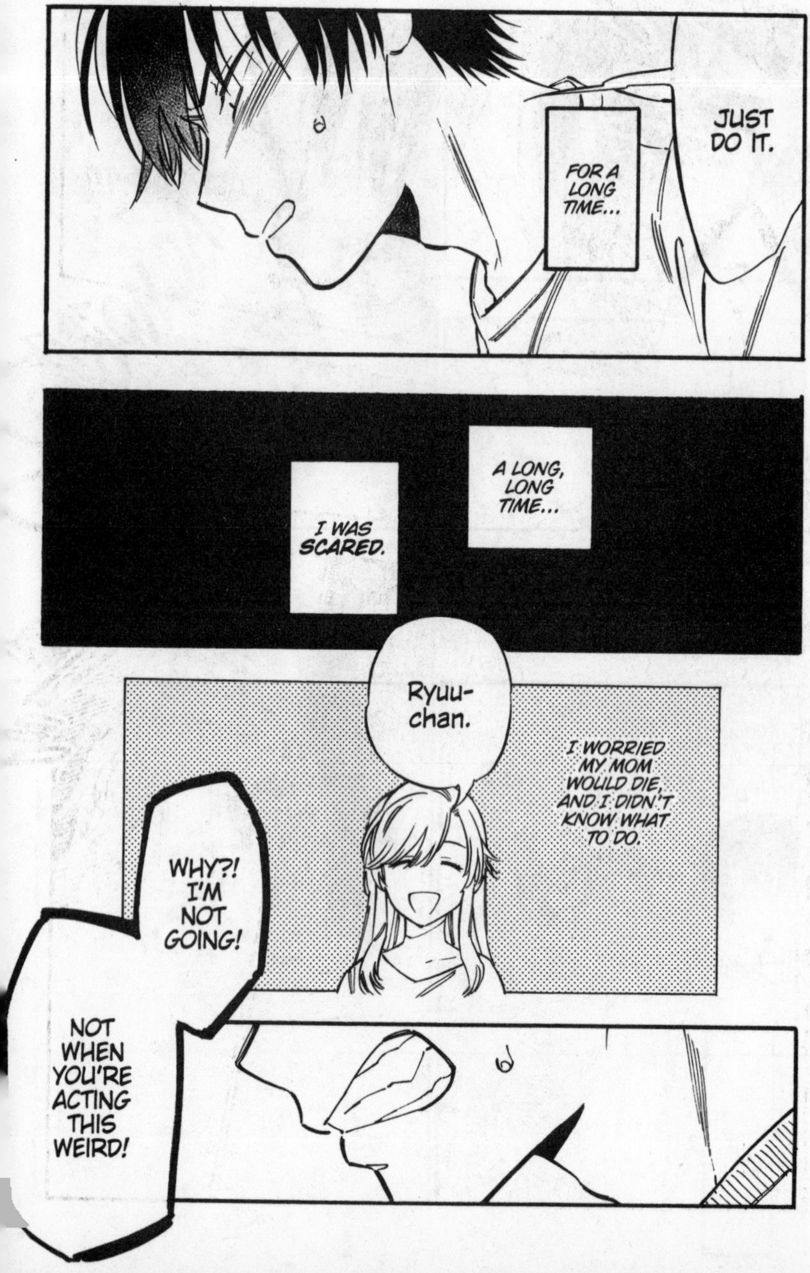
JUST DO IT.
FOR A LONG TIME...
A LONG, LONG TIME...
I WAS SCARED.
Ryuu-chan.
I WORRIED MY MOM WOULD DIE, AND I DIDN'T KNOW WHAT TO DO.
WHY?! I'M NOT GOING! NOT WHEN YOU'RE ACTING THIS WEIRD!

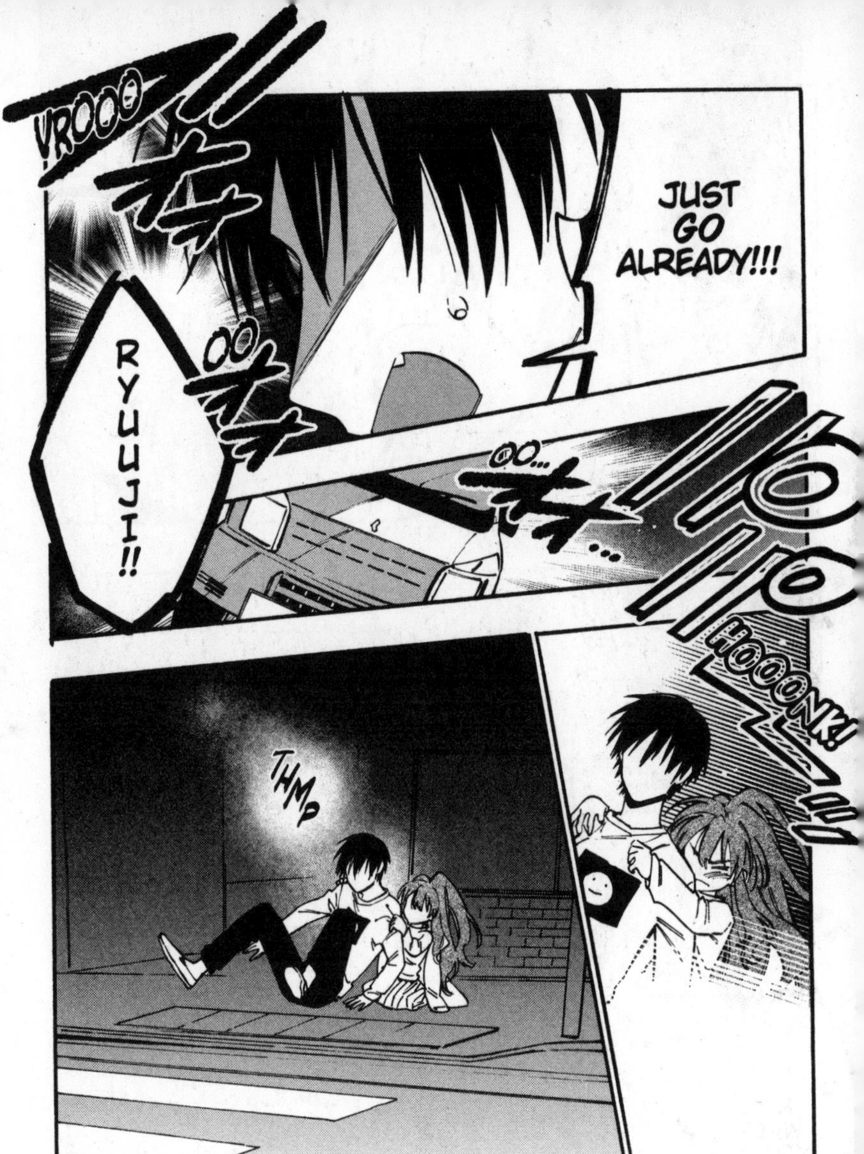
JUST GO ALREADY!!!
VROOO
RYUUJI!!
OO...
OO...
HOOOONK!!
THMP

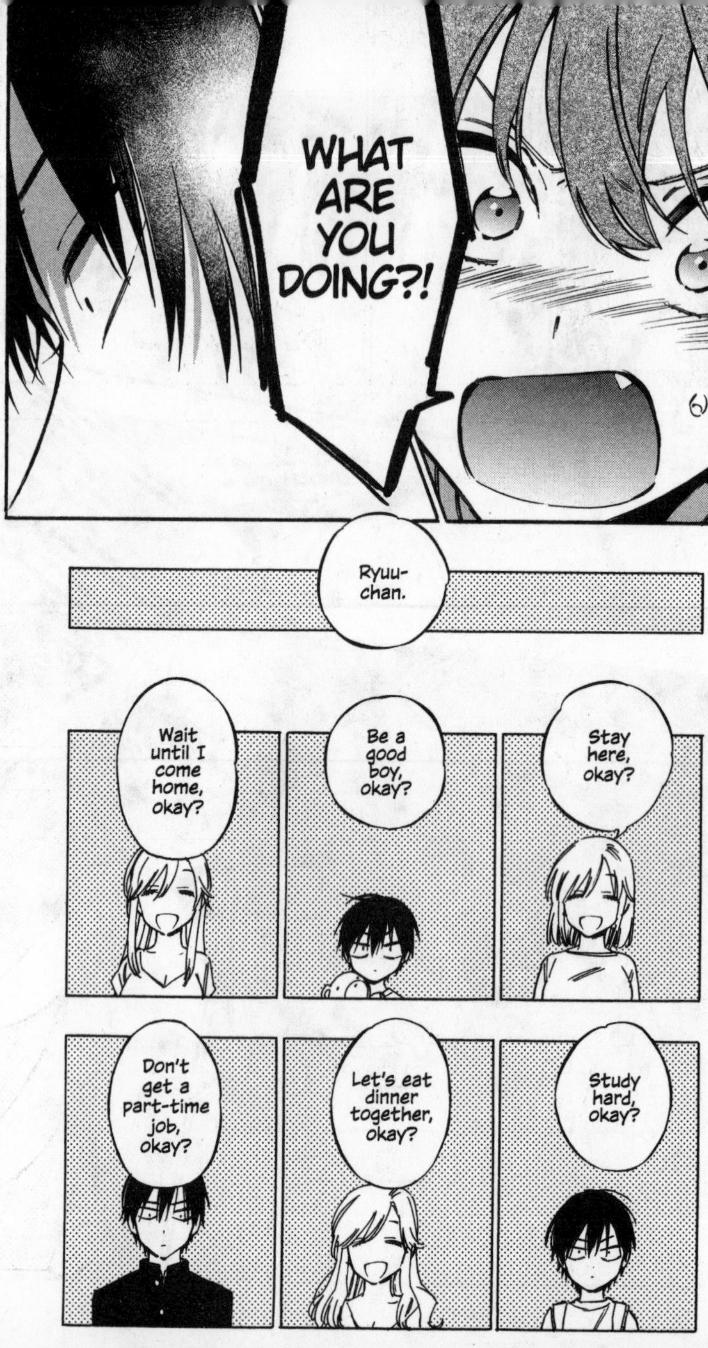
WHAT ARE YOU DOING?!
Ryuu-chan.
Stay here, okay?
Be a good boy, okay?
Wait until I come home, okay?
Study hard, okay?
Let's eat dinner together, okay?
Don't get a part-time job, okay?

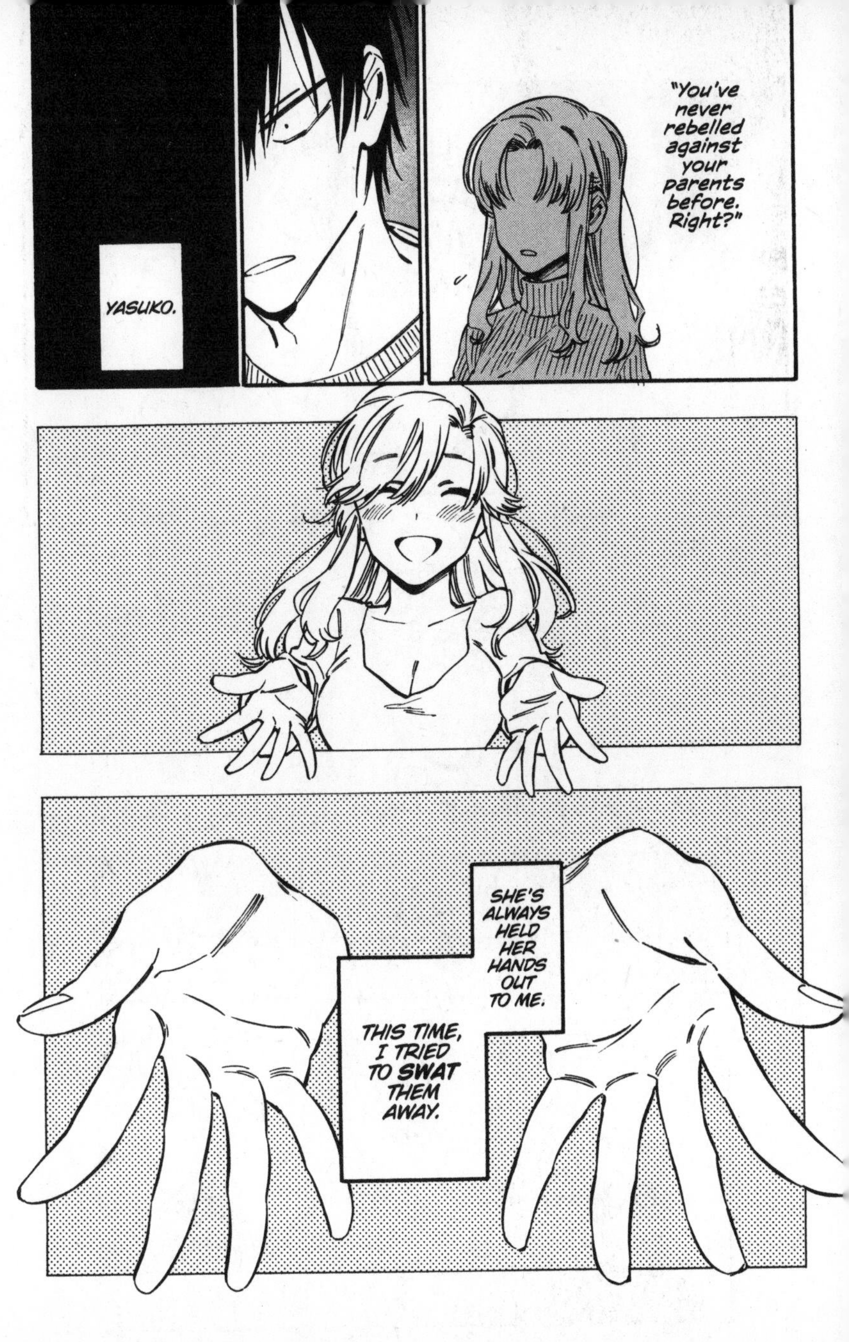
"You've never rebelled against your parents before. Right?"
YASUKO.
SHE'S ALWAYS HELD HER HANDS OUT TO ME.
THIS TIME, I TRIED TO **SWAT** THEM AWAY.

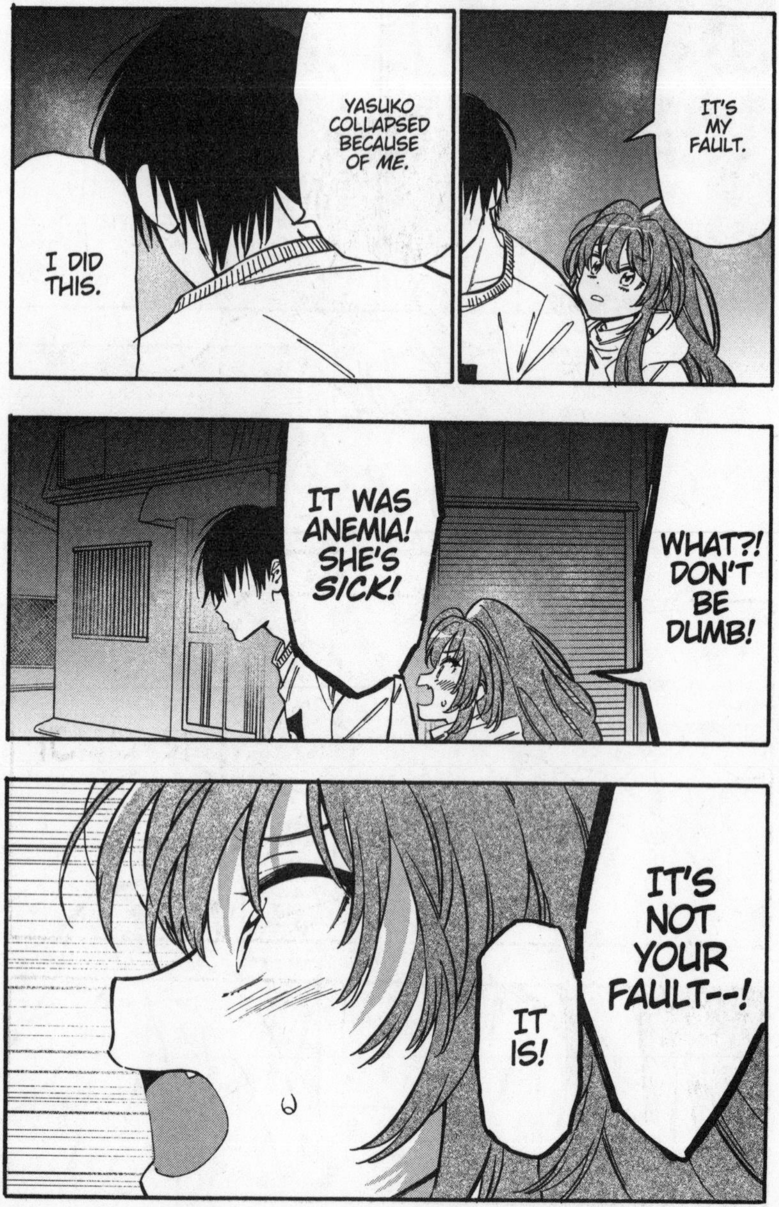
IT'S MY FAULT.
YASUKO COLLAPSED BECAUSE OF ME.
I DID THIS.
WHAT?! DON'T BE DUMB!
IT WAS ANEMIA! SHE'S SICK!
IT'S NOT YOUR FAULT--!
IT IS!

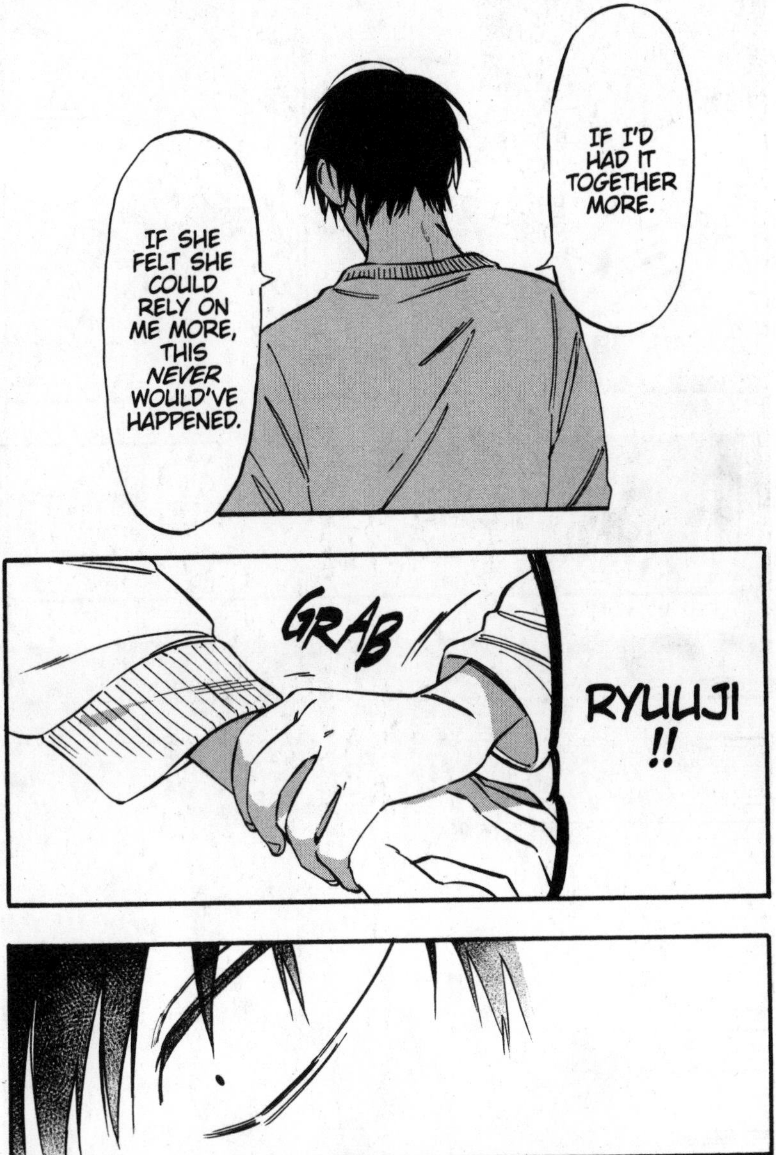
IF I'D HAD IT TOGETHER MORE.
IF SHE FELT SHE COULD RELY ON ME MORE, THIS *NEVER* WOULD'VE HAPPENED.
RYUUJI!!
GRAB

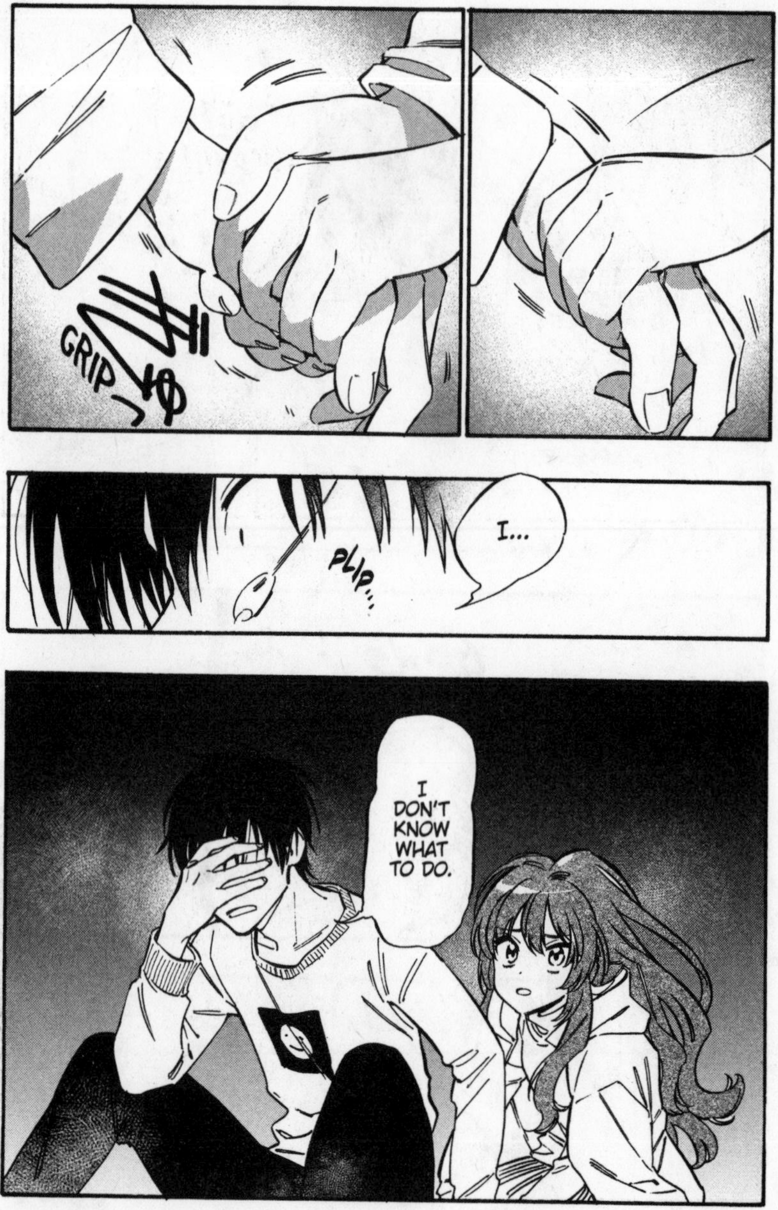
GRIP
I...
PLIP...
I DON'T KNOW WHAT TO DO.

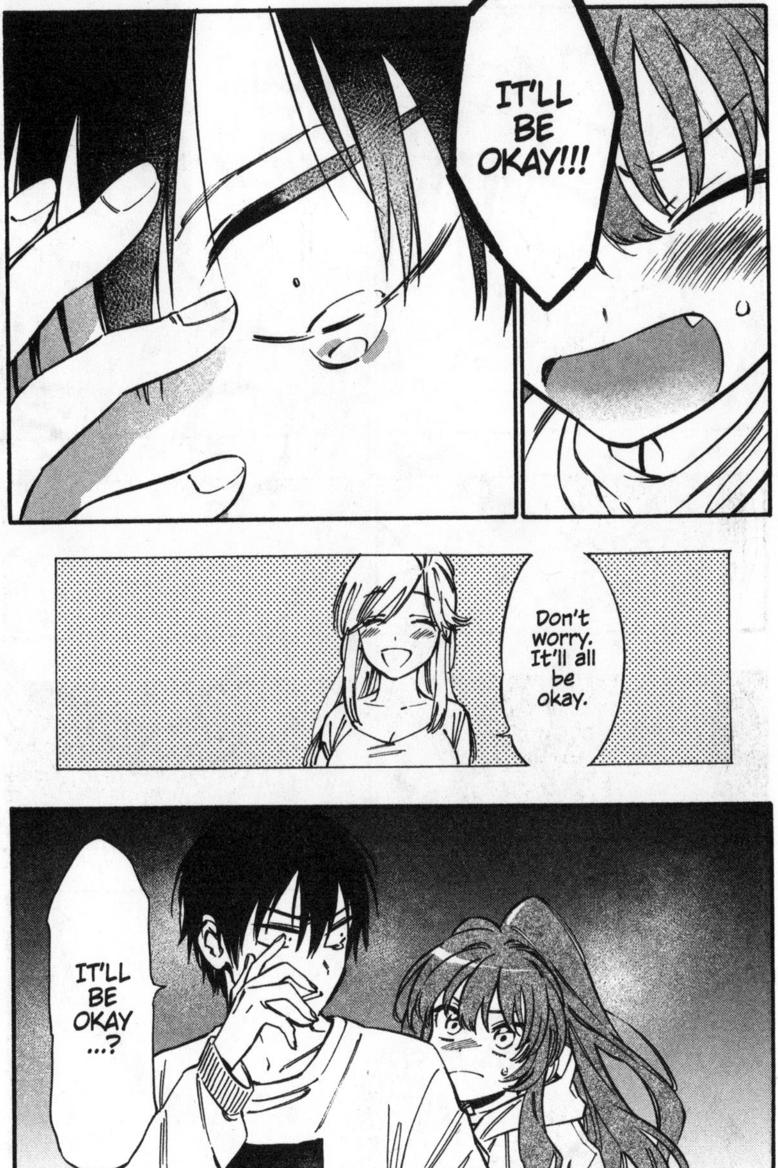
IT'LL BE OKAY!!!
Don't worry. It'll all be okay.
IT'LL BE OKAY ...?

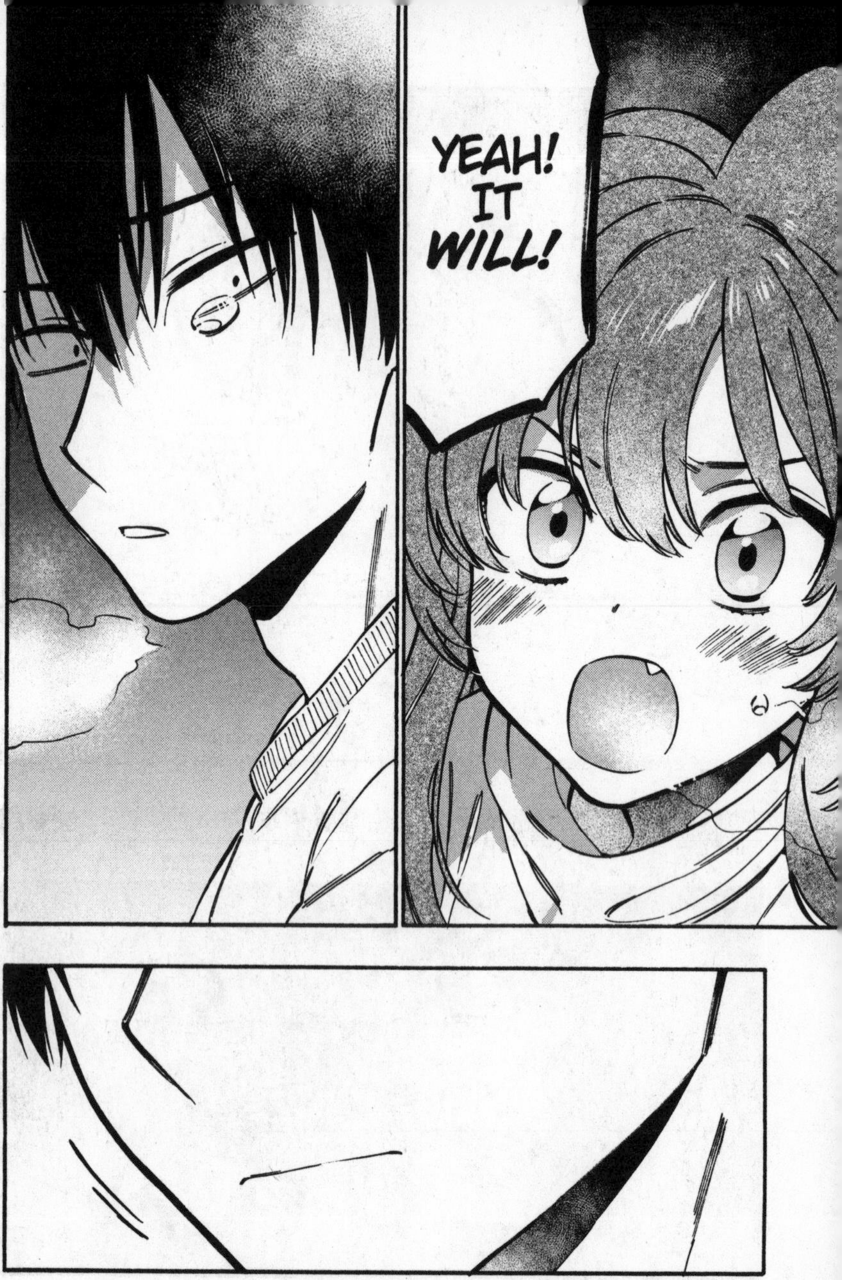
YEAH! IT WILL!

RYUUJI? LET'S GO HOME.

SWUF

NOT YET.

THERE'S SOMEWHERE I HAVE TO GO.

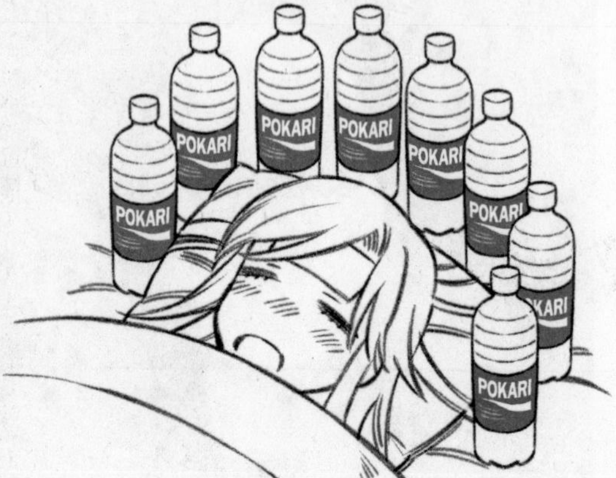
POKARI

# Chapter 92
# My First Part-Time Job

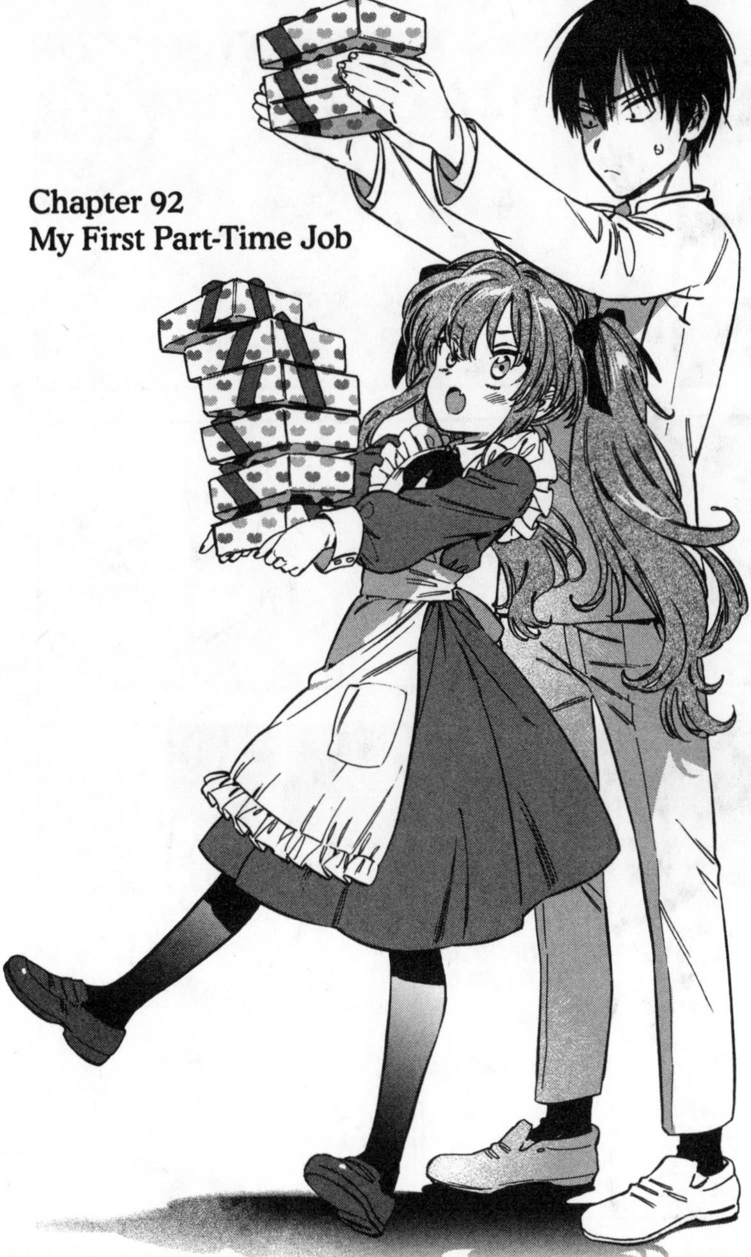

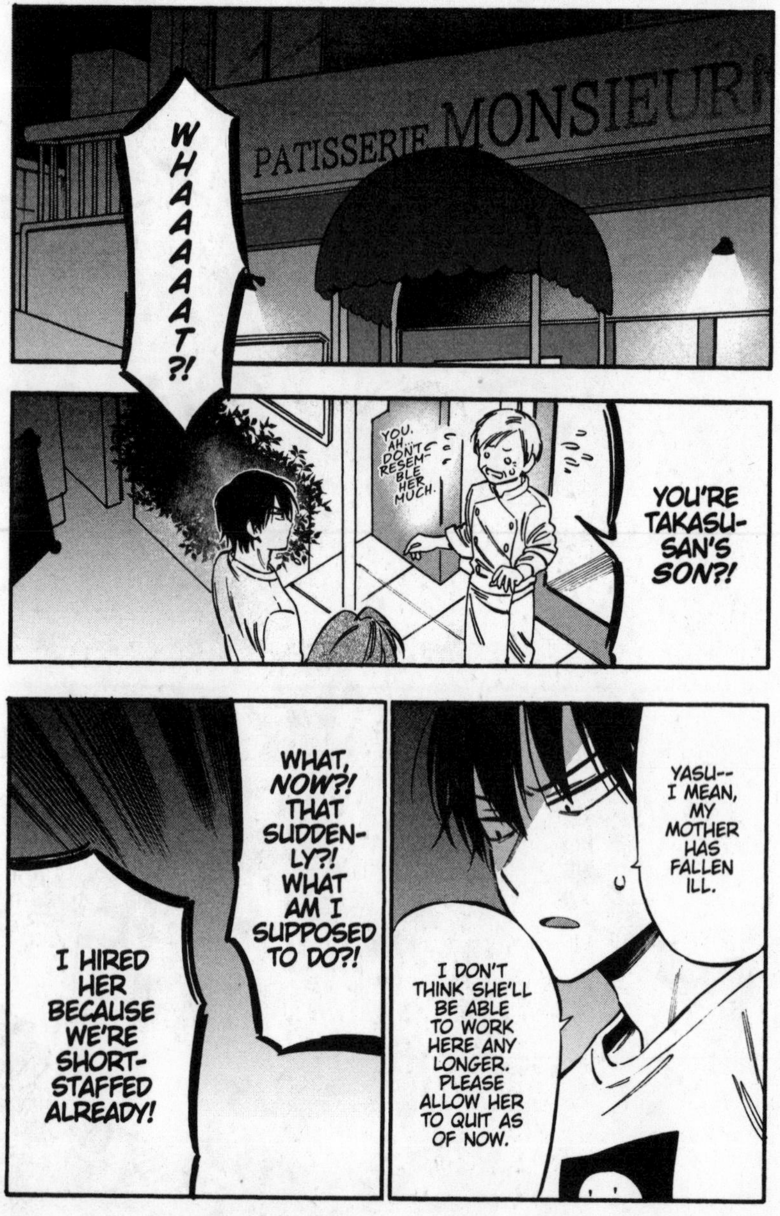
PATISSERIE MONSIEUR
WHAAAAAAT?!
YOU'RE TAKASU-SAN'S SON?!
YOU. AH... DON'T RESEMBLE HER MUCH.
YASU-- I MEAN, MY MOTHER HAS FALLEN ILL.
I DON'T THINK SHE'LL BE ABLE TO WORK HERE ANY LONGER. PLEASE ALLOW HER TO QUIT AS OF NOW.
WHAT, NOW?! THAT SUDDENLY?! WHAT AM I SUPPOSED TO DO?!
I HIRED HER BECAUSE WE'RE SHORT-STAFFED ALREADY!

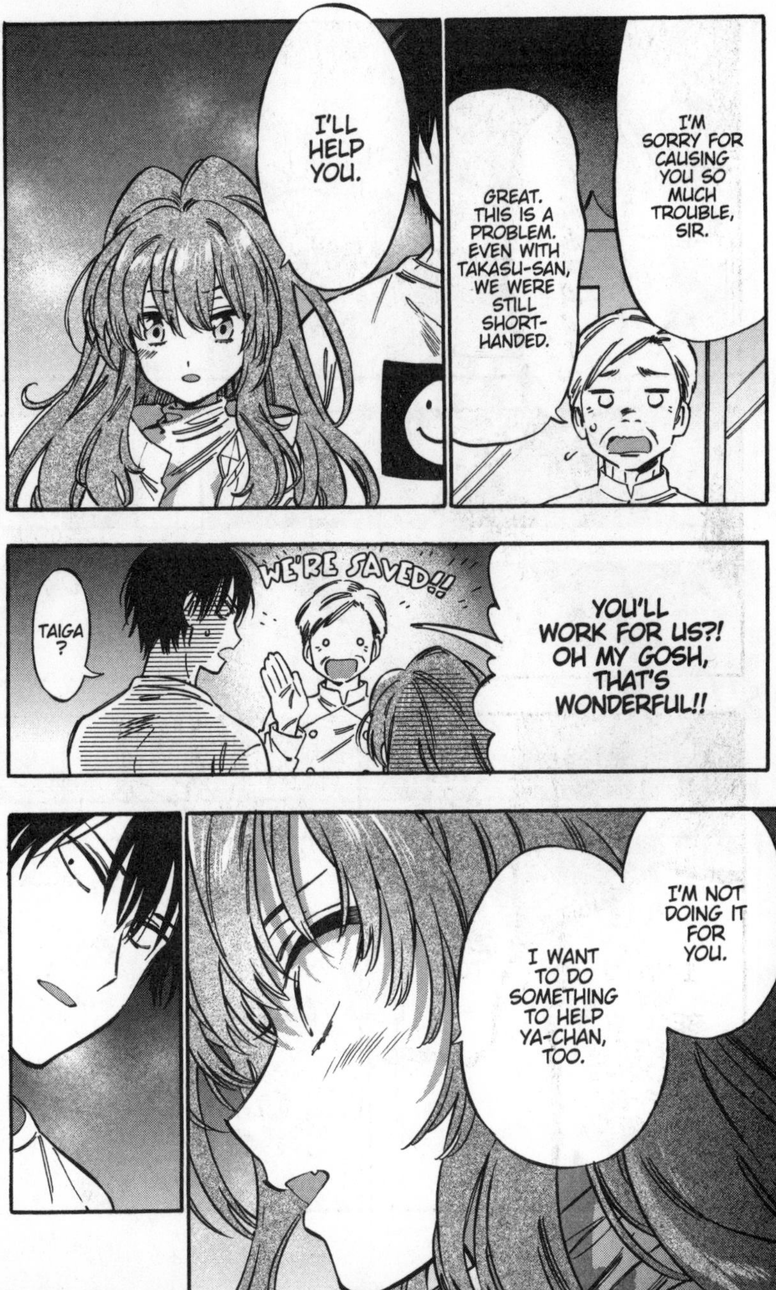
I'M SORRY FOR CAUSING YOU SO MUCH TROUBLE, SIR.
GREAT. THIS IS A PROBLEM. EVEN WITH TAKASU-SAN, WE WERE STILL SHORT-HANDED.
I'LL HELP YOU.
YOU'LL WORK FOR US?! OH MY GOSH, THAT'S WONDERFUL!!
WE'RE SAVED!!
TAIGA?
I'M NOT DOING IT FOR YOU.
I WANT TO DO SOMETHING TO HELP YA-CHAN, TOO.

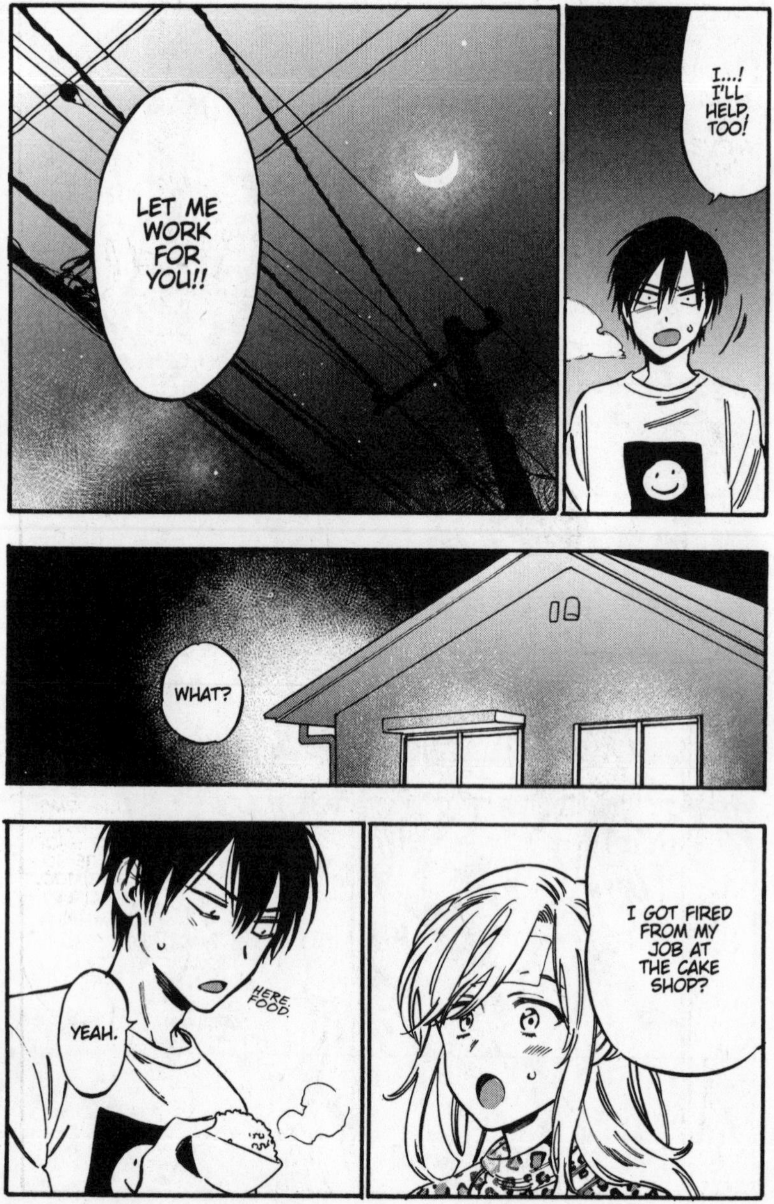
I...! I'LL HELP, TOO!
LET ME WORK FOR YOU!!
WHAT?
I GOT FIRED FROM MY JOB AT THE CAKE SHOP?
HERE. FOOD.
YEAH.

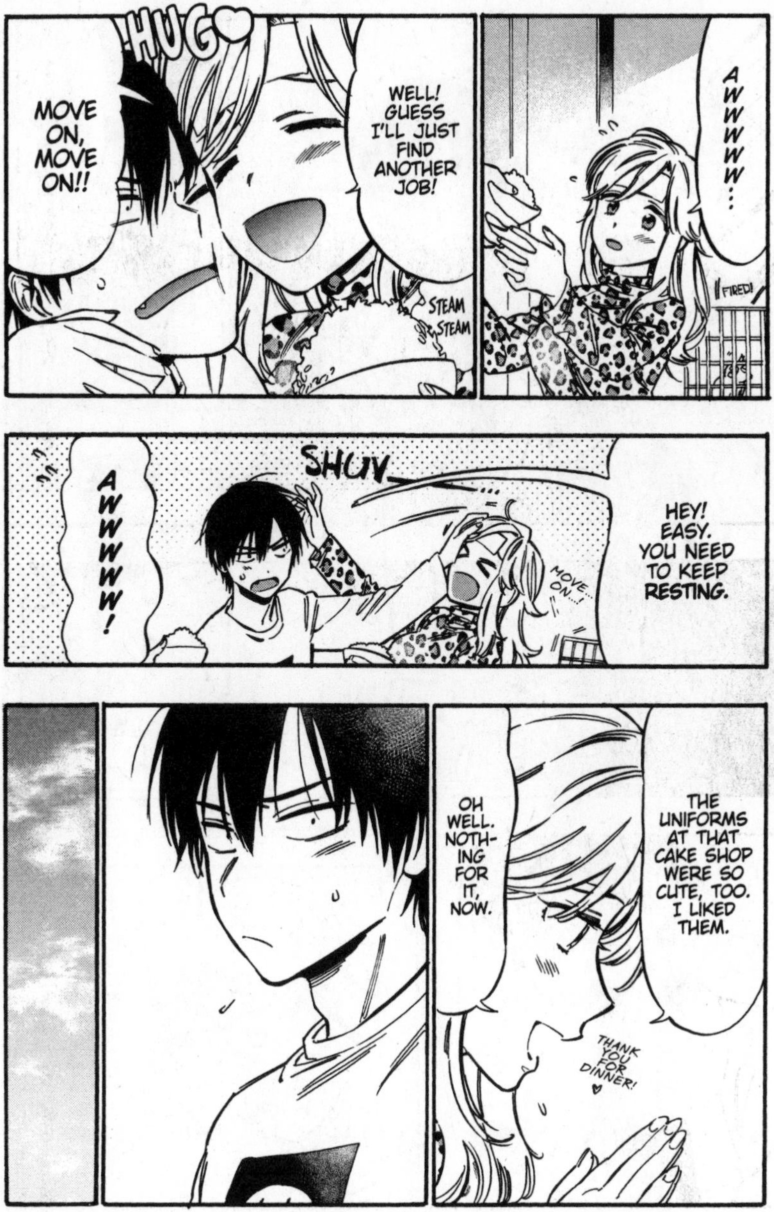
AWWWWW...
FIRED!
WELL! GUESS I'LL JUST FIND ANOTHER JOB!
HUG
MOVE ON, MOVE ON!!
STEAM STEAM
HEY! EASY. YOU NEED TO KEEP RESTING.
SHUV
MOVE ON...!
AWWWWWW!
THE UNIFORMS AT THAT CAKE SHOP WERE SO CUTE, TOO. I LIKED THEM.
OH WELL. NOTHING FOR IT, NOW.
THANK YOU FOR DINNER! ♥

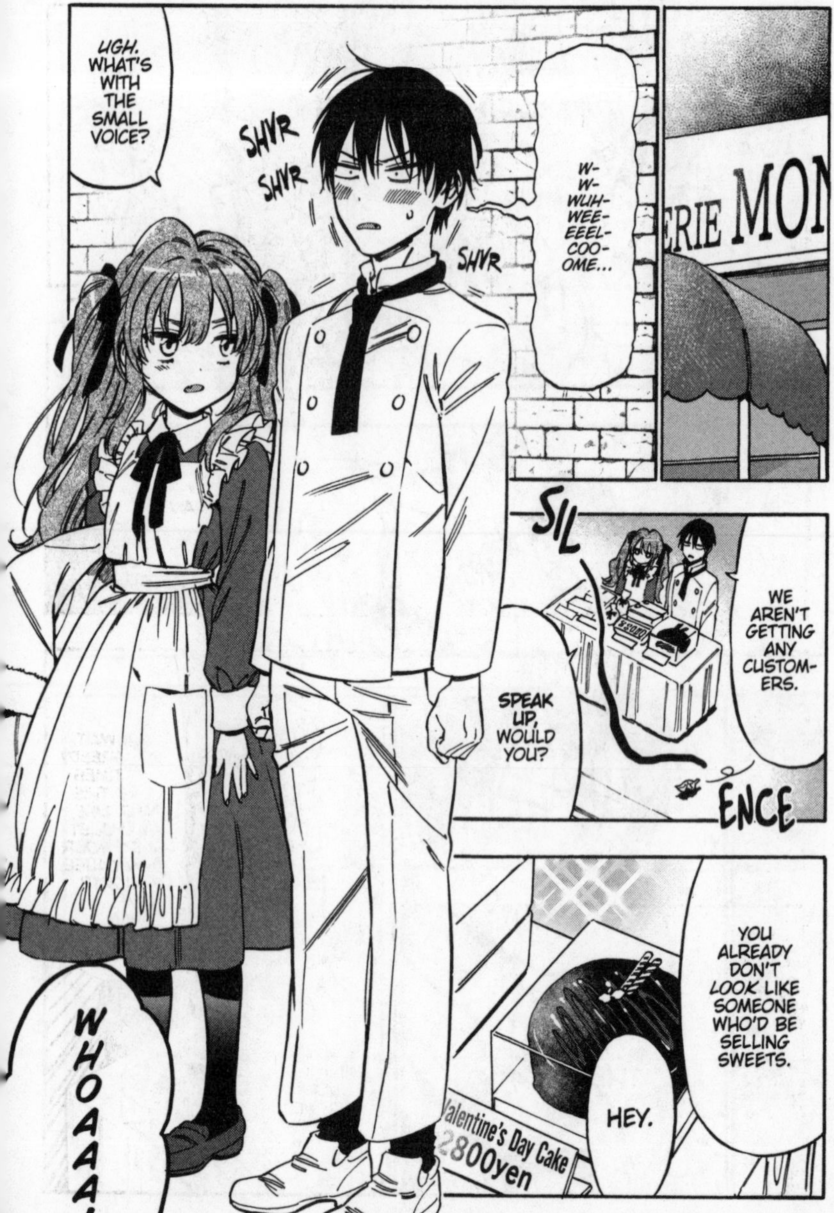

ERIE MON
W-W-WUH-WEEEL-COO-OME...
SHVR
SHVR
SHVR
UGH. WHAT'S WITH THE SMALL VOICE?
SPEAK UP, WOULD YOU?
WE AREN'T GETTING ANY CUSTOMERS.
SILENCE
HEY.
YOU ALREADY DON'T LOOK LIKE SOMEONE WHO'D BE SELLING SWEETS.
Valentine's Day Cake 2800yen
WHOAAA!

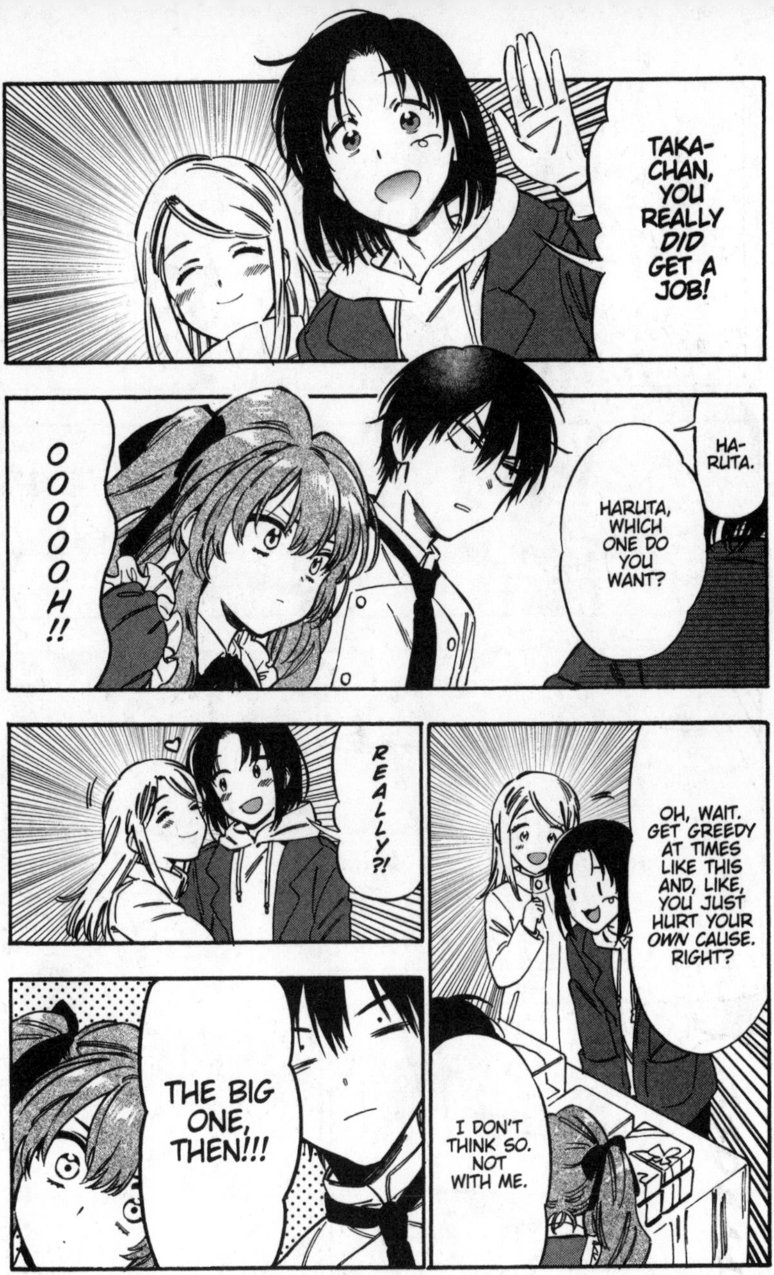
TAKA-CHAN, YOU REALLY *DID* GET A JOB!
HA-RUTA.
HARUTA, WHICH ONE DO YOU WANT?
OOOOOOOH!!
OH, WAIT. GET GREEDY AT TIMES LIKE THIS AND, LIKE, YOU JUST HURT YOUR *OWN* CAUSE. RIGHT?
I DON'T THINK SO. NOT WITH ME.
REALLY?!
THE BIG ONE, THEN!!!

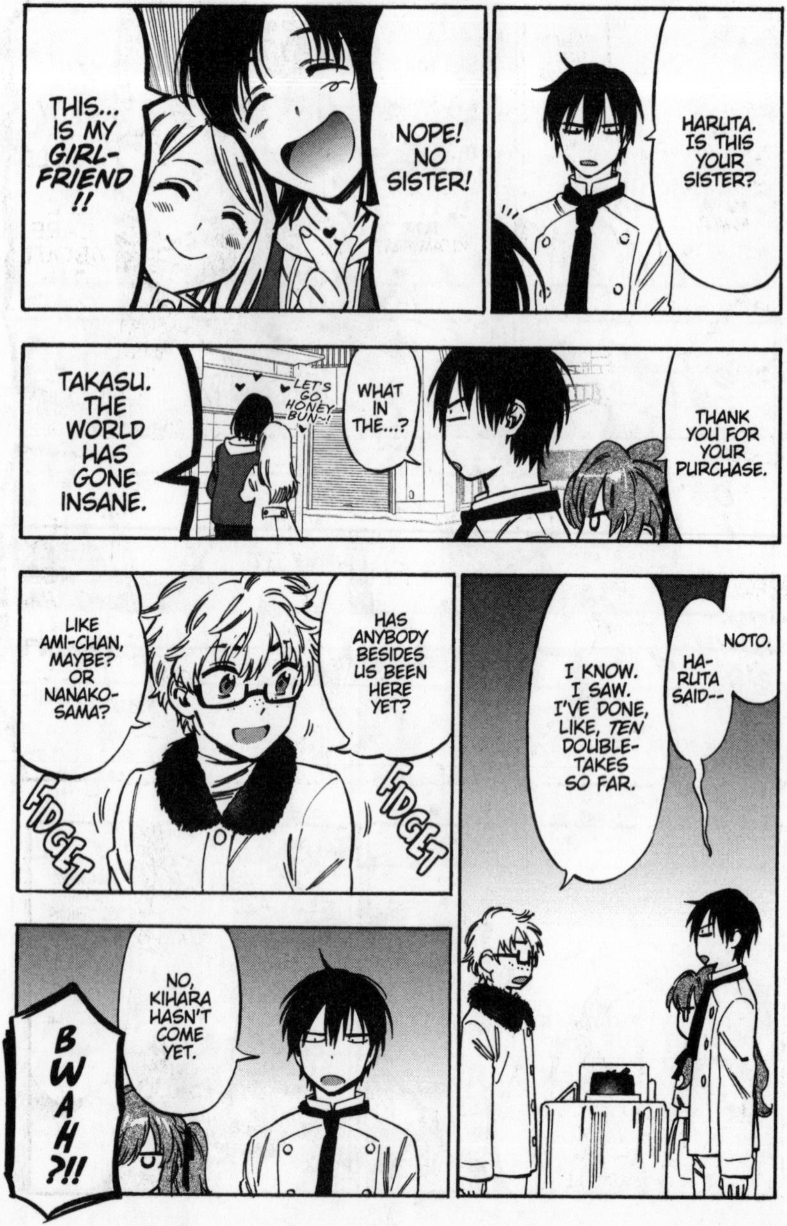
HARUTA. IS THIS YOUR SISTER?
NOPE! NO SISTER!
THIS... IS MY *GIRLFRIEND*!!
THANK YOU FOR YOUR PURCHASE.
WHAT IN THE...?
LET'S GO HONEY BUN~!
TAKASU. THE WORLD HAS GONE INSANE.
NOTO.
HARUTA SAID--
I KNOW. I SAW. I'VE DONE, LIKE, *TEN* DOUBLE-TAKES SO FAR.
HAS ANYBODY BESIDES US BEEN HERE YET?
FIDGET
LIKE AMI-CHAN, MAYBE? OR NANAKO-SAMA?
FIDGET
NO, KIHARA HASN'T COME YET.
BWAH?!!

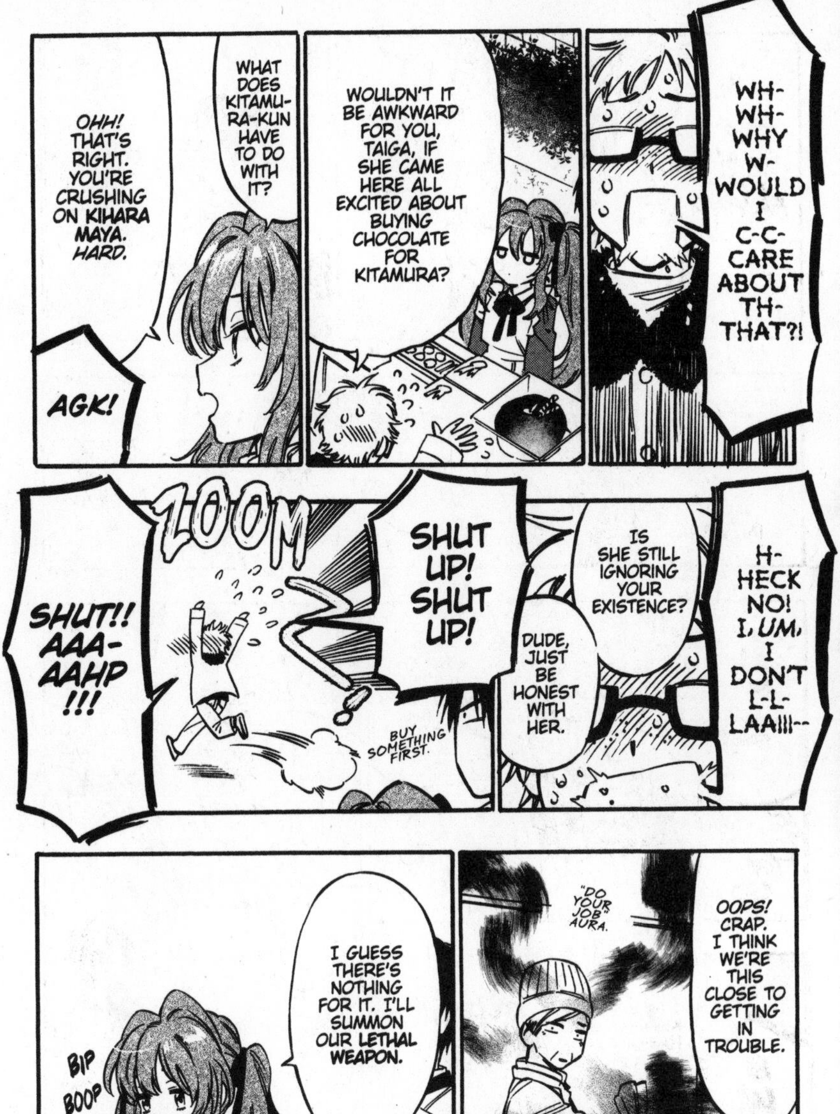
WH-WH-WHY W-WOULD I C-C-CARE ABOUT TH-THAT?!
WOULDN'T IT BE AWKWARD FOR YOU, TAIGA, IF SHE CAME HERE ALL EXCITED ABOUT BUYING CHOCOLATE FOR KITAMURA?
WHAT DOES KITAMURA-KUN HAVE TO DO WITH IT?
OHH! THAT'S RIGHT. YOU'RE CRUSHING ON KIHARA MAYA. HARD.
AGK!
H-HECK NO! I, UM, I DON'T L-L-LAAIII--
IS SHE STILL IGNORING YOUR EXISTENCE?
DUDE, JUST BE HONEST WITH HER.
SHUT UP! SHUT UP!
ZOOM
BUY SOMETHING FIRST.
SHUT!! AAA-AAHP!!!
OOPS! CRAP. I THINK WE'RE THIS CLOSE TO GETTING IN TROUBLE.
"DO YOUR JOB" AURA.
I GUESS THERE'S NOTHING FOR IT. I'LL SUMMON OUR LETHAL WEAPON.
BIP BOOP BEEP

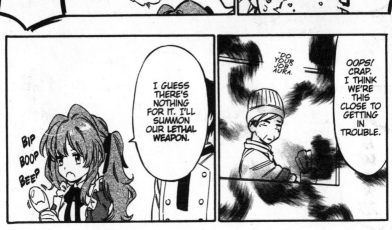

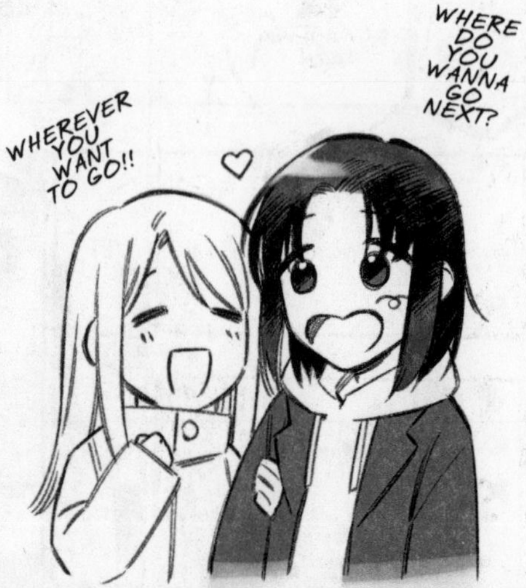
WHERE DO YOU WANNA GO NEXT?
WHEREVER YOU WANT TO GO!!

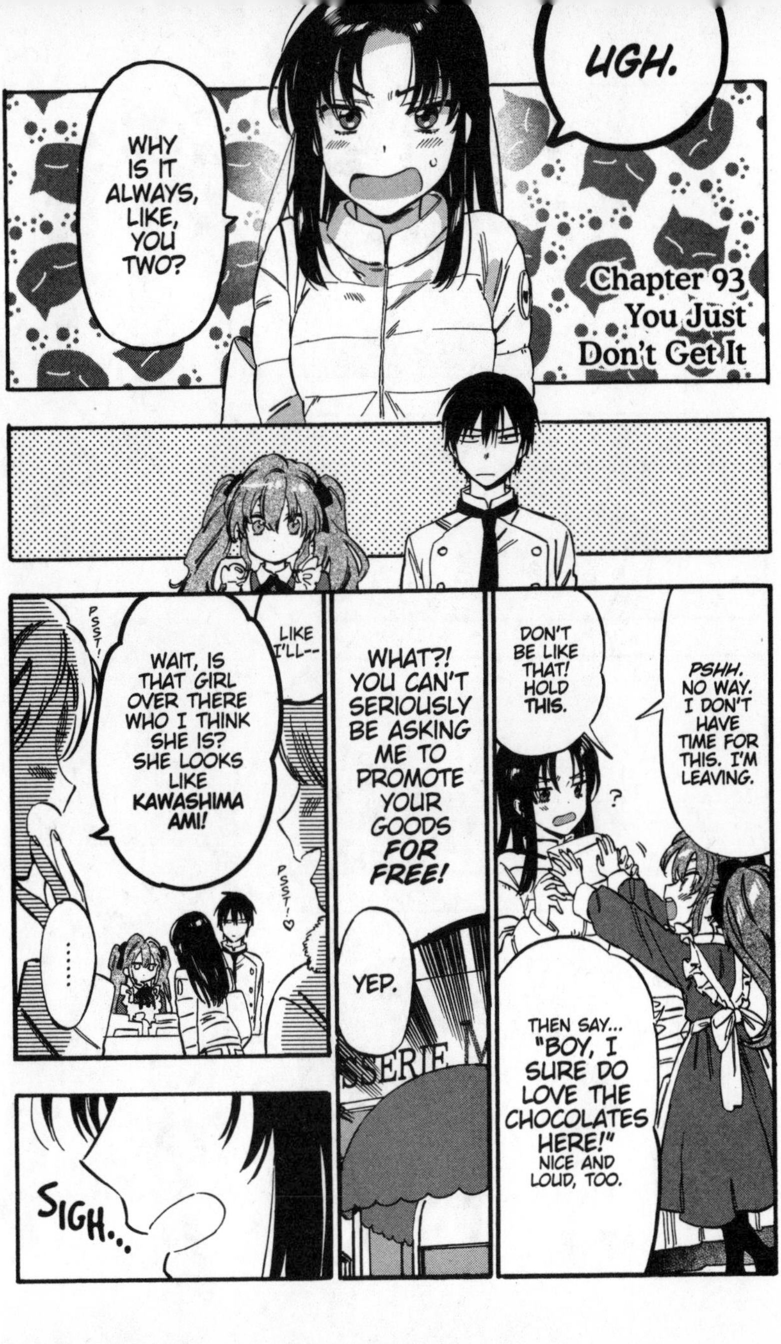
UGH.
WHY IS IT ALWAYS, LIKE, YOU TWO?
Chapter 93
You Just Don't Get It
PSHH. NO WAY. I DON'T HAVE TIME FOR THIS. I'M LEAVING.
DON'T BE LIKE THAT! HOLD THIS.
?
THEN SAY... "BOY, I SURE DO LOVE THE CHOCOLATES HERE!" NICE AND LOUD, TOO.
WHAT?! YOU CAN'T SERIOUSLY BE ASKING ME TO PROMOTE YOUR GOODS FOR FREE!
YEP.
SSERIE M
LIKE I'LL--
WAIT, IS THAT GIRL OVER THERE WHO I THINK SHE IS? SHE LOOKS LIKE KAWASHIMA AMI!
PSST!
PSST!♡
......
SIGH...

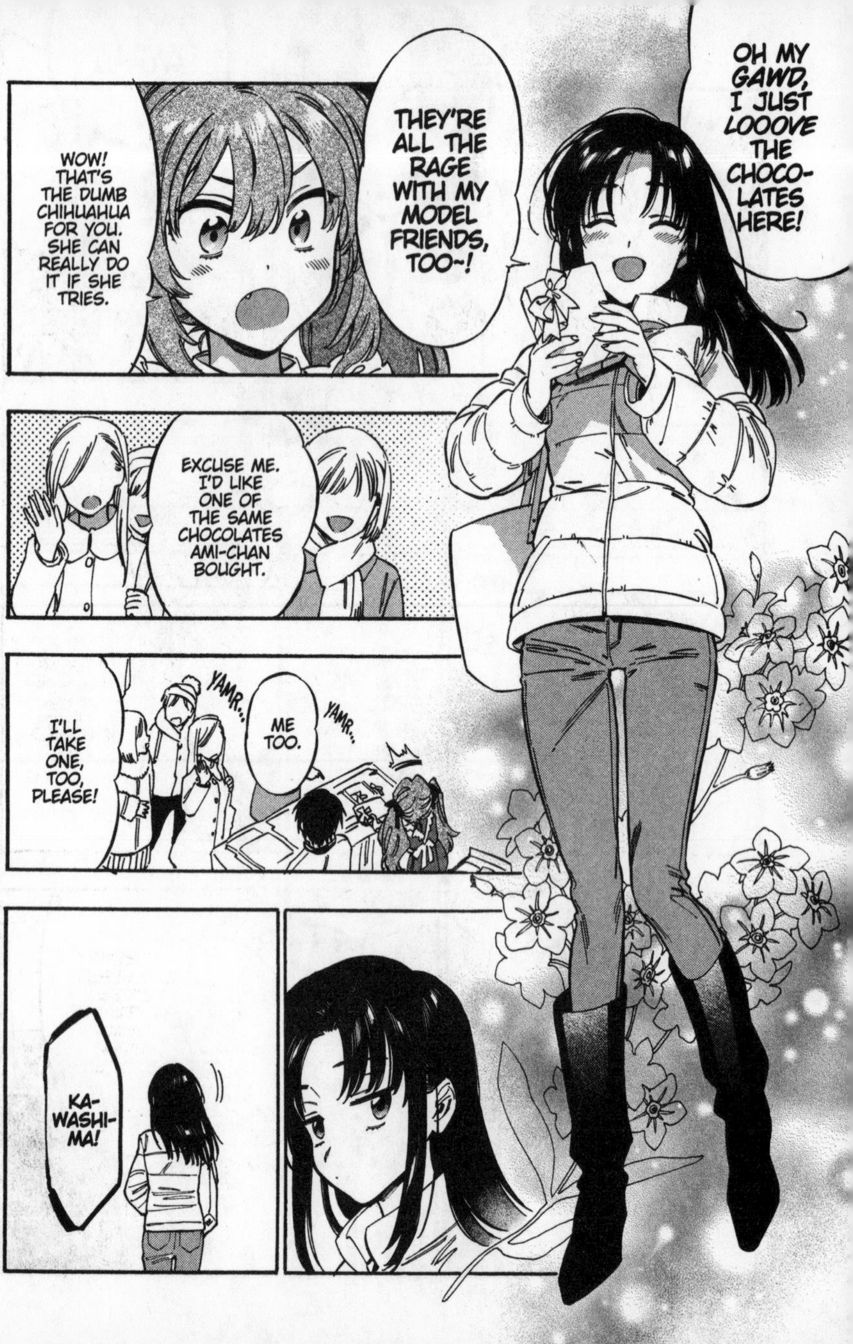
OH MY GAWD, I JUST LOOOVE THE CHOCO-LATES HERE!
THEY'RE ALL THE RAGE WITH MY MODEL FRIENDS, TOO~!
WOW! THAT'S THE DUMB CHIHUAHUA FOR YOU. SHE CAN REALLY DO IT IF SHE TRIES.
EXCUSE ME. I'D LIKE ONE OF THE SAME CHOCOLATES AMI-CHAN BOUGHT.
YAMR...
YAMR...
ME TOO.
I'LL TAKE ONE, TOO, PLEASE!
KA-WASHI-MA!

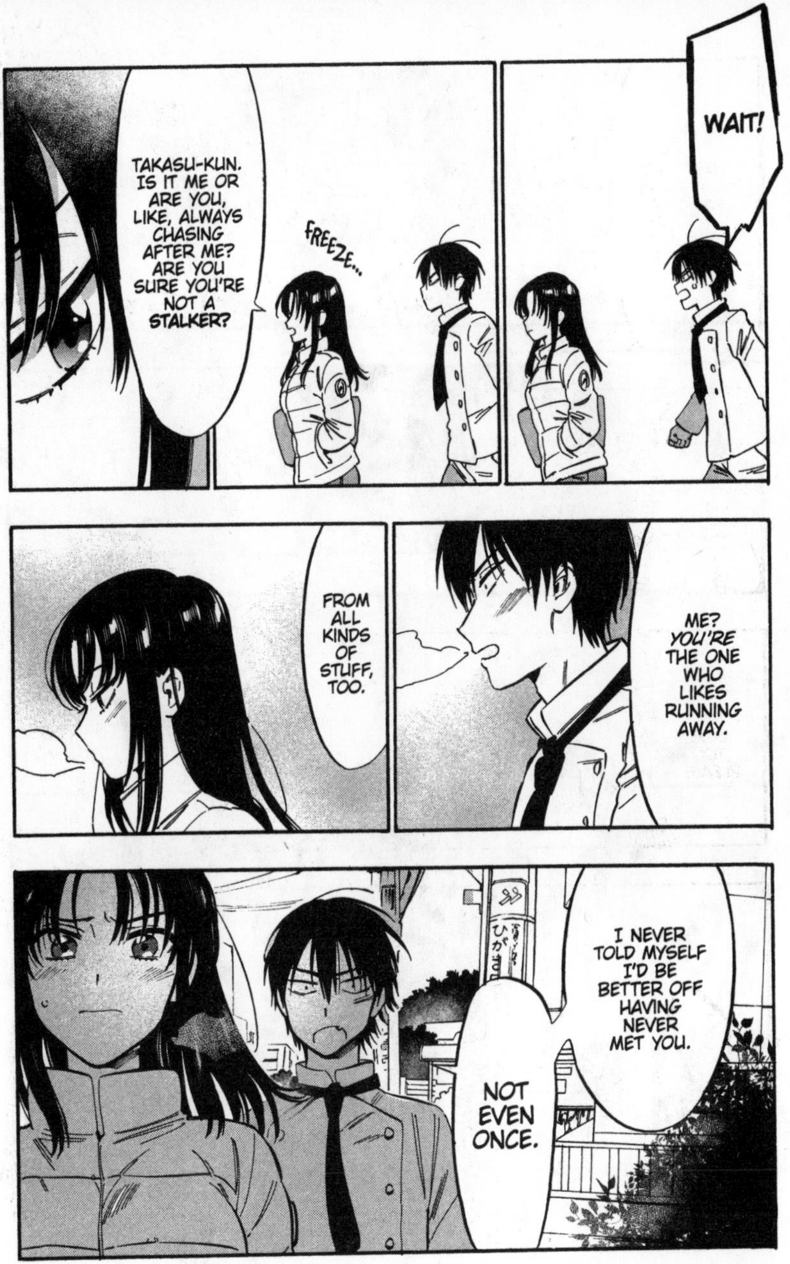
WAIT!
FREEZE...
TAKASU-KUN. IS IT ME OR ARE YOU, LIKE, ALWAYS CHASING AFTER ME? ARE YOU SURE YOU'RE NOT A STALKER?
ME? *YOU'RE* THE ONE WHO LIKES RUNNING AWAY.
FROM ALL KINDS OF STUFF, TOO.
I NEVER TOLD MYSELF I'D BE BETTER OFF HAVING NEVER MET YOU.
NOT EVEN ONCE.

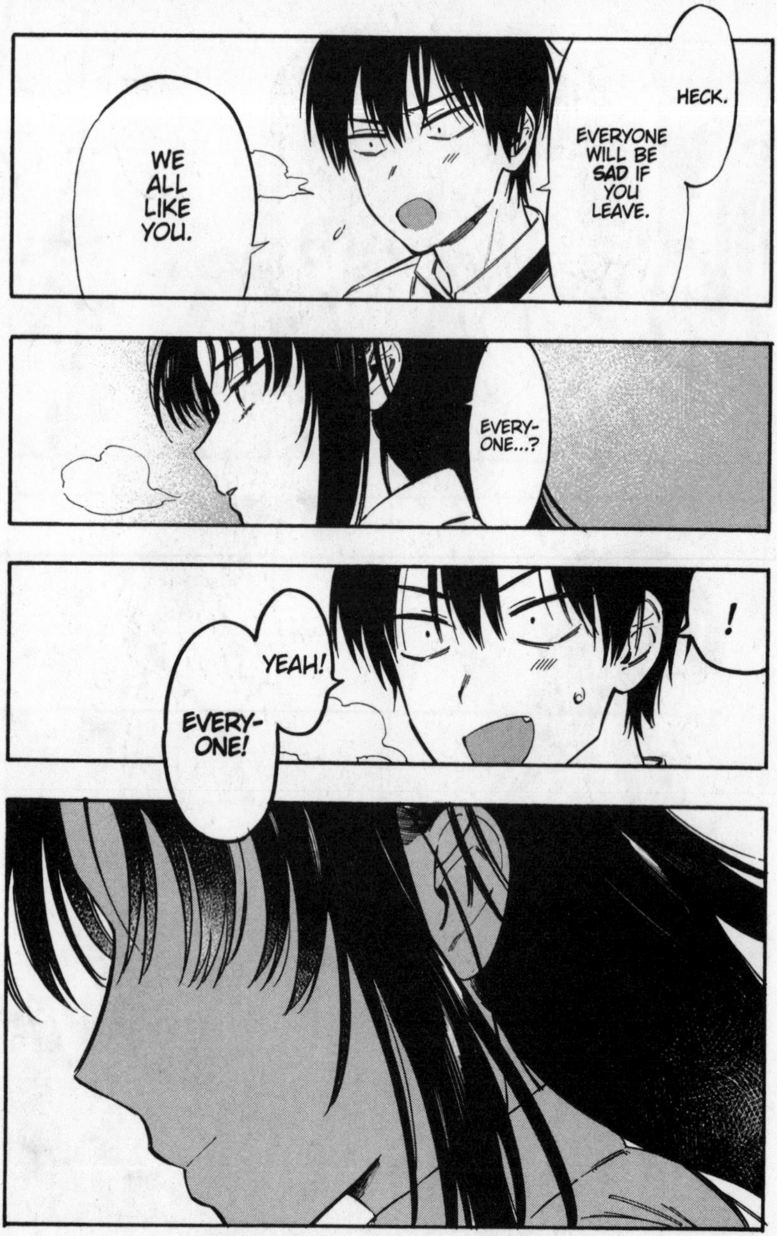
HECK.
EVERYONE WILL BE SAD IF YOU LEAVE.
WE ALL LIKE YOU.
EVERY-ONE...?
!
YEAH!
EVERY-ONE!

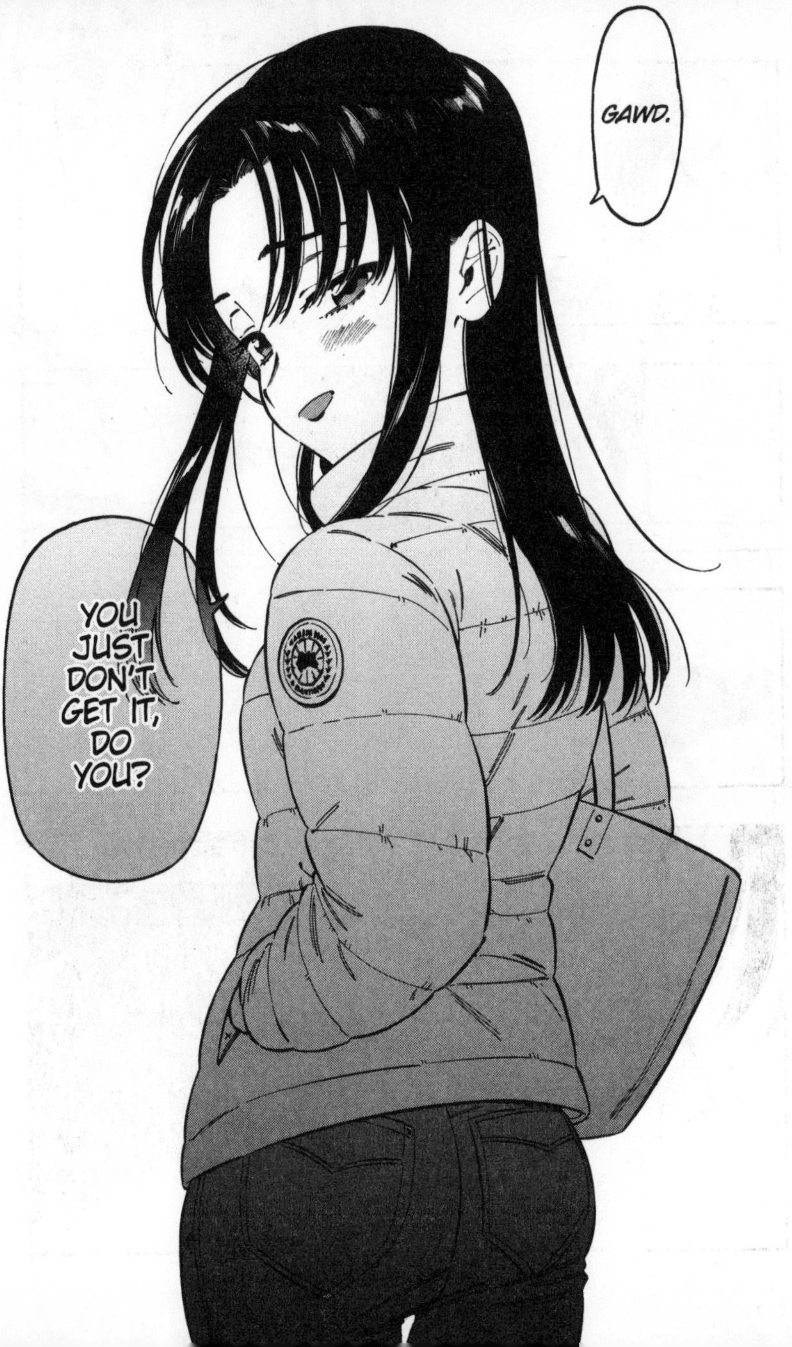
GAWD.
YOU JUST DON'T GET IT, DO YOU?

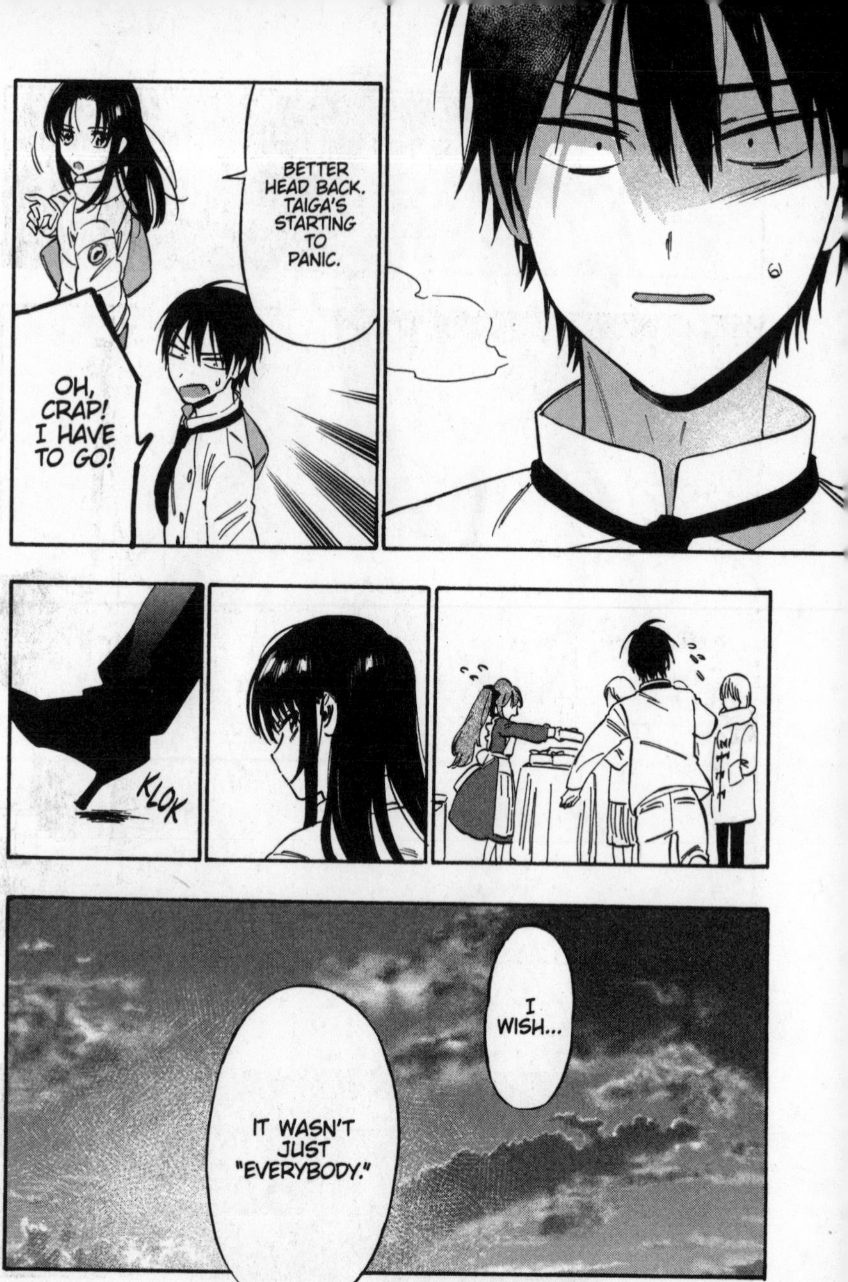
BETTER HEAD BACK. TAIGA'S STARTING TO PANIC.
OH, CRAP! I HAVE TO GO!
KLOK
I WISH...
IT WASN'T JUST "EVERYBODY."

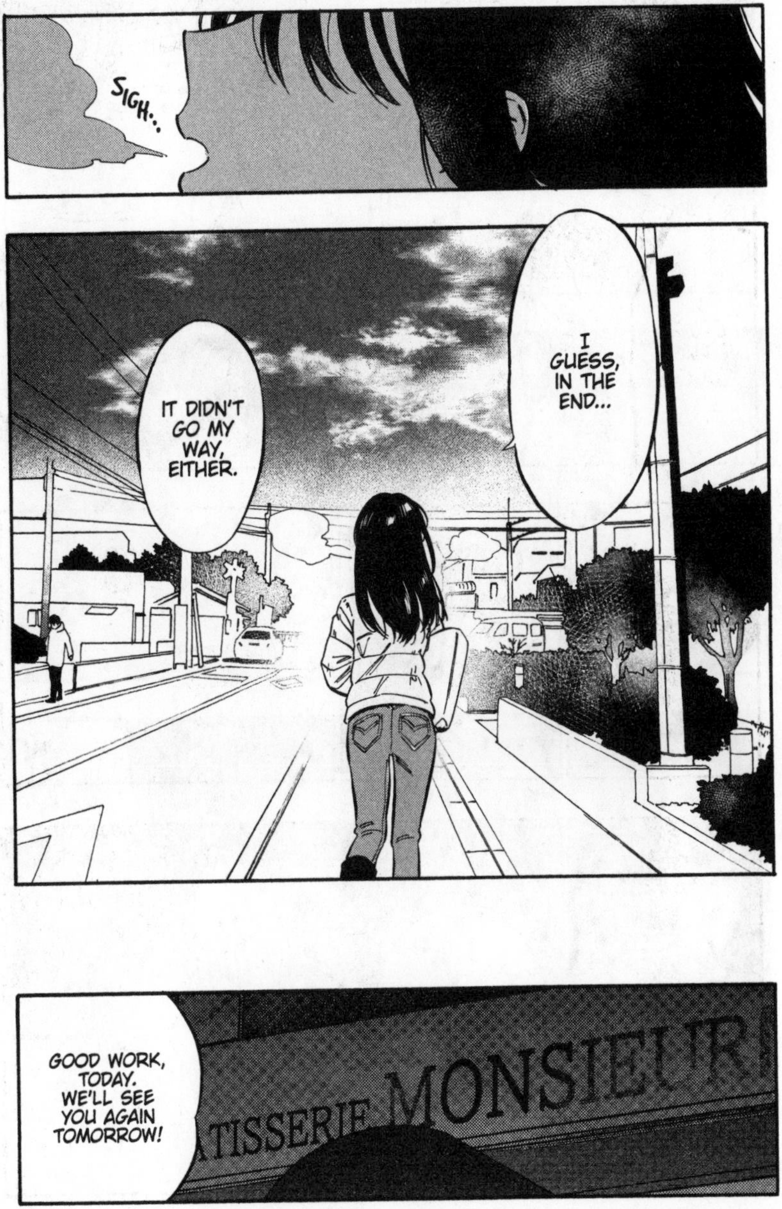
SIGH...
I GUESS, IN THE END...
IT DIDN'T GO MY WAY, EITHER.
GOOD WORK, TODAY. WE'LL SEE YOU AGAIN TOMORROW!
ATISSERIE MONSIEUR

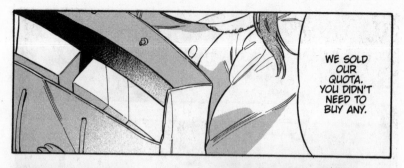

WE SOLD OUR QUOTA. YOU DIDN'T NEED TO BUY ANY.

I CAUSED EVERYONE A LOT OF TROUBLE ON THE SCHOOL TRIP. THESE ARE APOLOGY CHOCOLATES.

I WANTED TO.

AND...

ONE FOR KITAMURA-KUN. ONE FOR MINORIN.

ONE FOR THE CHIHUAHUA, TOO.

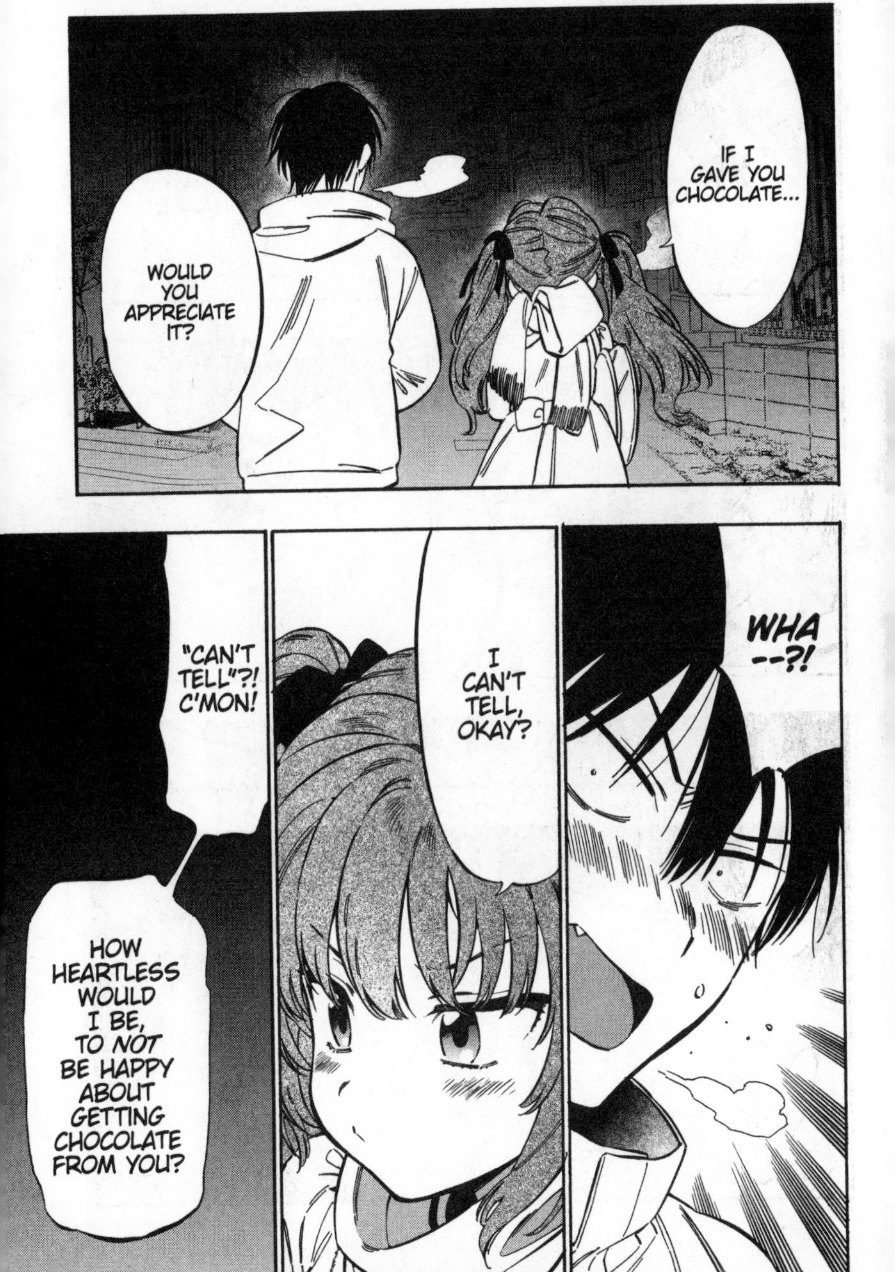
IF I GAVE YOU CHOCOLATE...
WOULD YOU APPRECIATE IT?
WHA--?!
I CAN'T TELL, OKAY?
"CAN'T TELL"?! C'MON!
HOW HEARTLESS WOULD I BE, TO *NOT* BE HAPPY ABOUT GETTING CHOCOLATE FROM YOU?

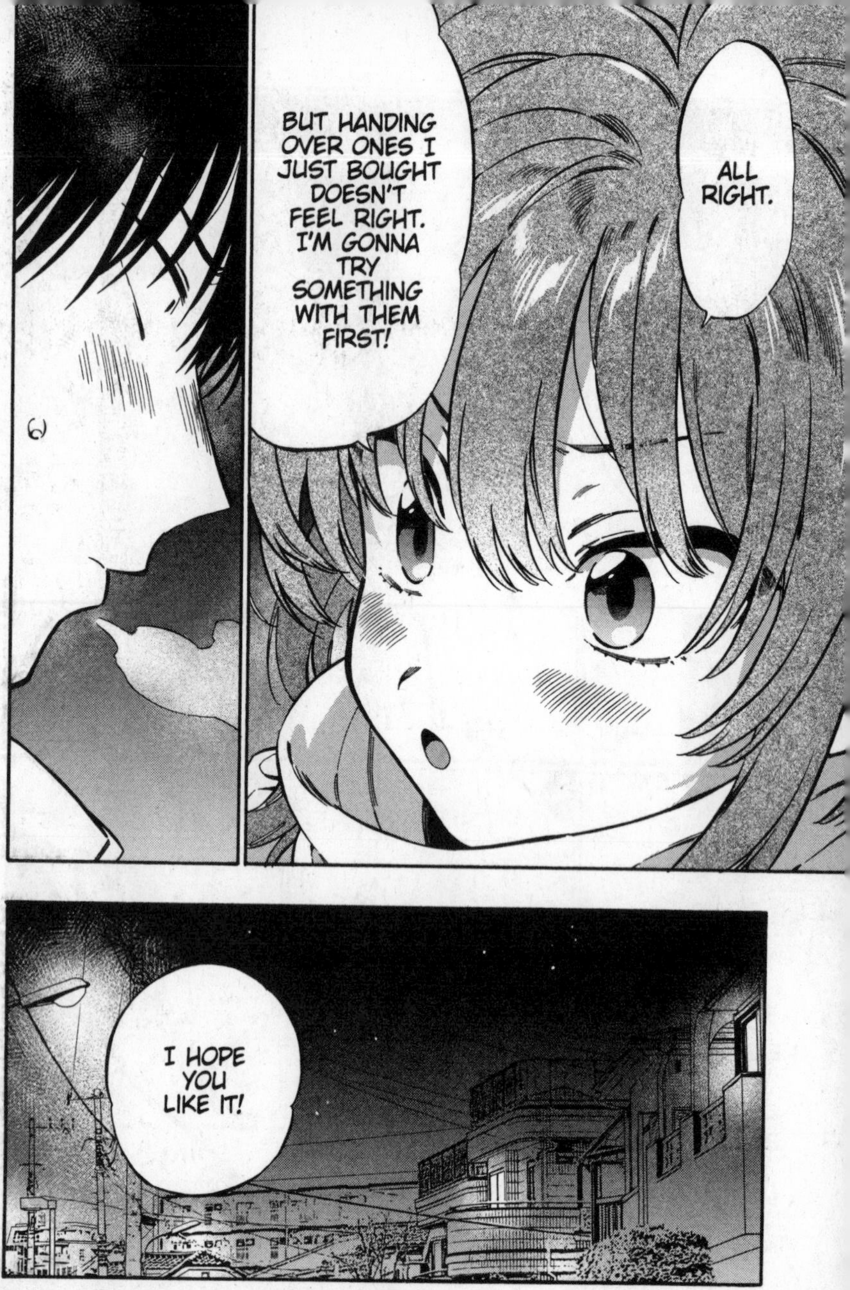
ALL RIGHT.
BUT HANDING OVER ONES I JUST BOUGHT DOESN'T FEEL RIGHT. I'M GONNA TRY SOMETHING WITH THEM FIRST!
I HOPE YOU LIKE IT!

Toradora!

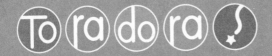

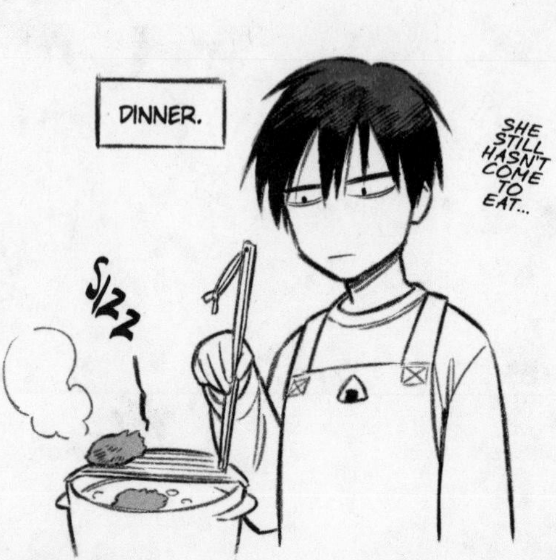
DINNER.
SHE STILL HASN'T COME TO EAT...
SIZZ

# Chapter 94
# Valentines

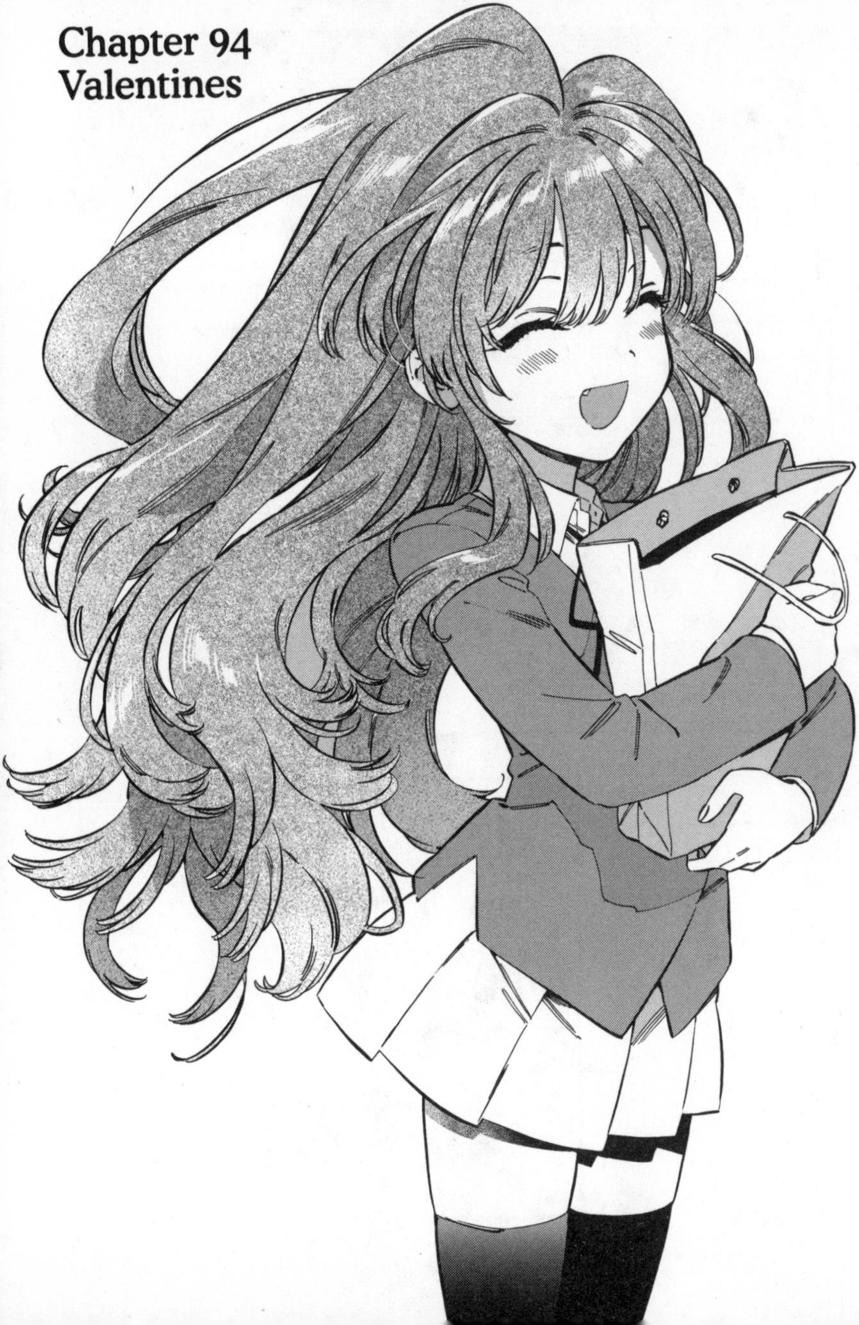

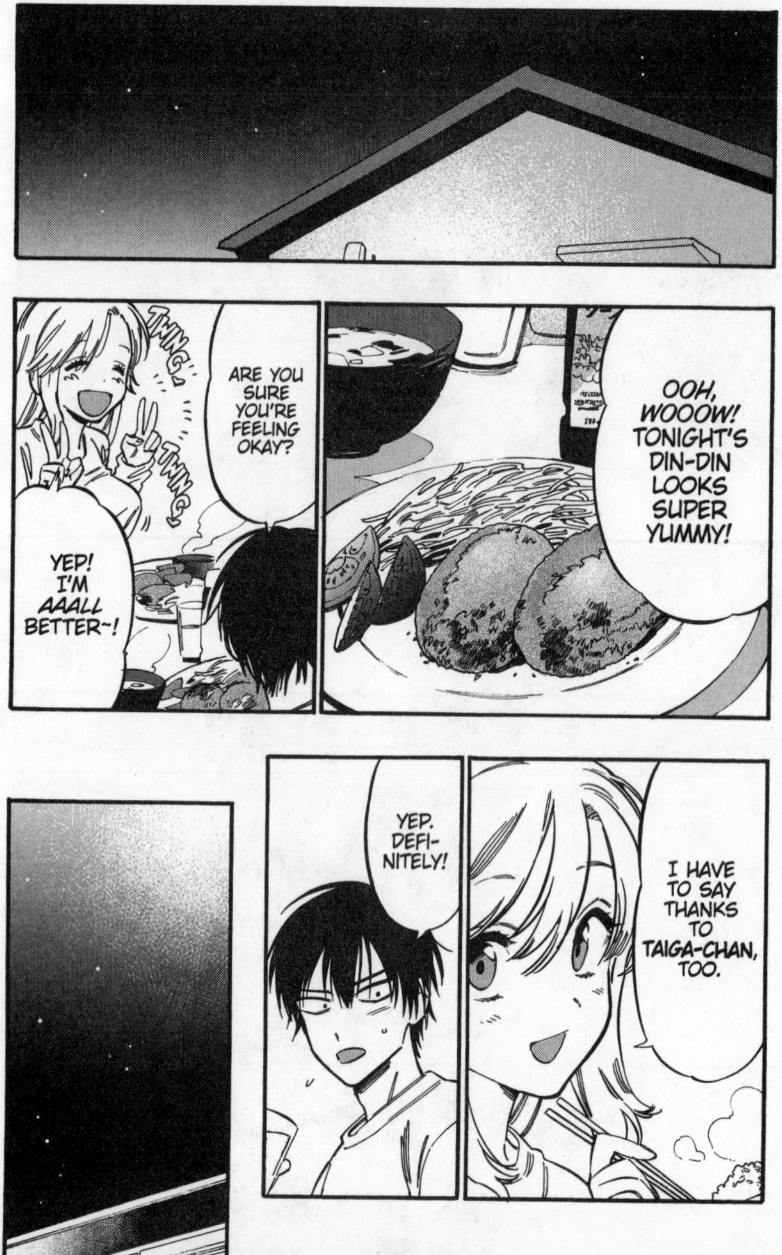
OOH, WOOOW! TONIGHT'S DIN-DIN LOOKS SUPER YUMMY!
ARE YOU SURE YOU'RE FEELING OKAY?
TWING TWING
YEP! I'M AAALL BETTER~!
I HAVE TO SAY THANKS TO TAIGA-CHAN, TOO.
YEP. DEFI-NITELY!

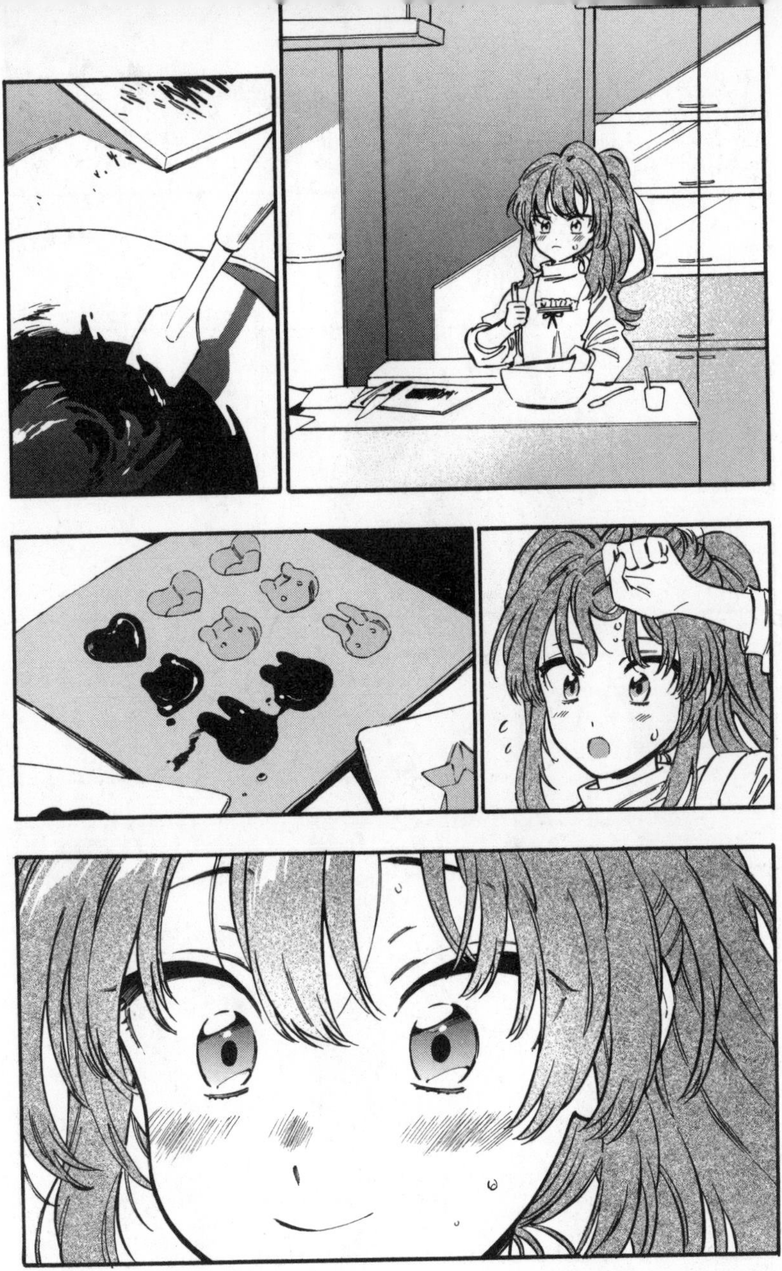

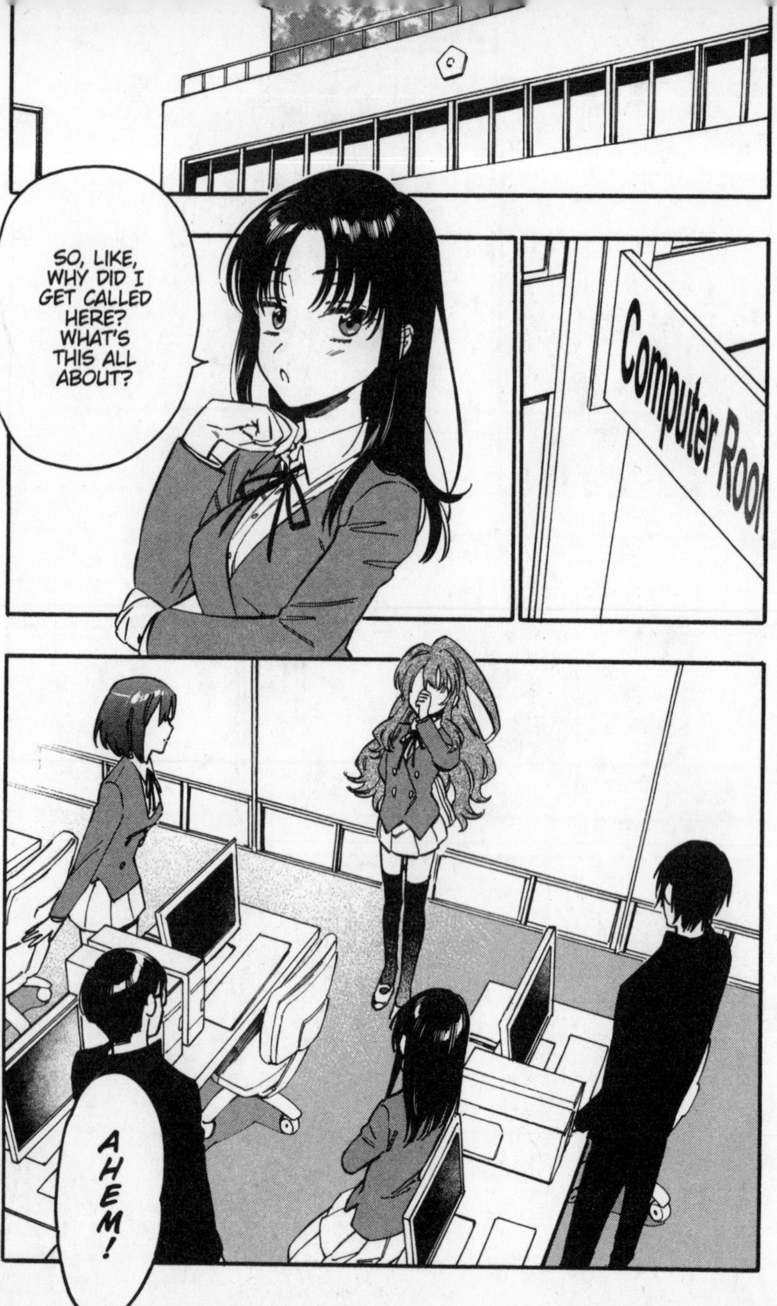
Computer Roo
SO, LIKE, WHY DID I GET CALLED HERE? WHAT'S THIS ALL ABOUT?
AHEM!

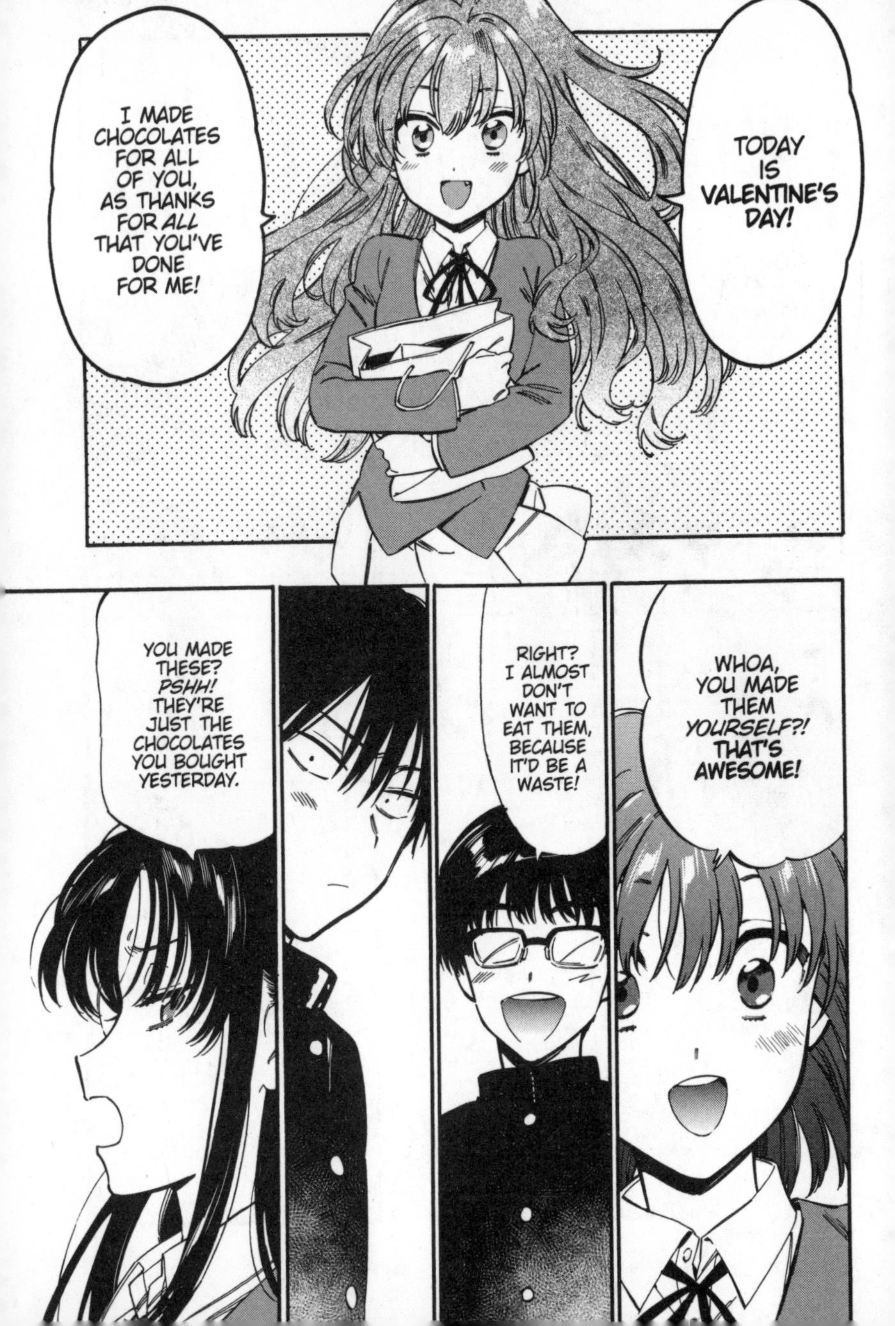
TODAY IS VALENTINE'S DAY!
I MADE CHOCOLATES FOR ALL OF YOU, AS THANKS FOR *ALL* THAT YOU'VE DONE FOR ME!
WHOA, YOU MADE THEM *YOURSELF*?! THAT'S AWESOME!
RIGHT? I ALMOST DON'T WANT TO EAT THEM, BECAUSE IT'D BE A WASTE!
YOU MADE THESE? *PSHH!* THEY'RE JUST THE CHOCOLATES YOU BOUGHT YESTERDAY.

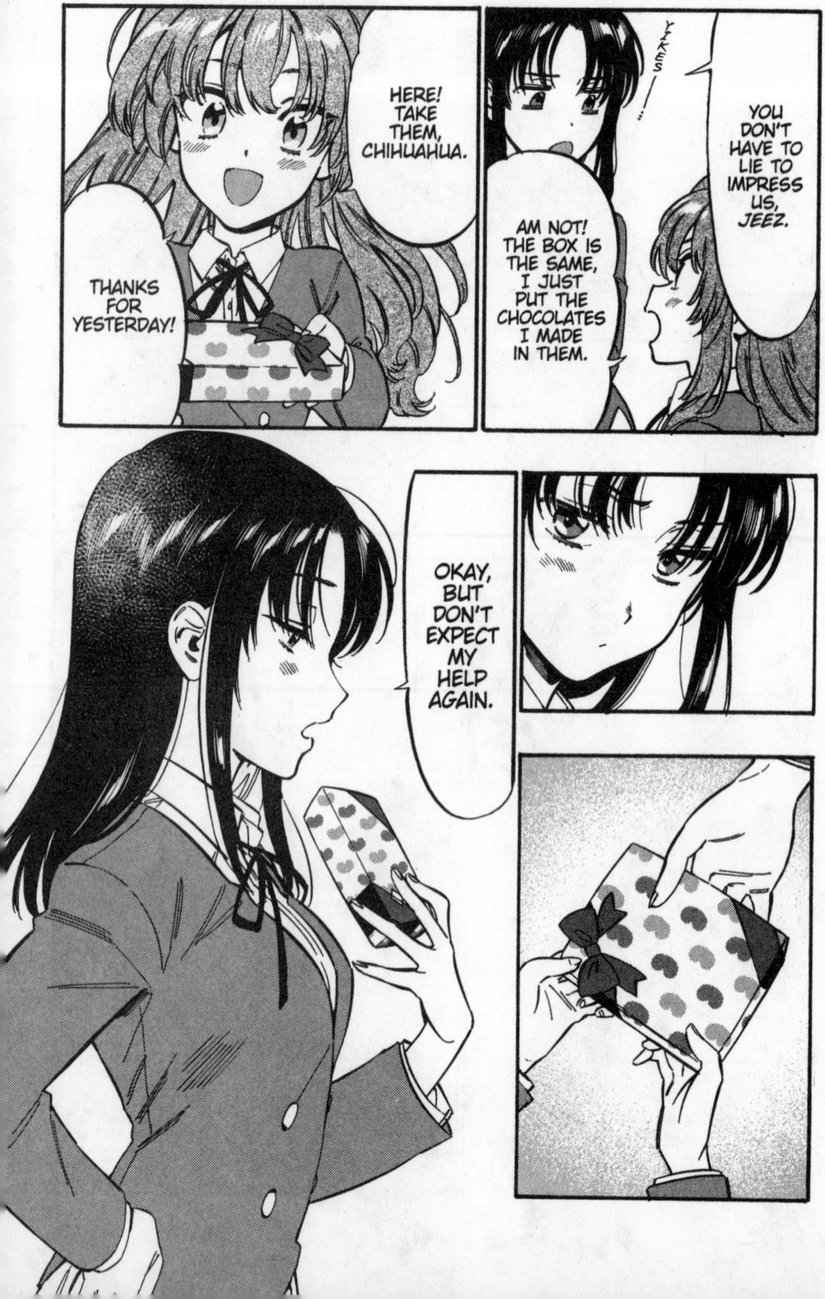
YIKES—...
YOU DON'T HAVE TO LIE TO IMPRESS US, JEEZ.
AM NOT! THE BOX IS THE SAME, I JUST PUT THE CHOCOLATES I MADE IN THEM.
HERE! TAKE THEM, CHIHUAHUA.
THANKS FOR YESTERDAY!
OKAY, BUT DON'T EXPECT MY HELP AGAIN.

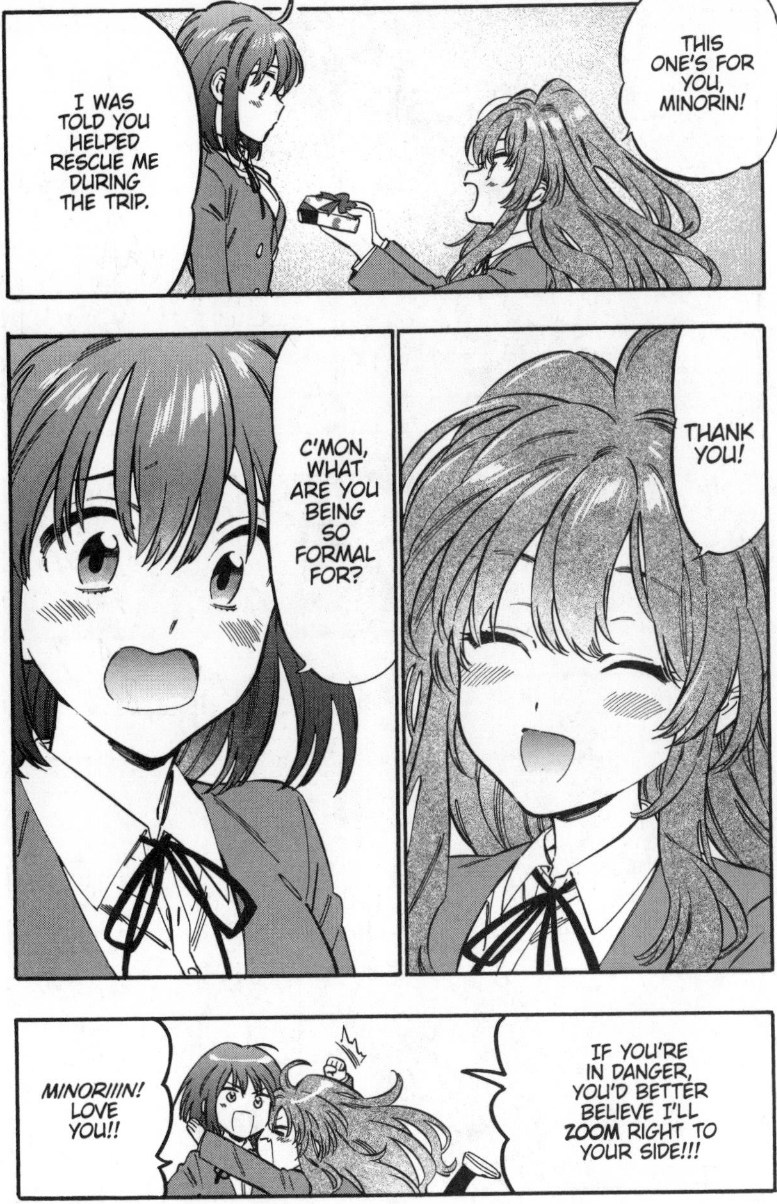
THIS ONE'S FOR YOU, MINORIN!
I WAS TOLD YOU HELPED RESCUE ME DURING THE TRIP.
THANK YOU!
C'MON, WHAT ARE YOU BEING SO FORMAL FOR?
IF YOU'RE IN DANGER, YOU'D BETTER BELIEVE I'LL ZOOM RIGHT TO YOUR SIDE!!!
MINORIIIN! LOVE YOU!!

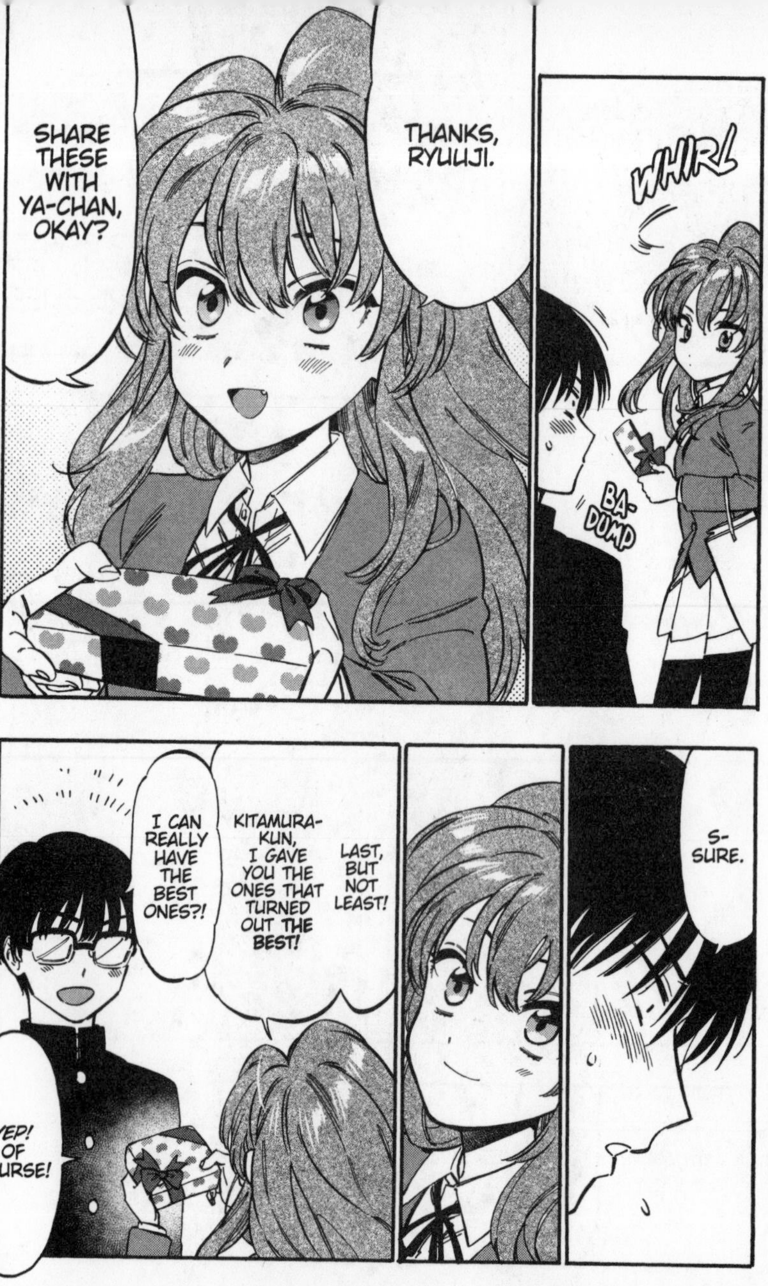
WHIRL
BA-DUMP
THANKS, RYUUJI.
SHARE THESE WITH YA-CHAN, OKAY?
S-SURE.
LAST, BUT NOT LEAST!
KITAMURA-KUN, I GAVE YOU THE ONES THAT TURNED OUT THE BEST!
I CAN REALLY HAVE THE BEST ONES?!
YEP! OF COURSE!

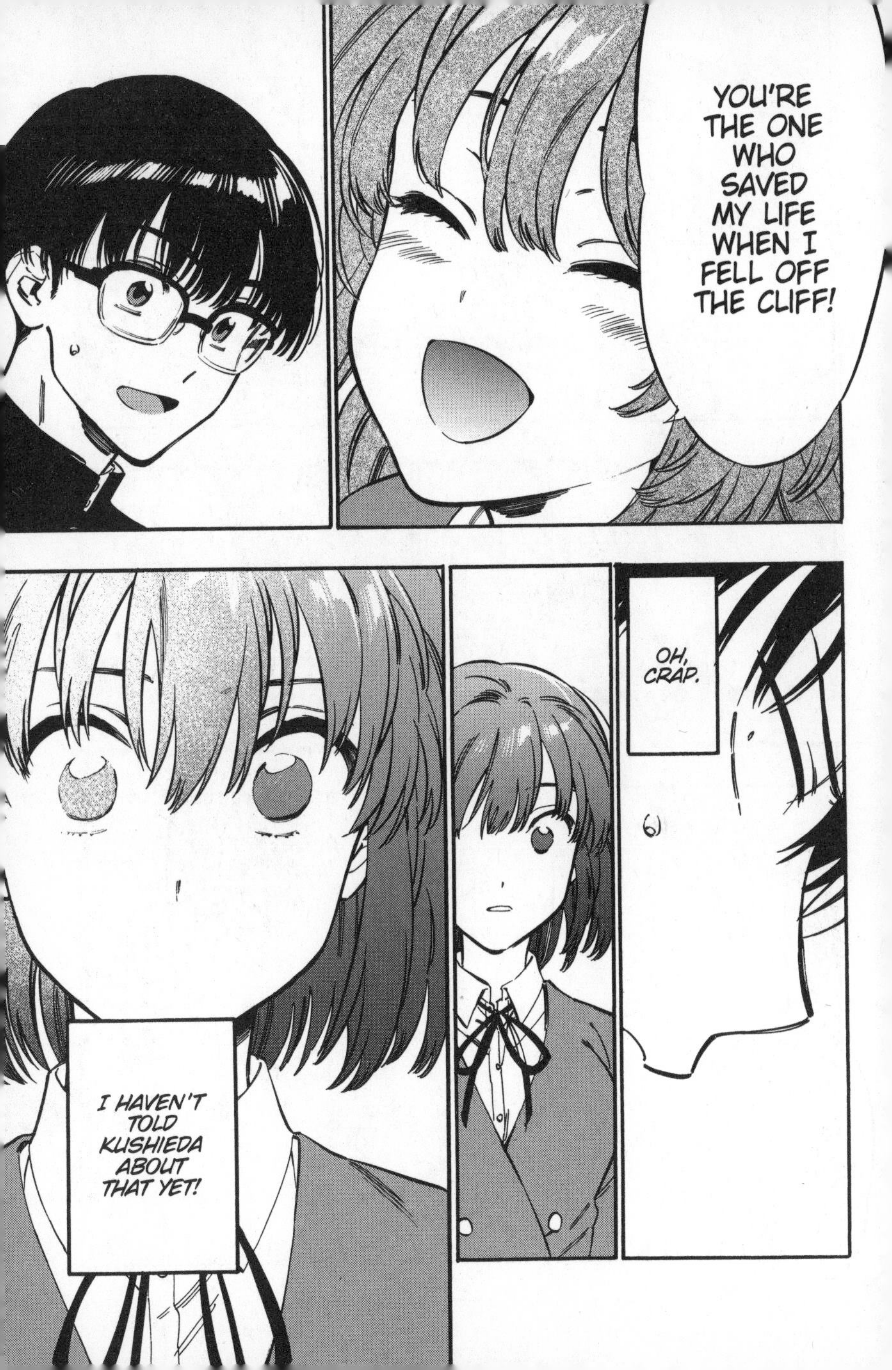
YOU'RE THE ONE WHO SAVED MY LIFE WHEN I FELL OFF THE CLIFF!
OH, CRAP.
I HAVEN'T TOLD KUSHIEDA ABOUT THAT YET!

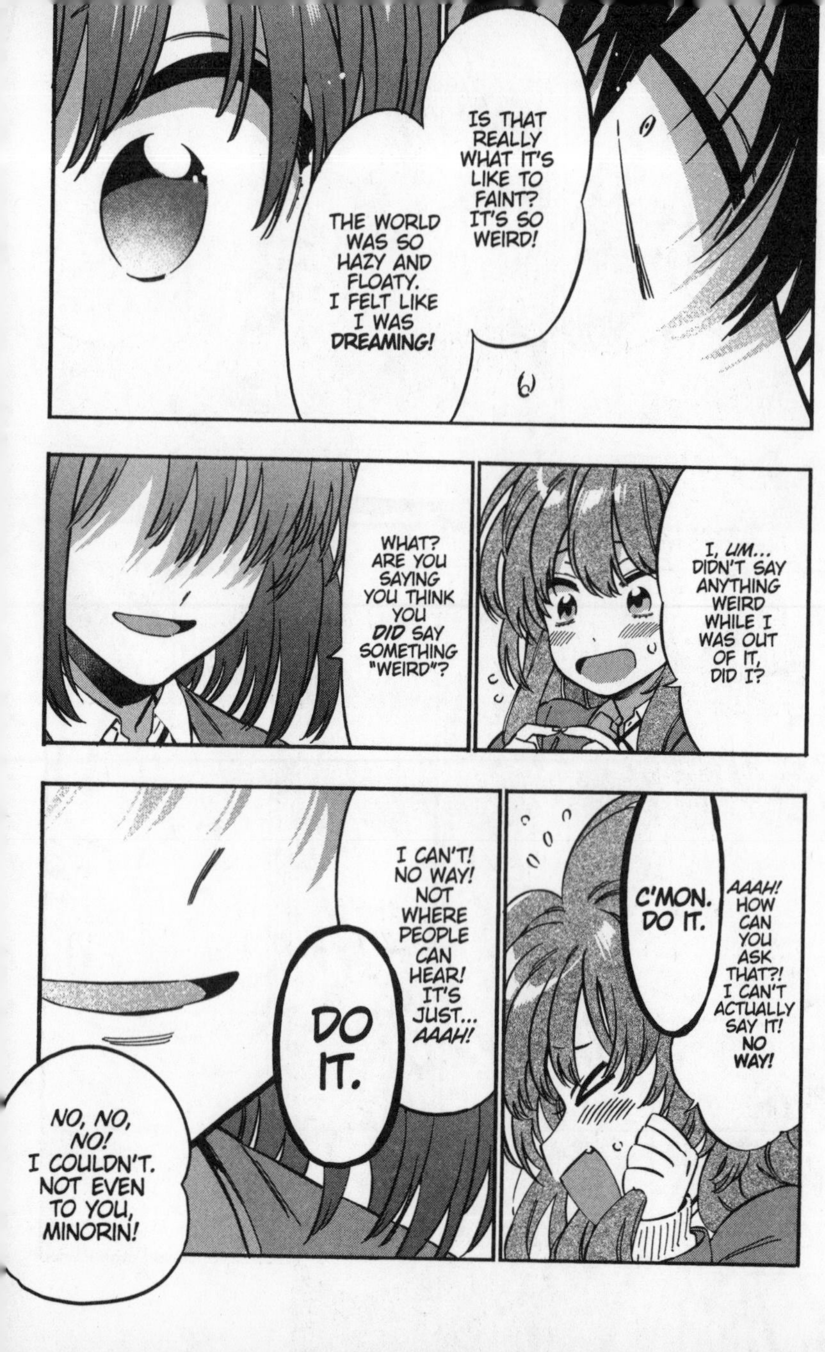
IS THAT REALLY WHAT IT'S LIKE TO FAINT? IT'S SO WEIRD!
THE WORLD WAS SO HAZY AND FLOATY. I FELT LIKE I WAS **DREAMING!**
I, *UM*... DIDN'T SAY ANYTHING WEIRD WHILE I WAS OUT OF IT, DID I?
WHAT? ARE YOU SAYING YOU THINK YOU *DID* SAY SOMETHING "WEIRD"?
C'MON. DO IT.
*AAAH!* HOW CAN YOU ASK THAT?! I CAN'T ACTUALLY SAY IT! NO WAY!
I CAN'T! NO WAY! NOT WHERE PEOPLE CAN HEAR! IT'S JUST... *AAAH!*
DO IT.
*NO, NO, NO!* I COULDN'T. NOT EVEN TO YOU, MINORIN!

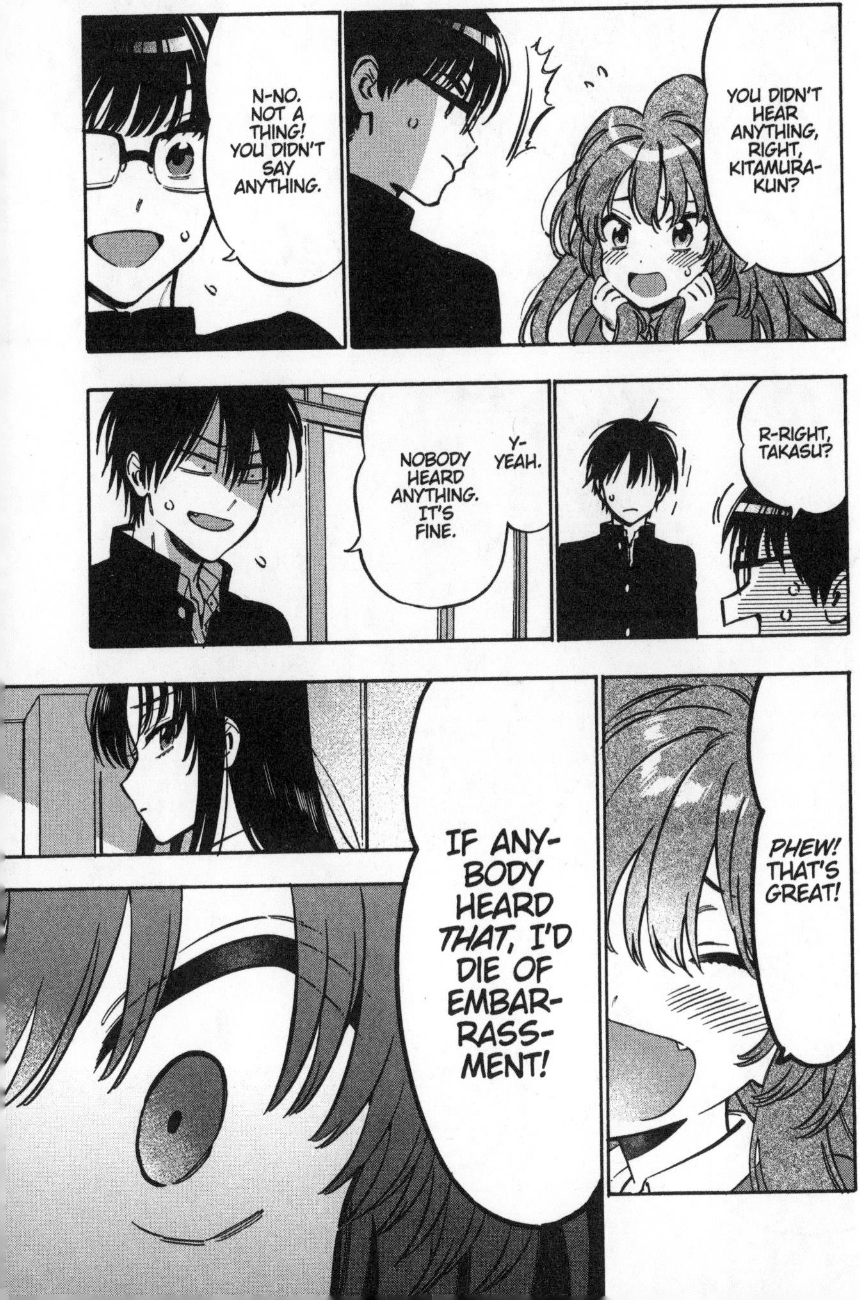
YOU DIDN'T HEAR ANYTHING, RIGHT, KITAMURA-KUN?
N-NO. NOT A THING! YOU DIDN'T SAY ANYTHING.
R-RIGHT, TAKASU?
Y-YEAH.
NOBODY HEARD ANYTHING. IT'S FINE.
*PHEW!* THAT'S GREAT!
IF ANYBODY HEARD *THAT*, I'D DIE OF EMBARRASSMENT!

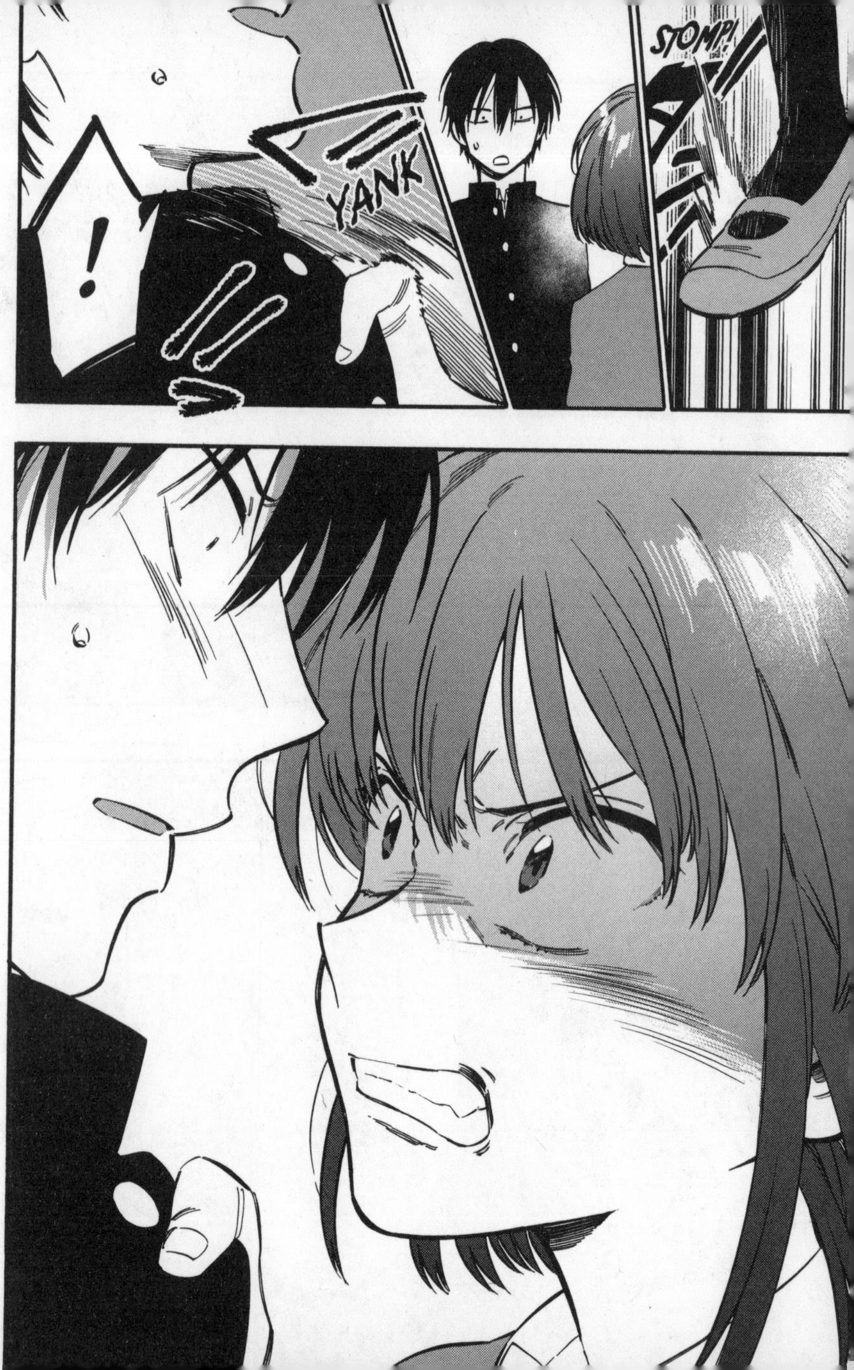
STOMP!
YANK
!

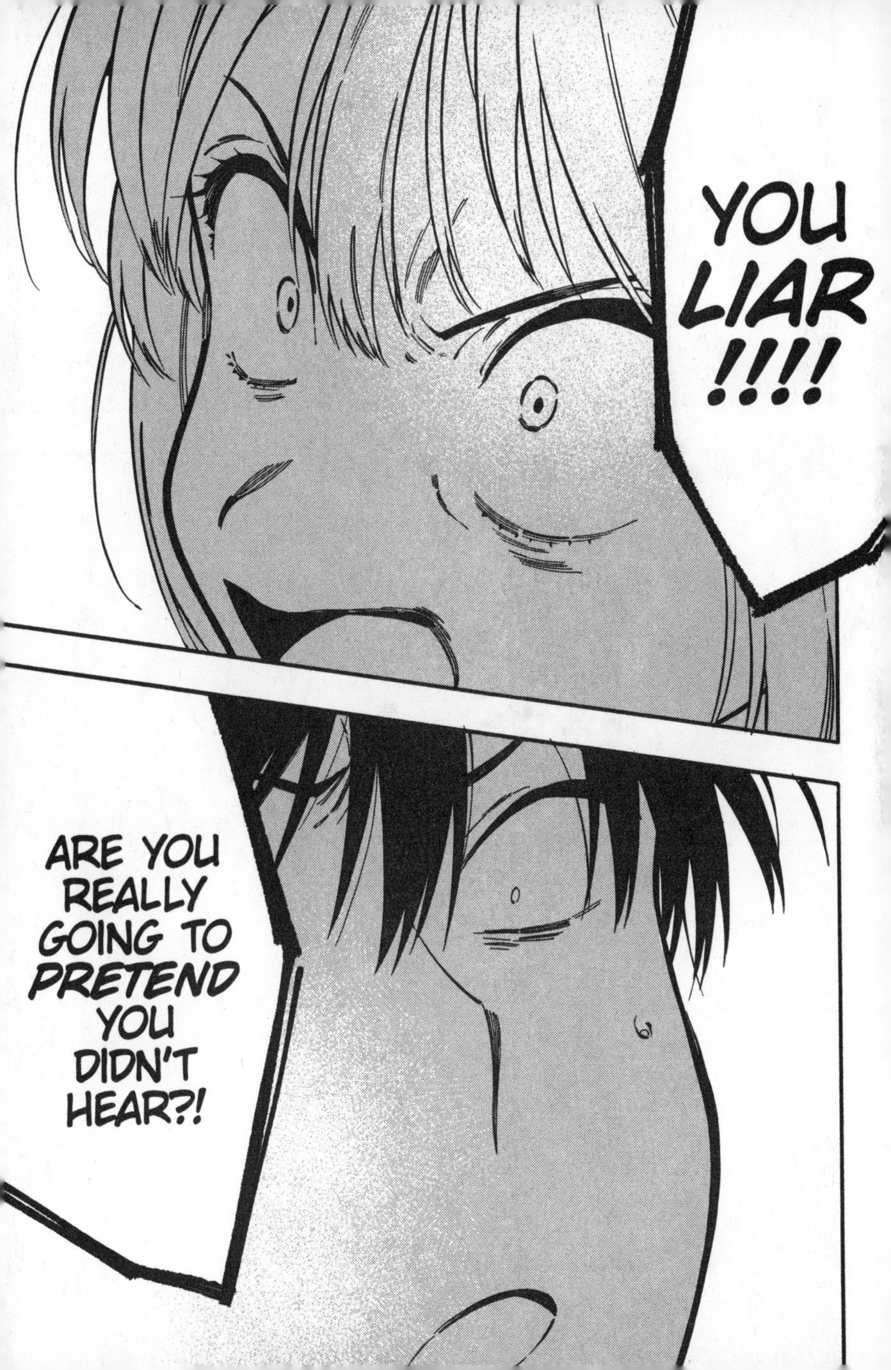
YOU LIAR !!!!
ARE YOU REALLY GOING TO PRETEND YOU DIDN'T HEAR?!

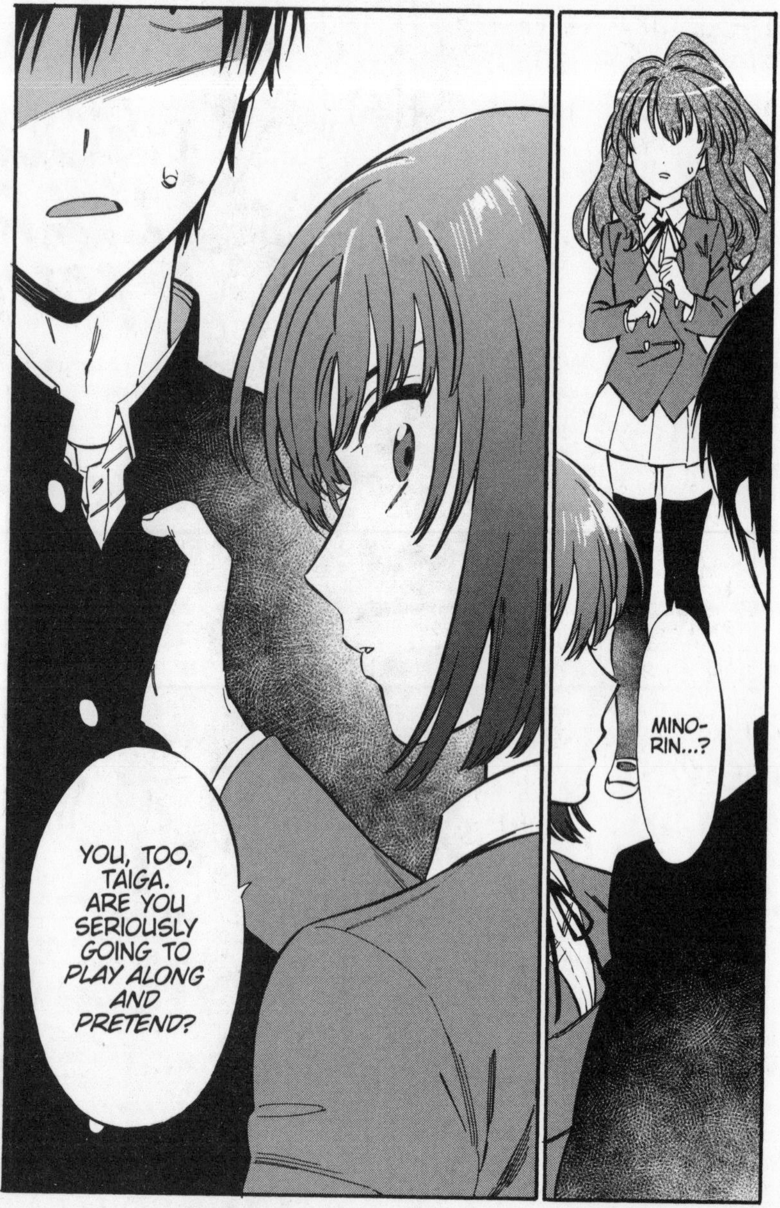
MINO-RIN...?
YOU, TOO, TAIGA. ARE YOU SERIOUSLY GOING TO *PLAY ALONG* AND *PRETEND?*

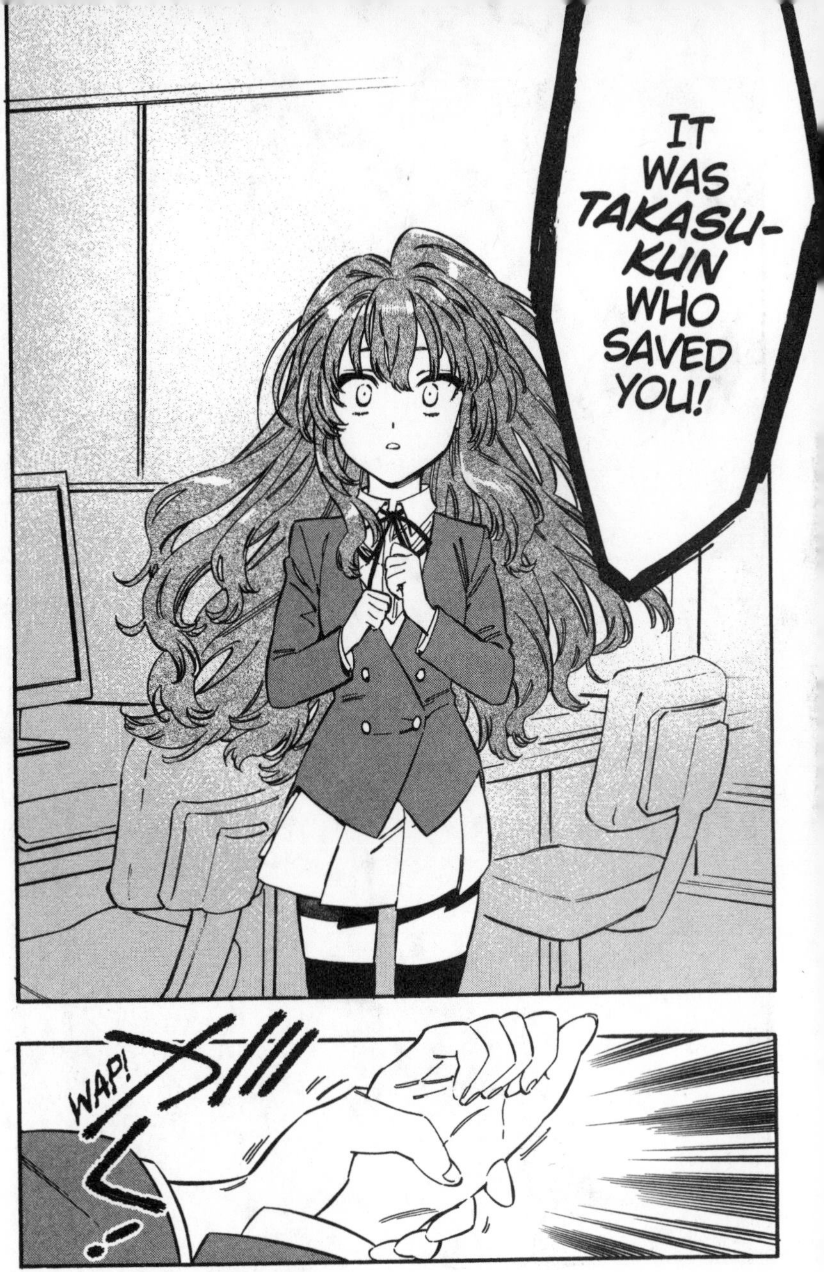
IT WAS TAKASU-KUN WHO SAVED YOU!
WAP!

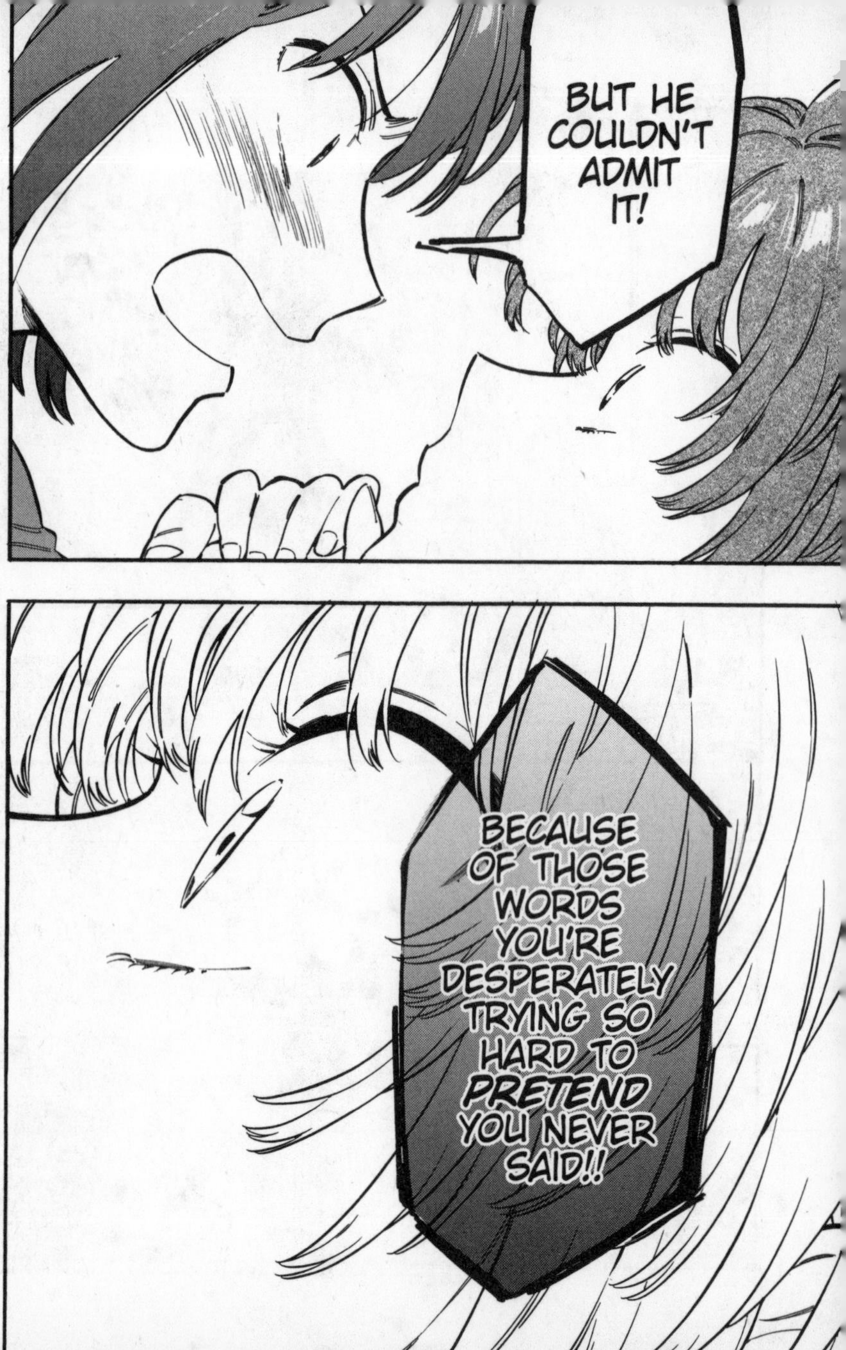
BUT HE COULDN'T ADMIT IT!
BECAUSE OF THOSE WORDS YOU'RE DESPERATELY TRYING SO HARD TO PRETEND YOU NEVER SAID!!

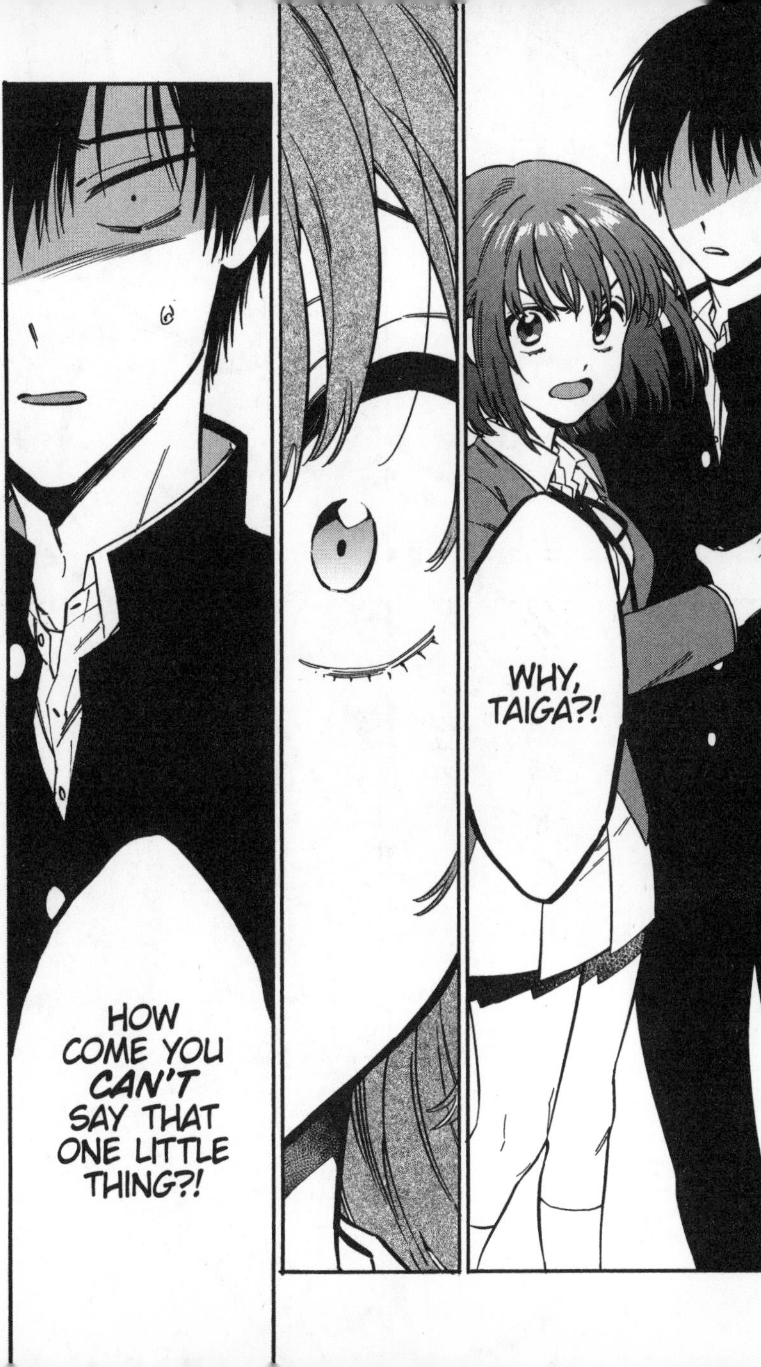
WHY, TAIGA?!
HOW COME YOU *CAN'T* SAY THAT ONE LITTLE THING?!

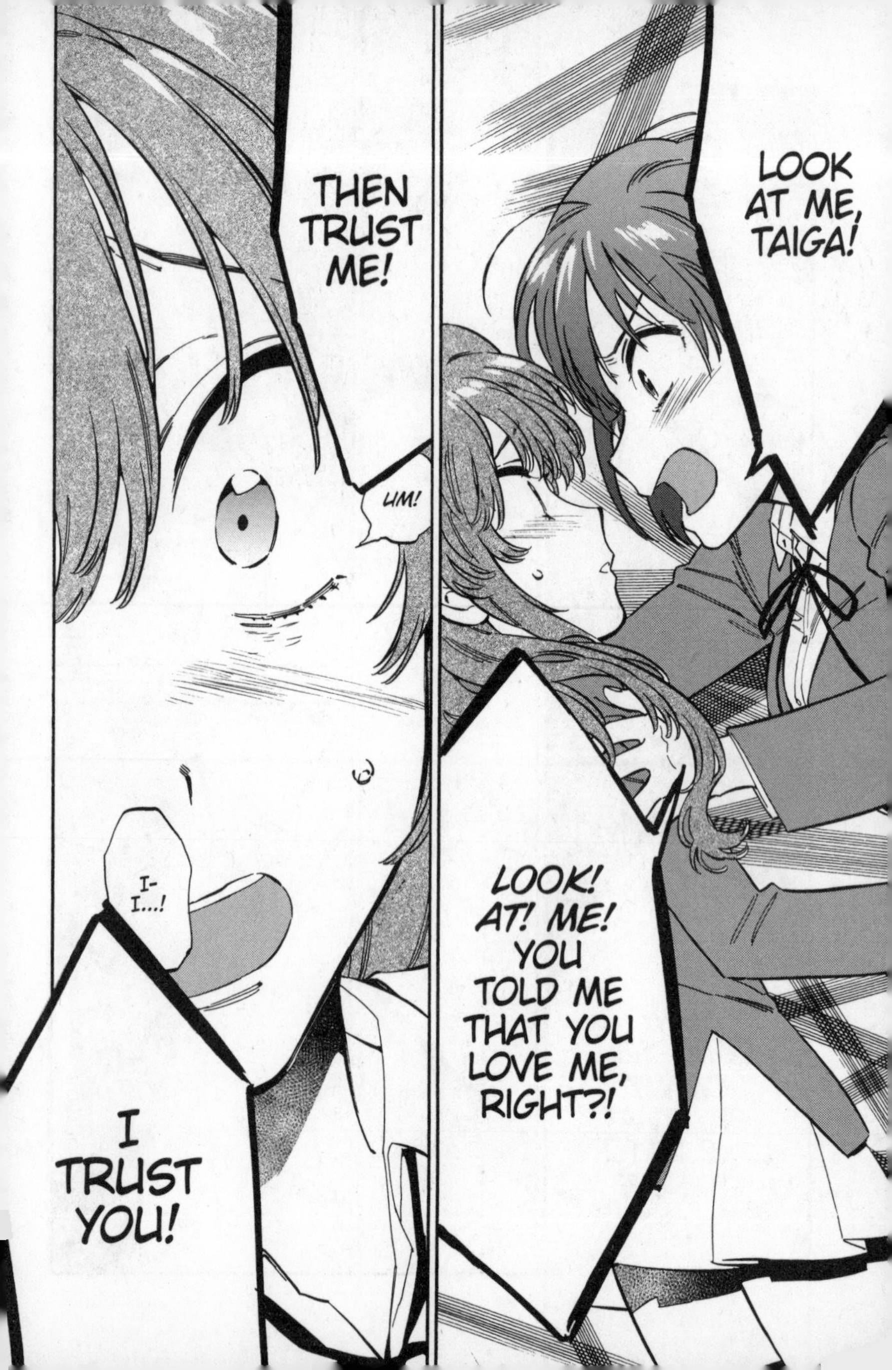
LOOK AT ME, TAIGA!
LOOK! AT! ME! YOU TOLD ME THAT YOU LOVE ME, RIGHT?!
THEN TRUST ME!
UM!
I- I...!
I TRUST YOU!

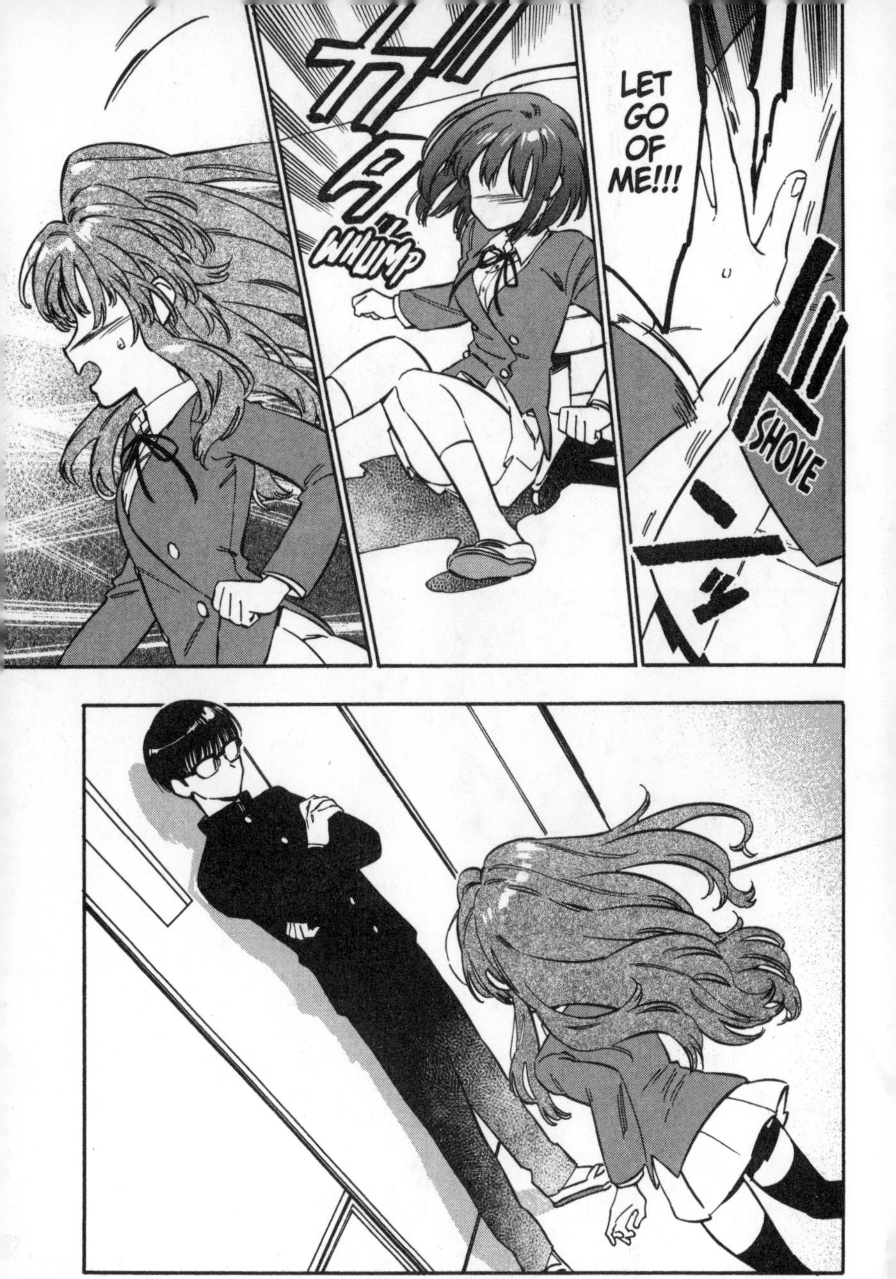
LET GO OF ME!!!
SHOVE
WHUMP

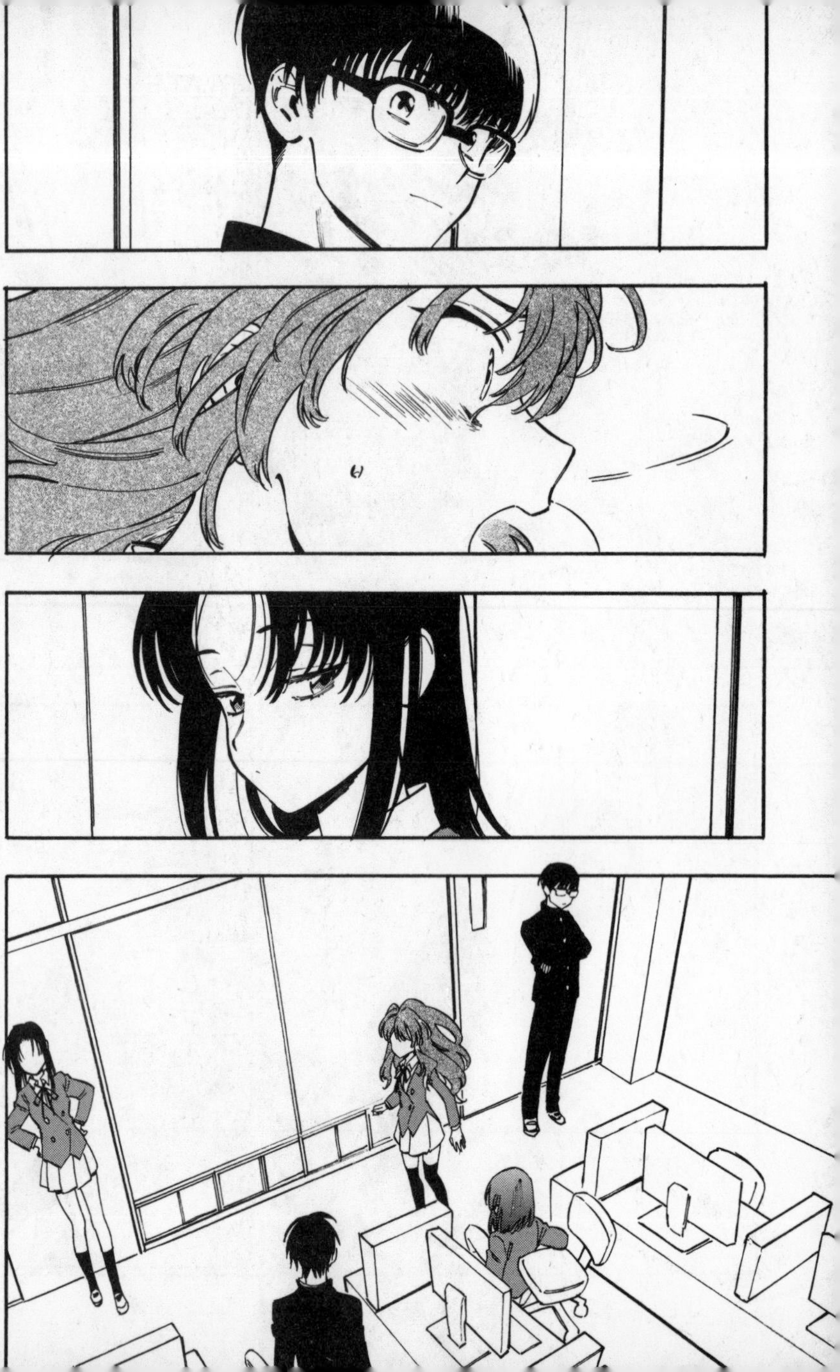

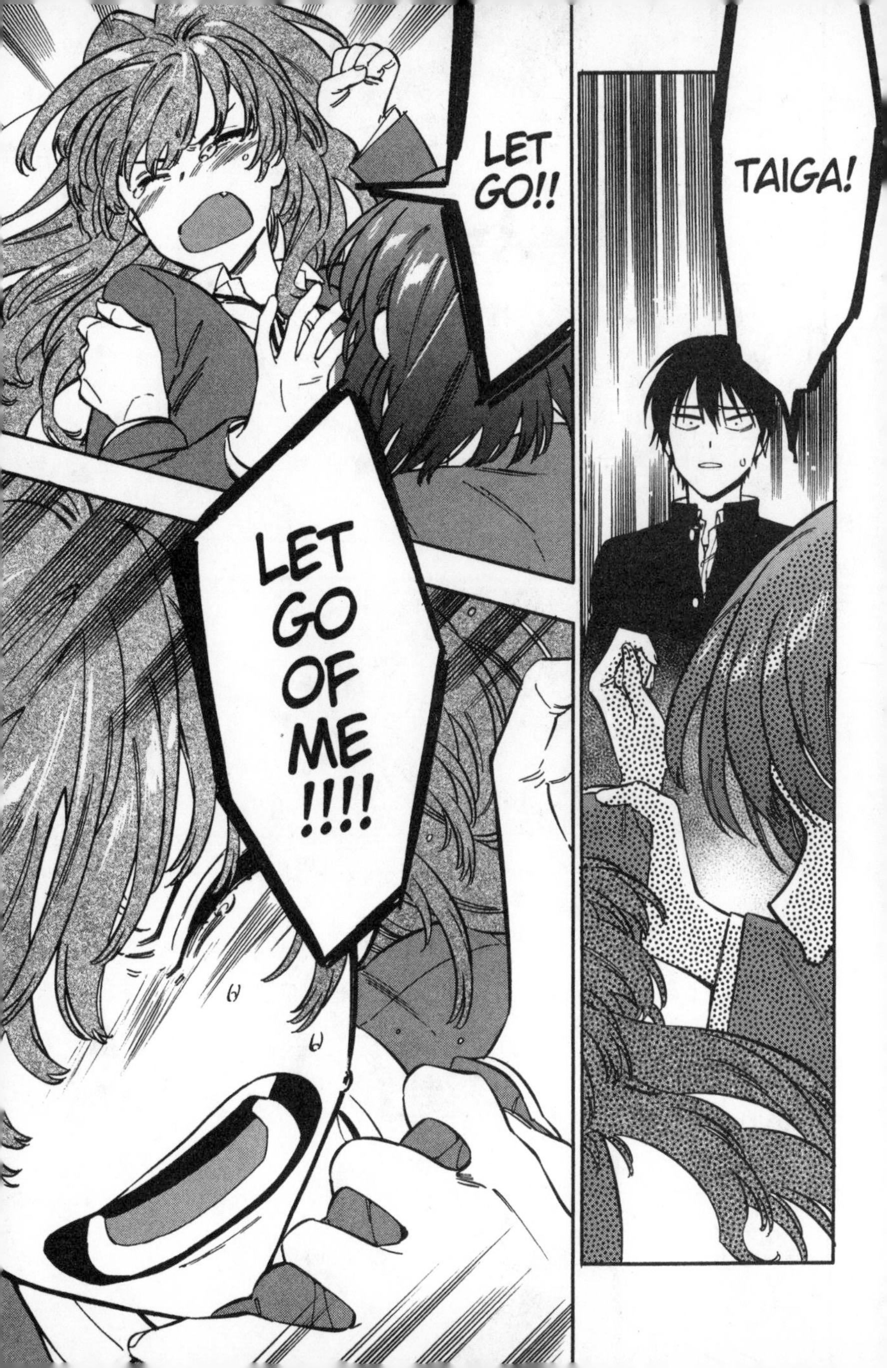
TAIGA!
LET GO!!
LET GO OF ME!!!!

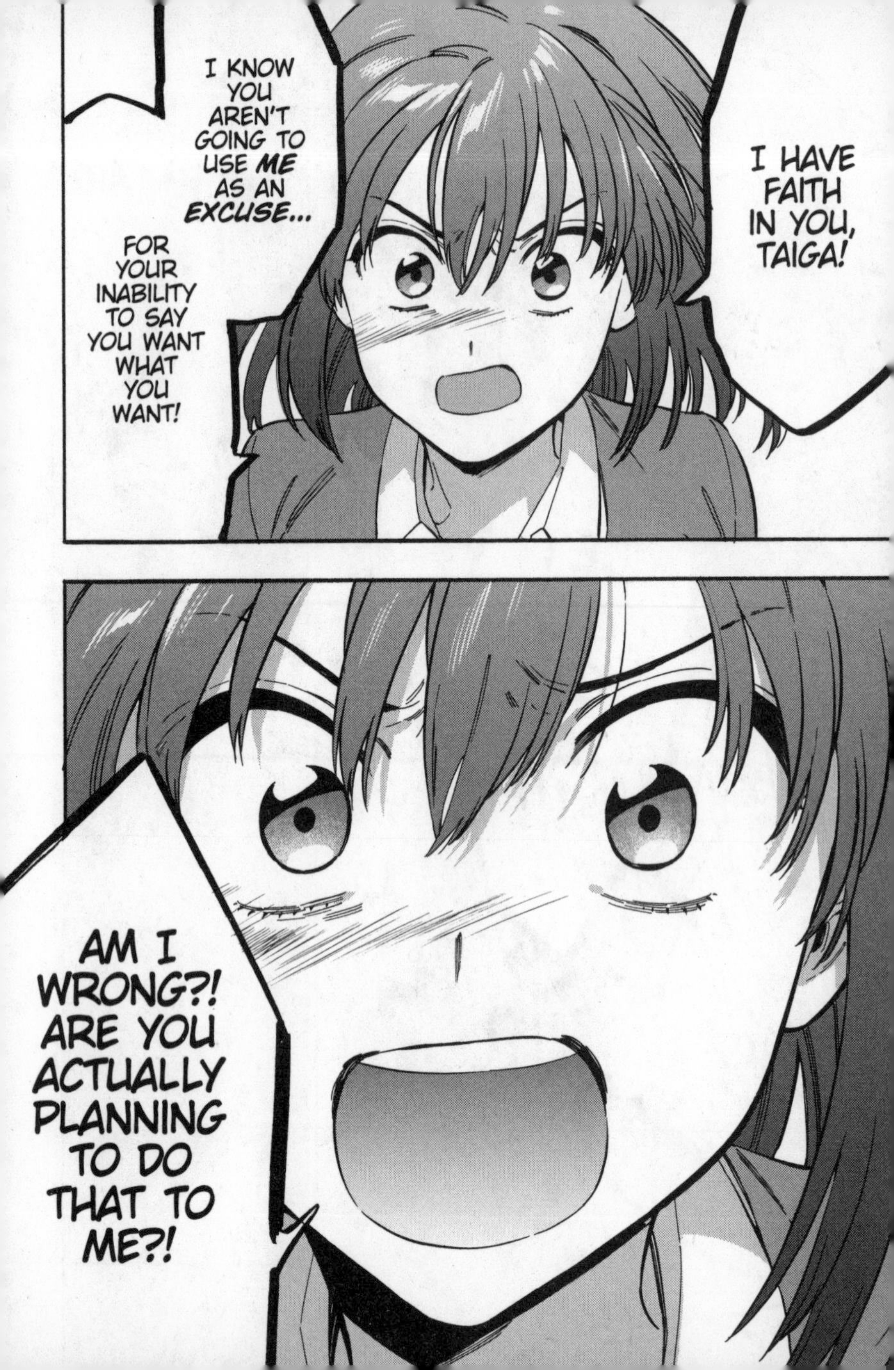
I HAVE FAITH IN YOU, TAIGA!
I KNOW YOU AREN'T GOING TO USE ME AS AN EXCUSE...
FOR YOUR INABILITY TO SAY YOU WANT WHAT YOU WANT!
AM I WRONG?! ARE YOU ACTUALLY PLANNING TO DO THAT TO ME?!

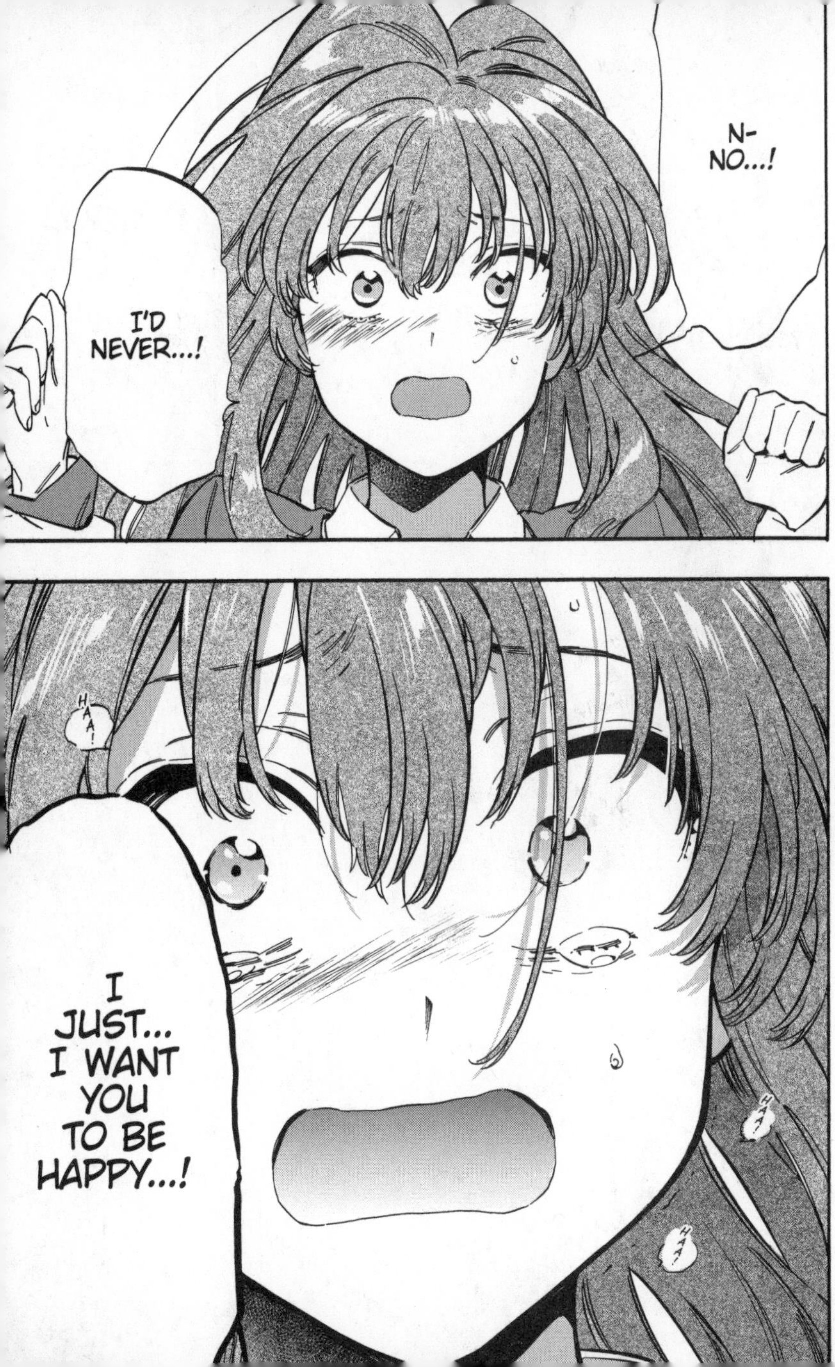
N- NO...!
I'D NEVER...!
HAA!
I JUST... I WANT YOU TO BE HAPPY...!
HAA!
HAA!

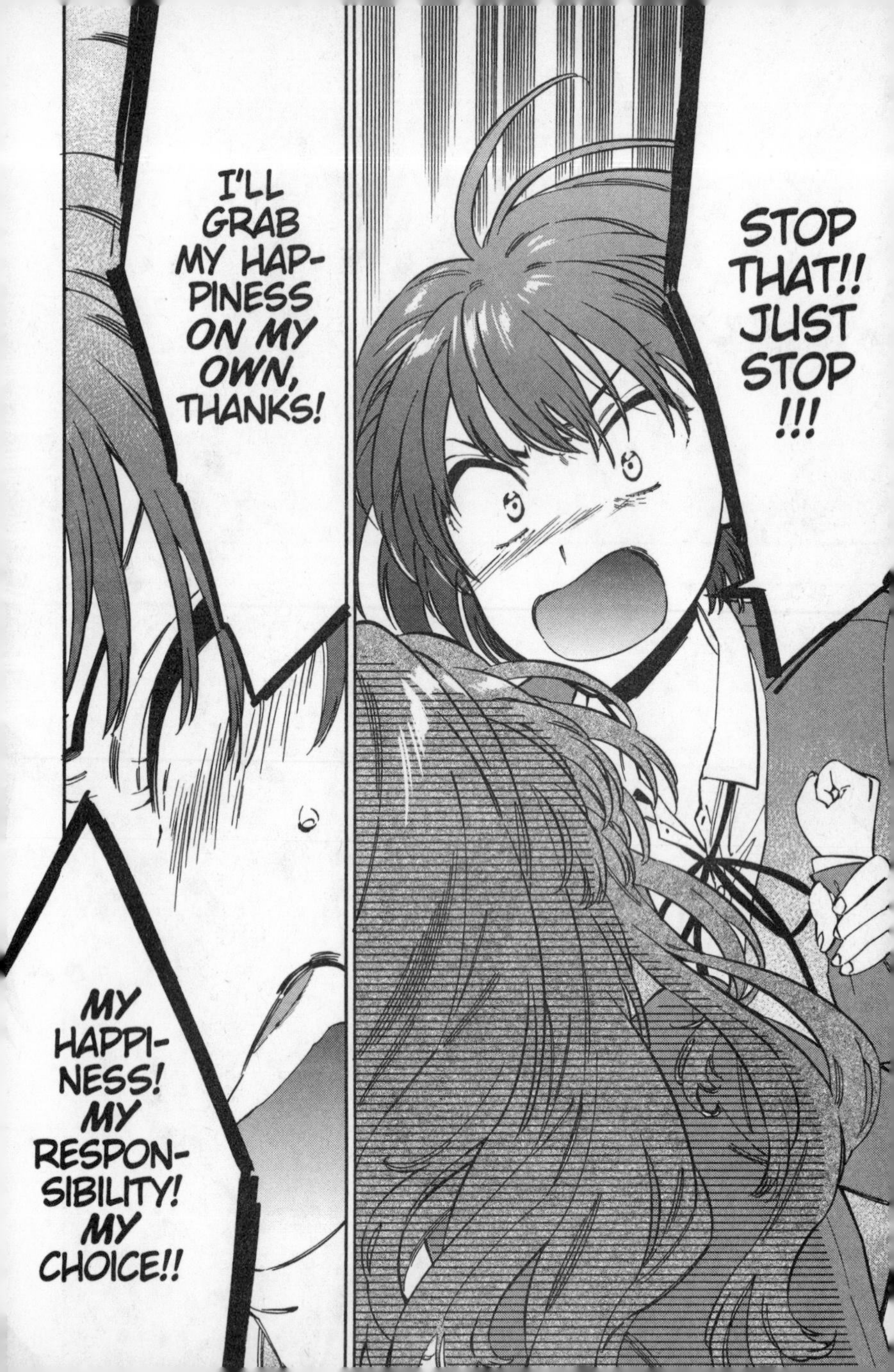
STOP THAT!! JUST STOP !!!
I'LL GRAB MY HAPPINESS ON MY OWN, THANKS!
MY HAPPINESS! MY RESPONSIBILITY! MY CHOICE!!

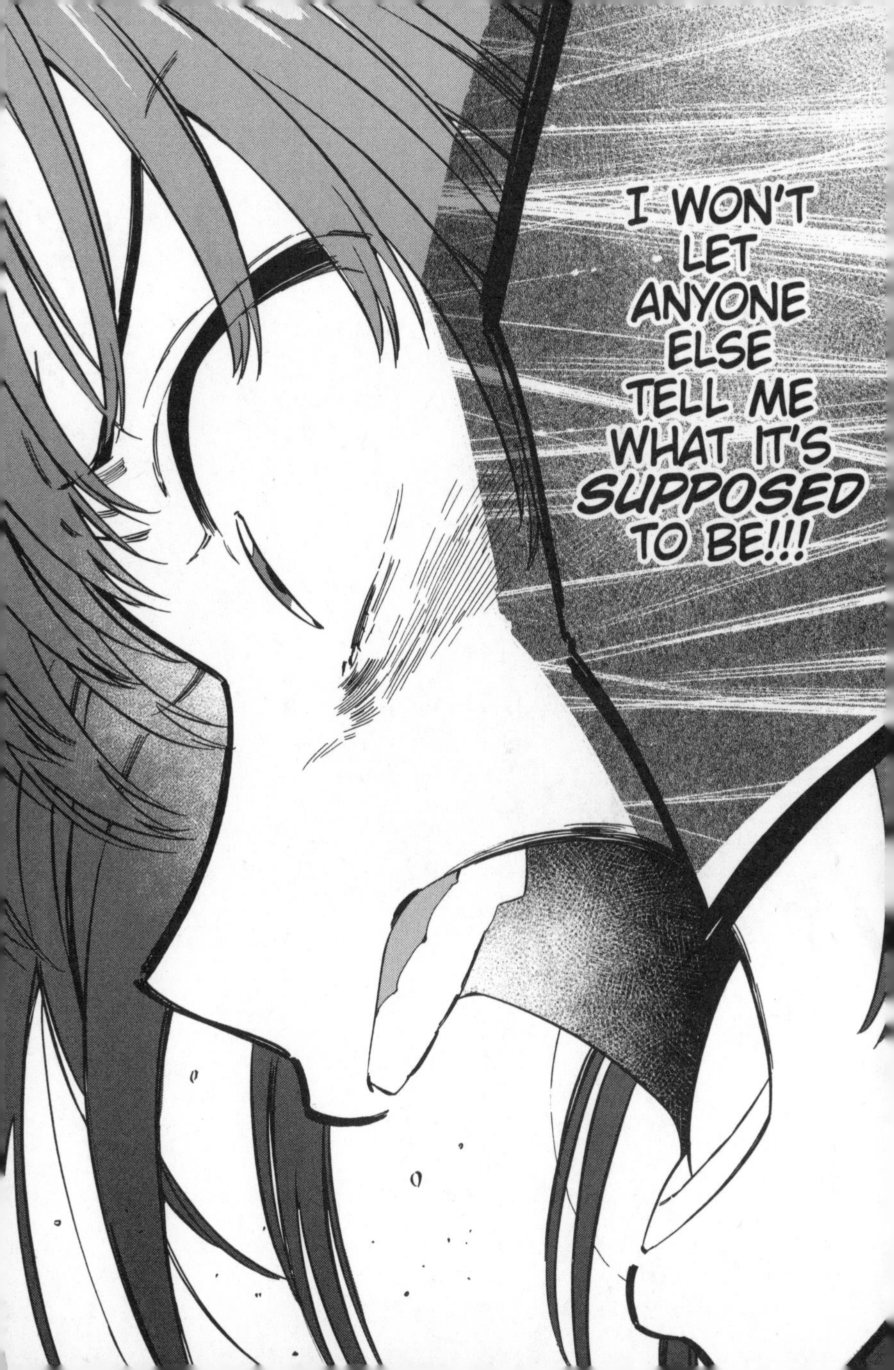
I WON'T LET ANYONE ELSE TELL ME WHAT IT'S *SUPPOSED* TO BE!!!

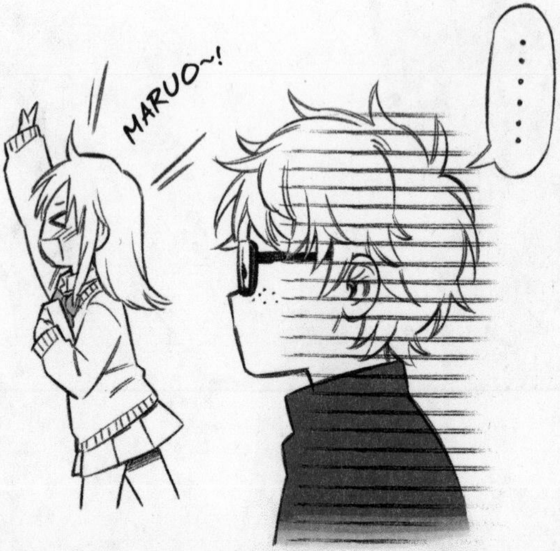
......
MARUO~!

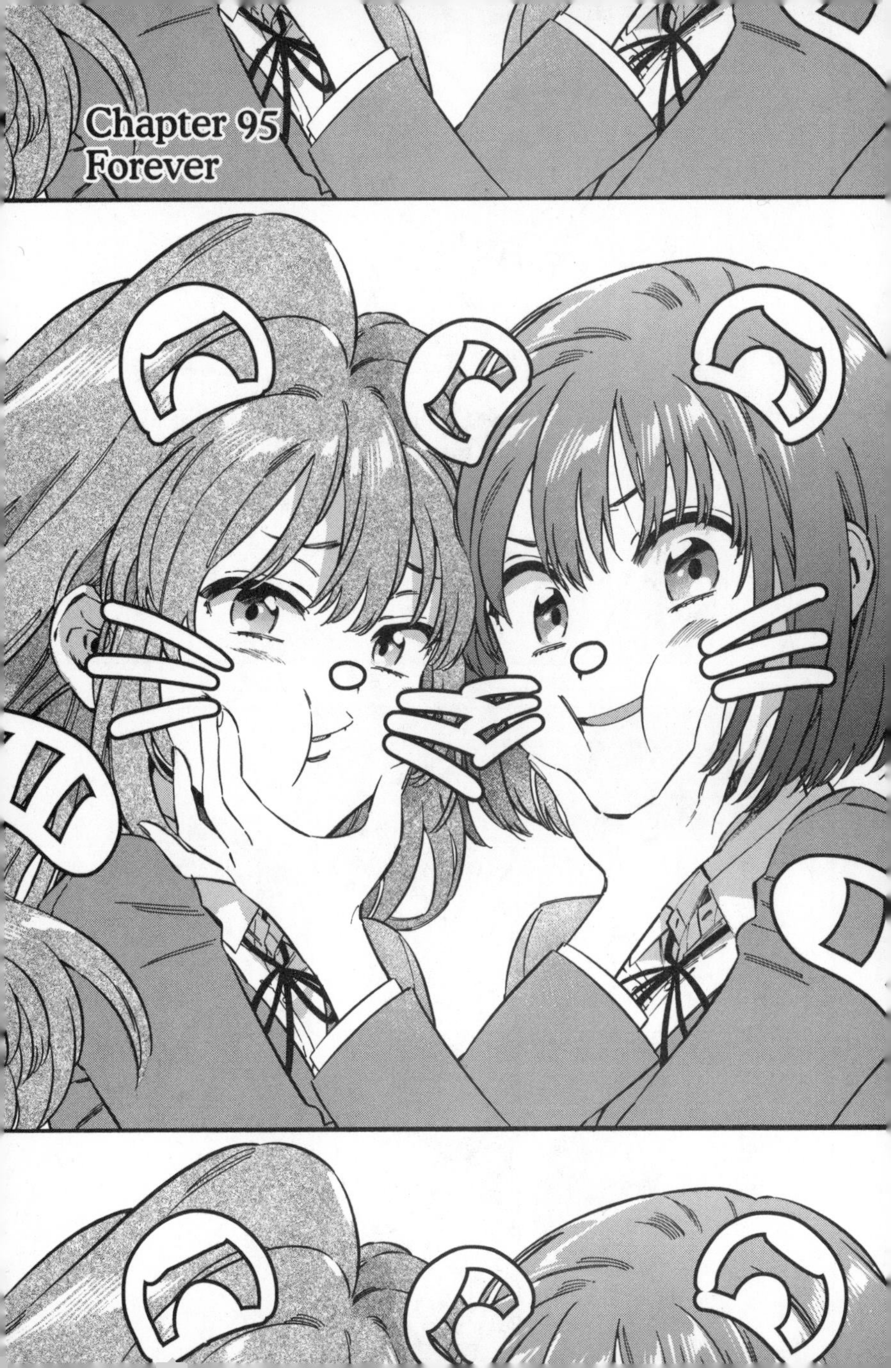
Chapter 95
Forever

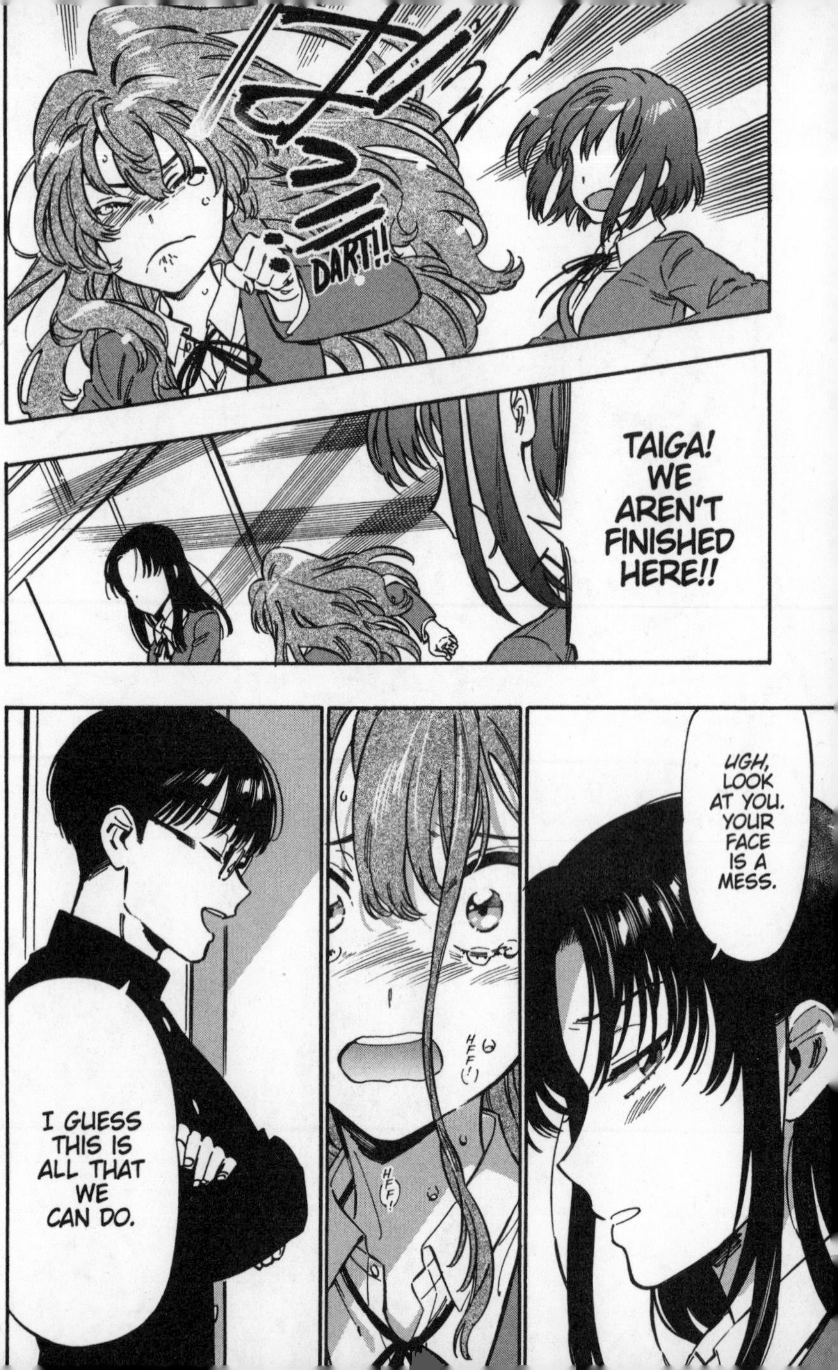
DART!!
TAIGA! WE AREN'T FINISHED HERE!!
UGH, LOOK AT YOU. YOUR FACE IS A MESS.
HFF(!)
HFF(!)
I GUESS THIS IS ALL THAT WE CAN DO.

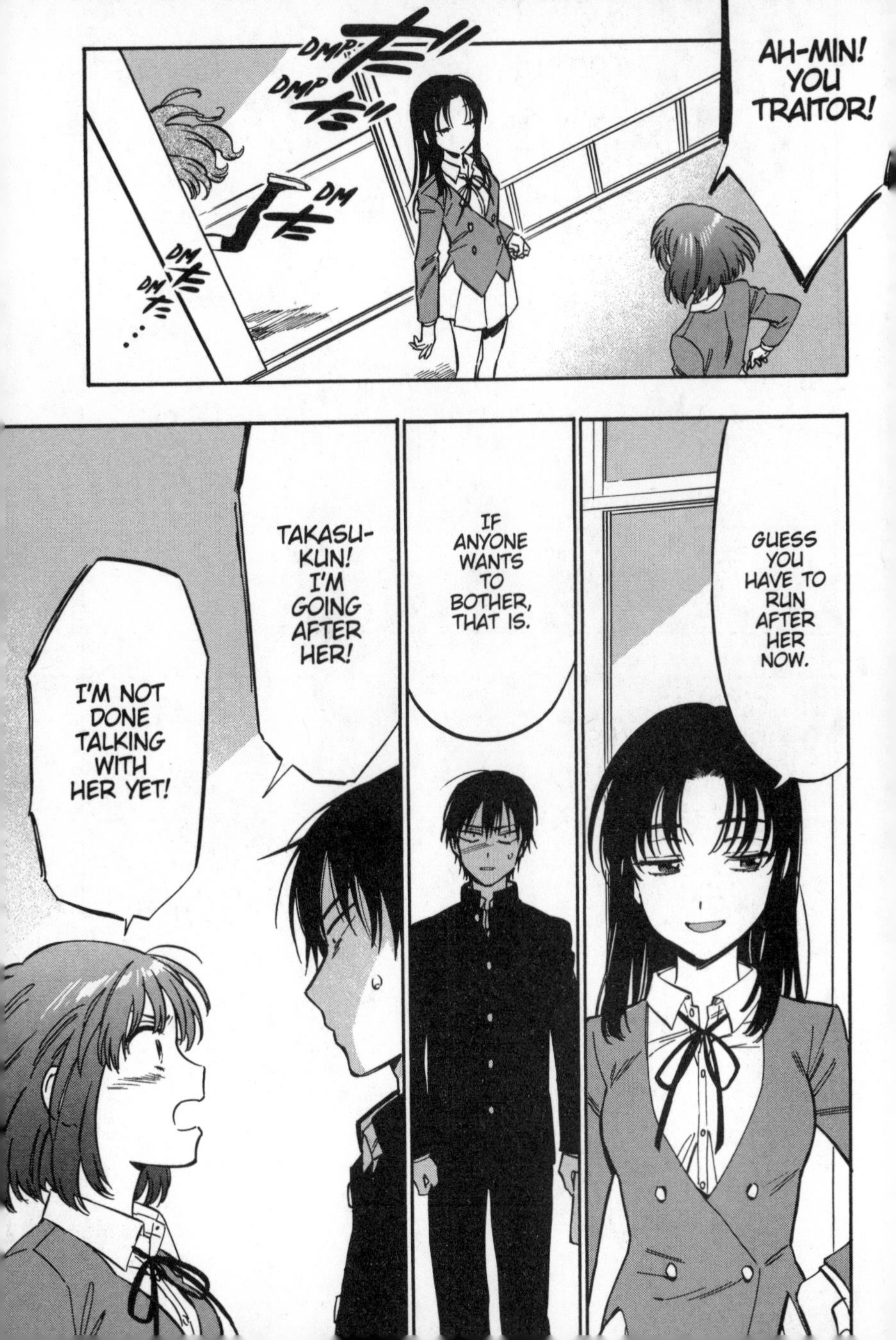
AH-MIN! YOU TRAITOR!
DMP
DMP
DM
DM
DM
...
GUESS YOU HAVE TO RUN AFTER HER NOW.
IF ANYONE WANTS TO BOTHER, THAT IS.
TAKASU-KUN! I'M GOING AFTER HER!
I'M NOT DONE TALKING WITH HER YET!

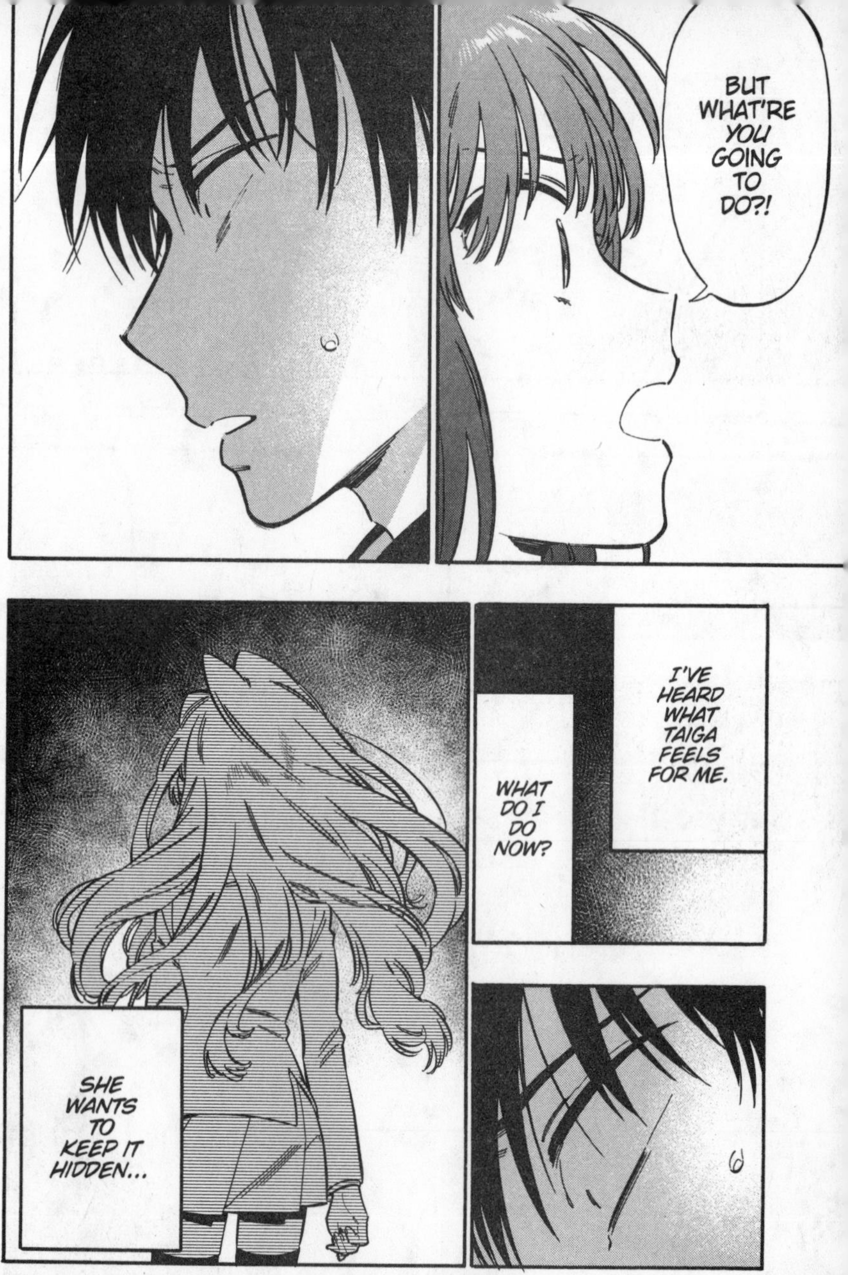
BUT WHAT'RE YOU GOING TO DO?!
I'VE HEARD WHAT TAIGA FEELS FOR ME.
WHAT DO I DO NOW?
SHE WANTS TO KEEP IT HIDDEN...

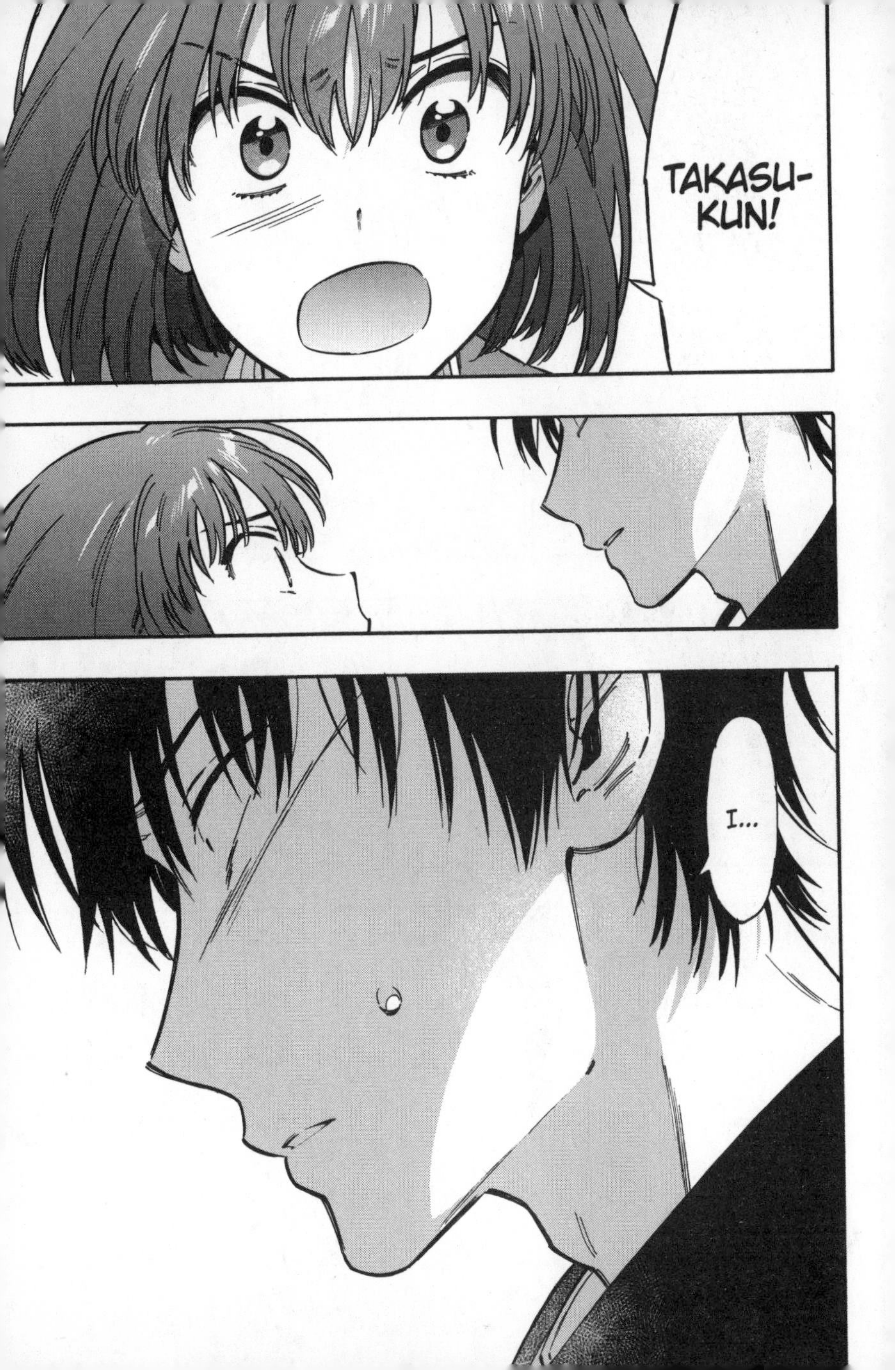
TAKASU-KUN!
I...

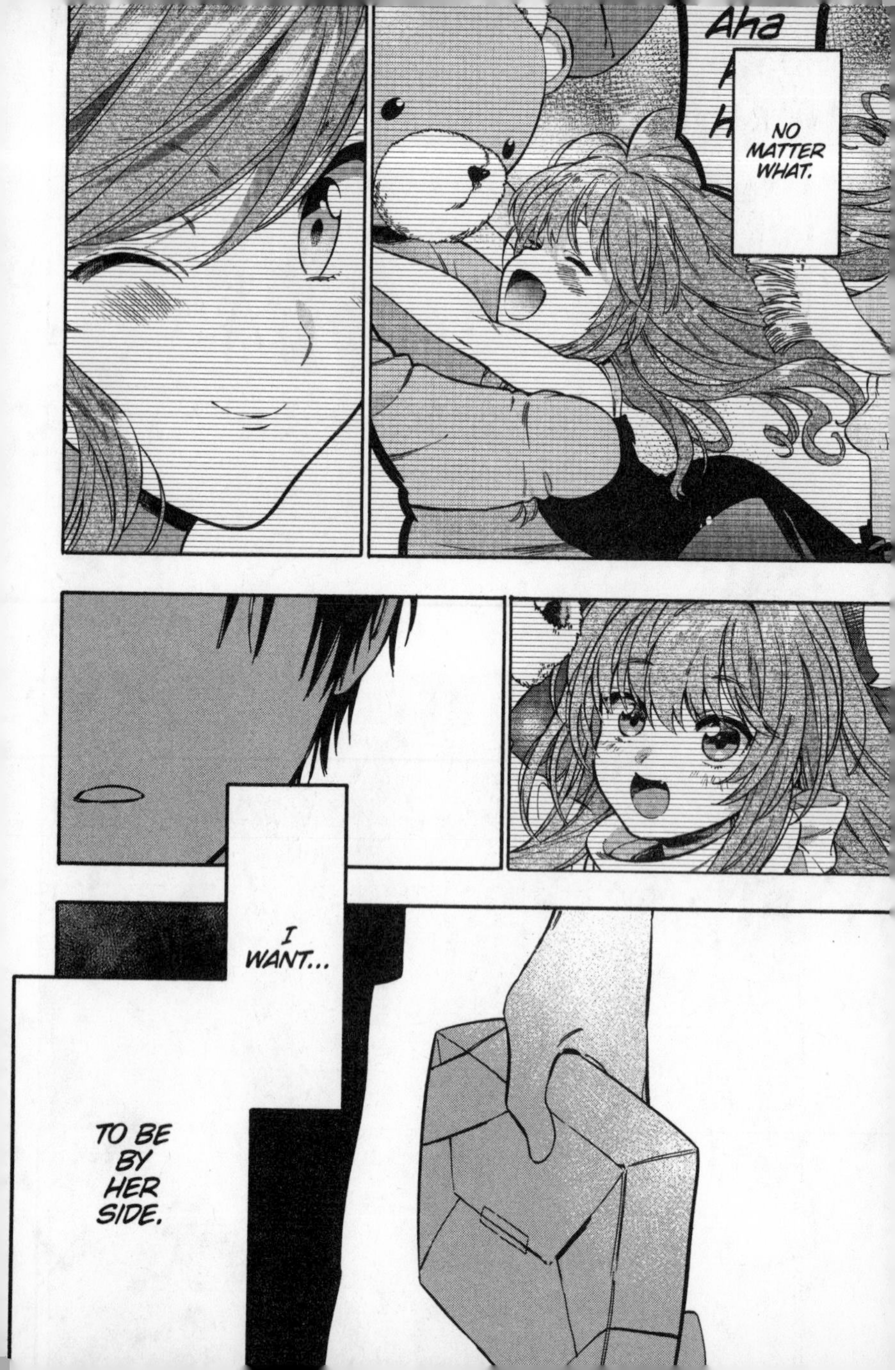

Aha
NO MATTER WHAT.
I WANT...
TO BE BY HER SIDE.

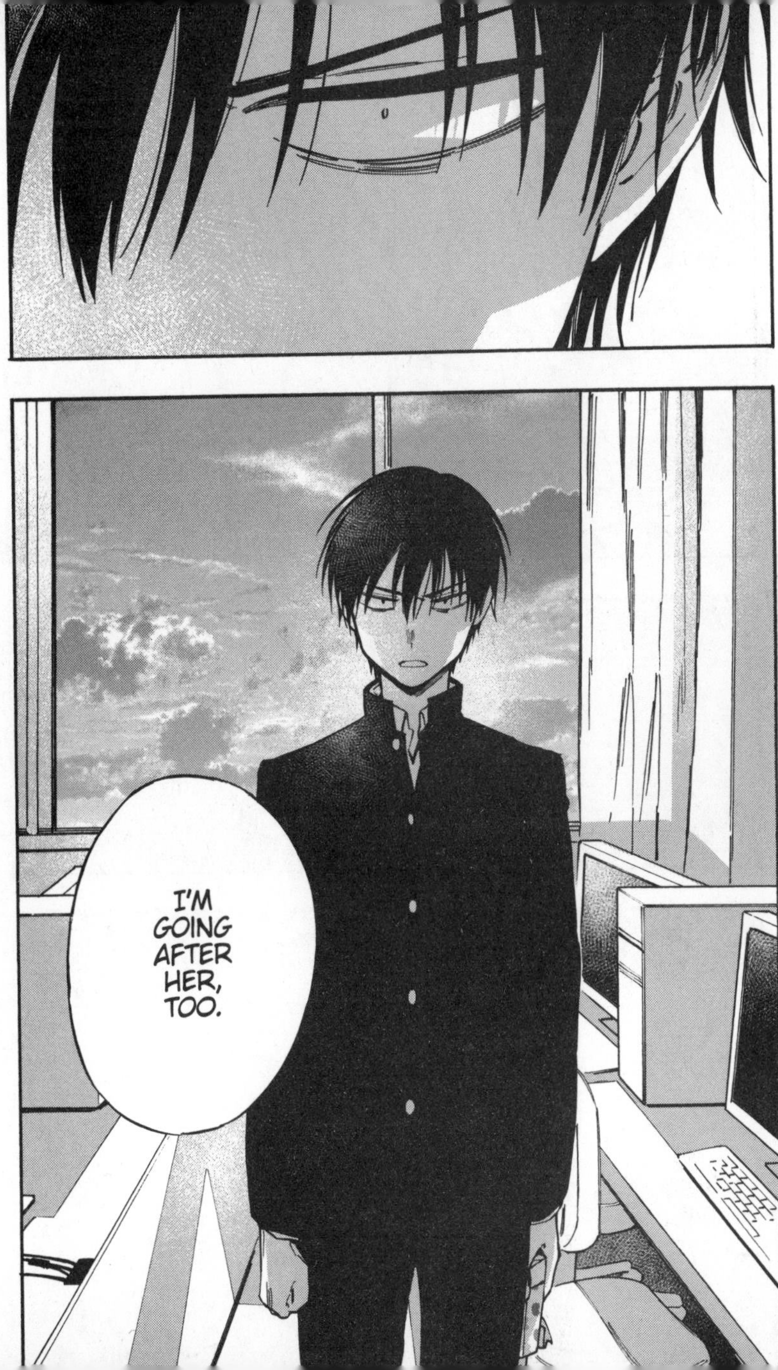
I'M GOING AFTER HER, TOO.

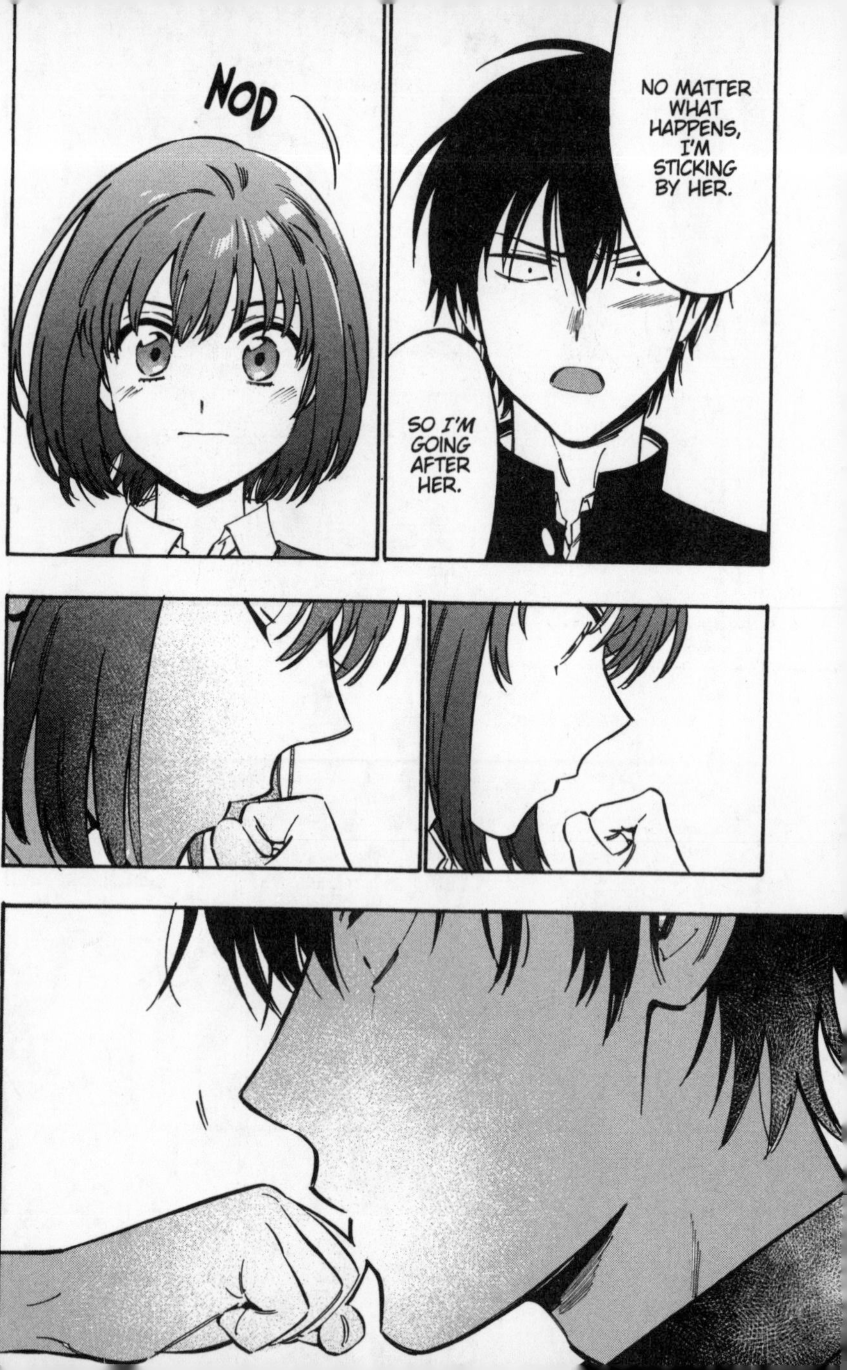
NO MATTER WHAT HAPPENS, I'M STICKING BY HER.
SO I'M GOING AFTER HER.
NOD

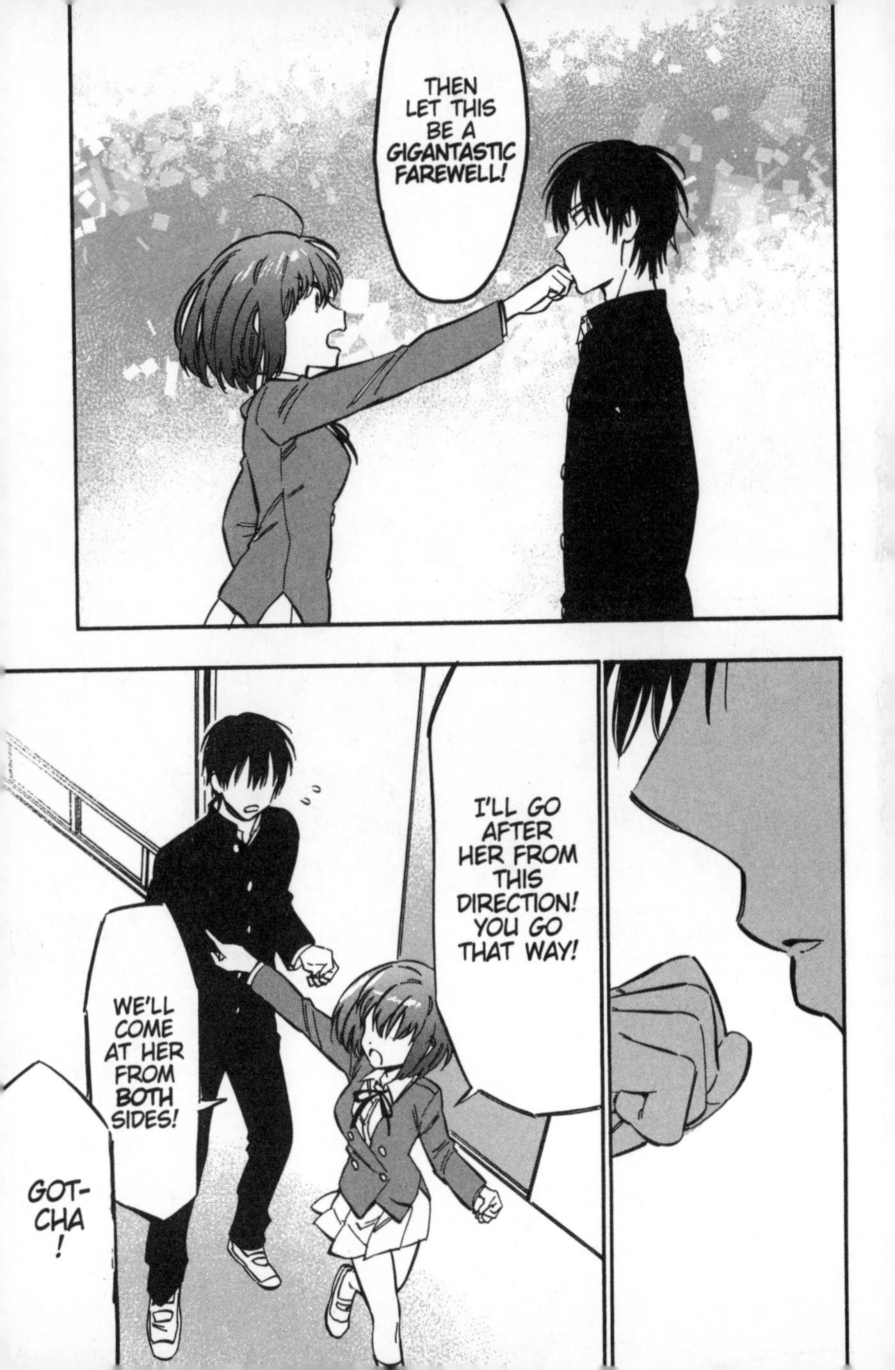
THEN LET THIS BE A GIGANTASTIC FAREWELL!
I'LL GO AFTER HER FROM THIS DIRECTION! YOU GO THAT WAY!
WE'LL COME AT HER FROM BOTH SIDES!
GOT-CHA!

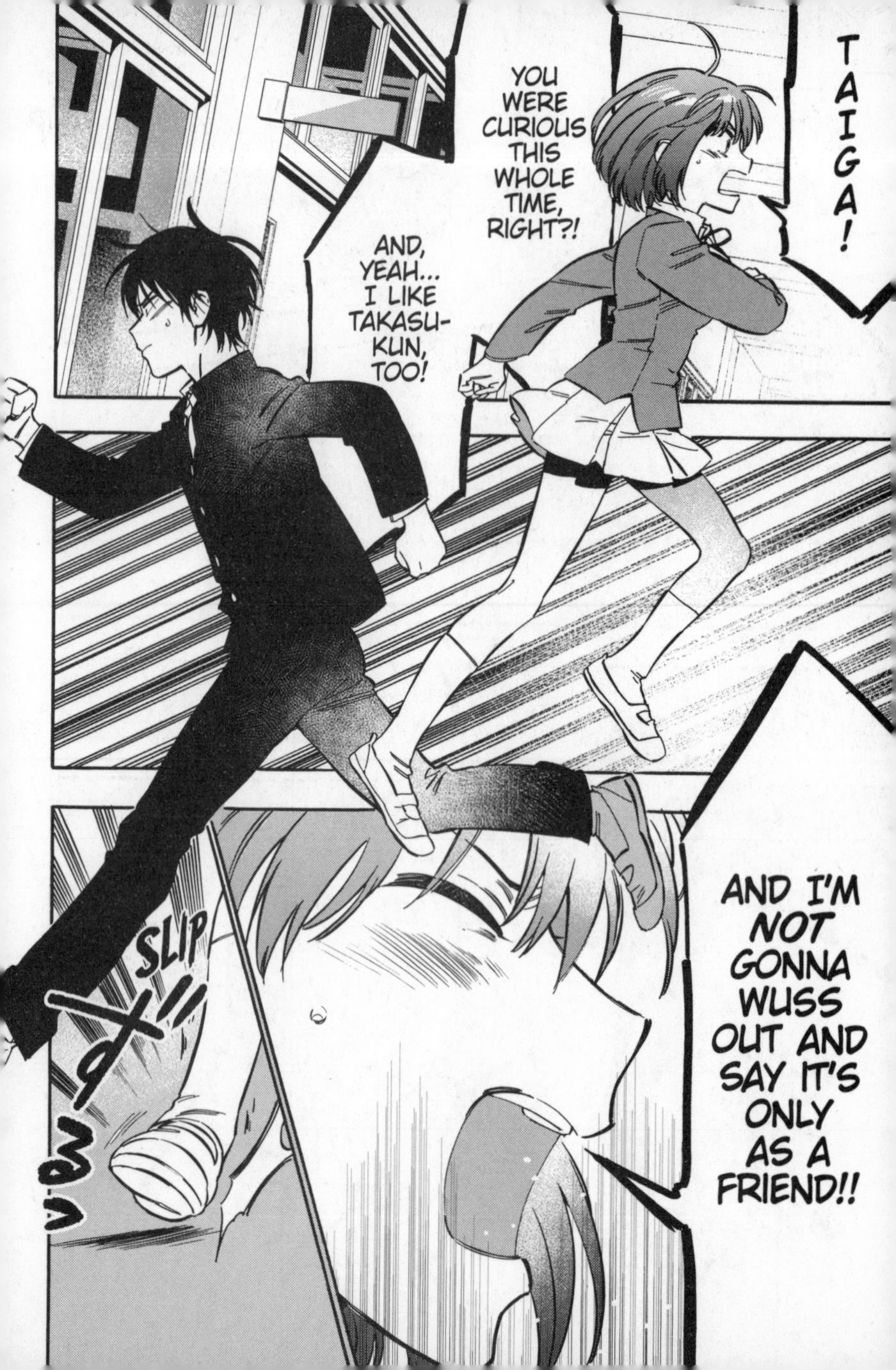
TAIGA!
YOU WERE CURIOUS THIS WHOLE TIME, RIGHT?!
AND, YEAH... I LIKE TAKASU-KUN, TOO!
AND I'M *NOT* GONNA WUSS OUT AND SAY IT'S ONLY AS A FRIEND!!
SLIP

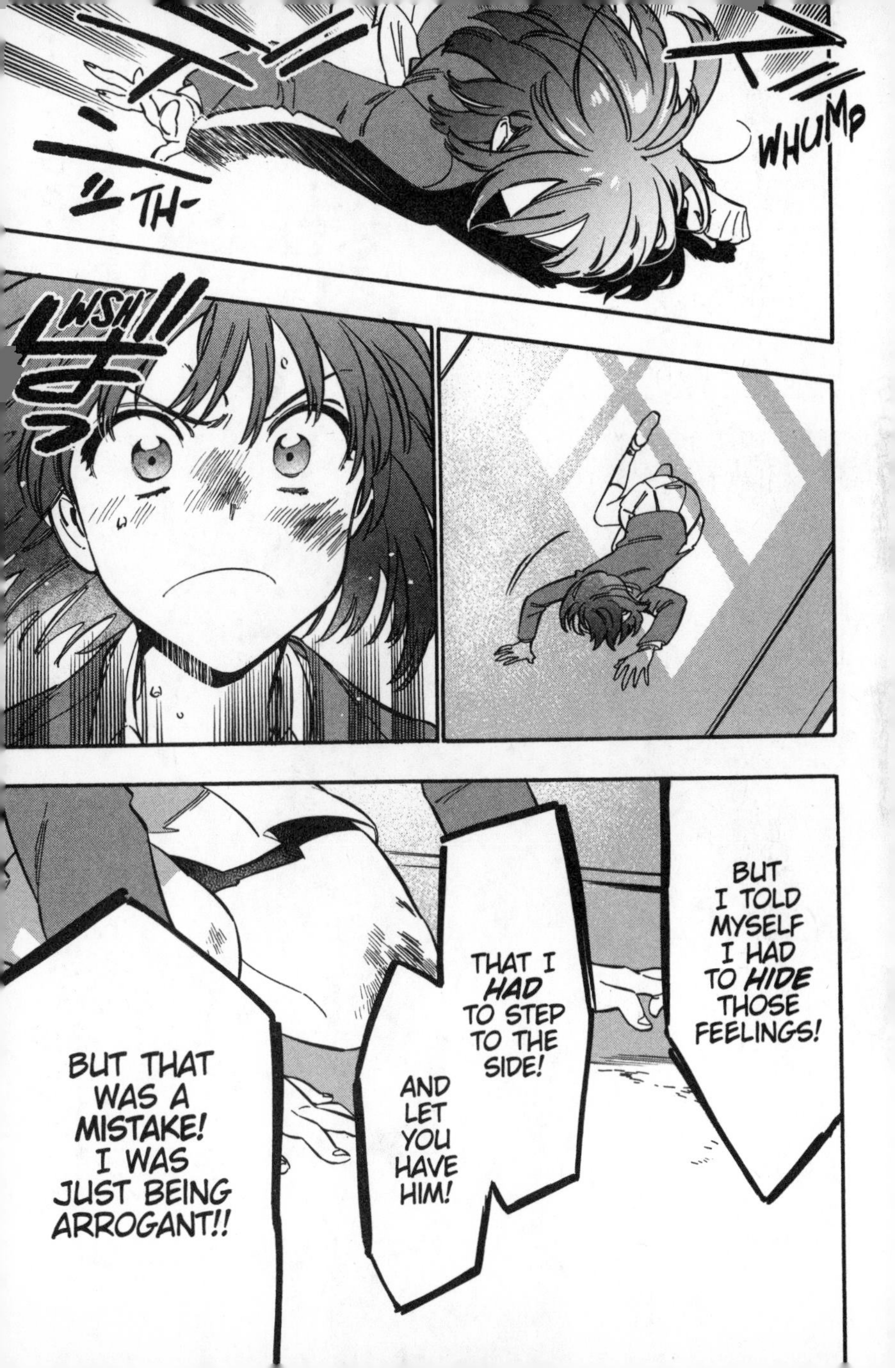
WHUMP
TH-
WSH!!
BUT I TOLD MYSELF I HAD TO *HIDE* THOSE FEELINGS!
THAT I *HAD* TO STEP TO THE SIDE!
AND LET YOU HAVE HIM!
BUT THAT WAS A MISTAKE! I WAS JUST BEING ARROGANT!!

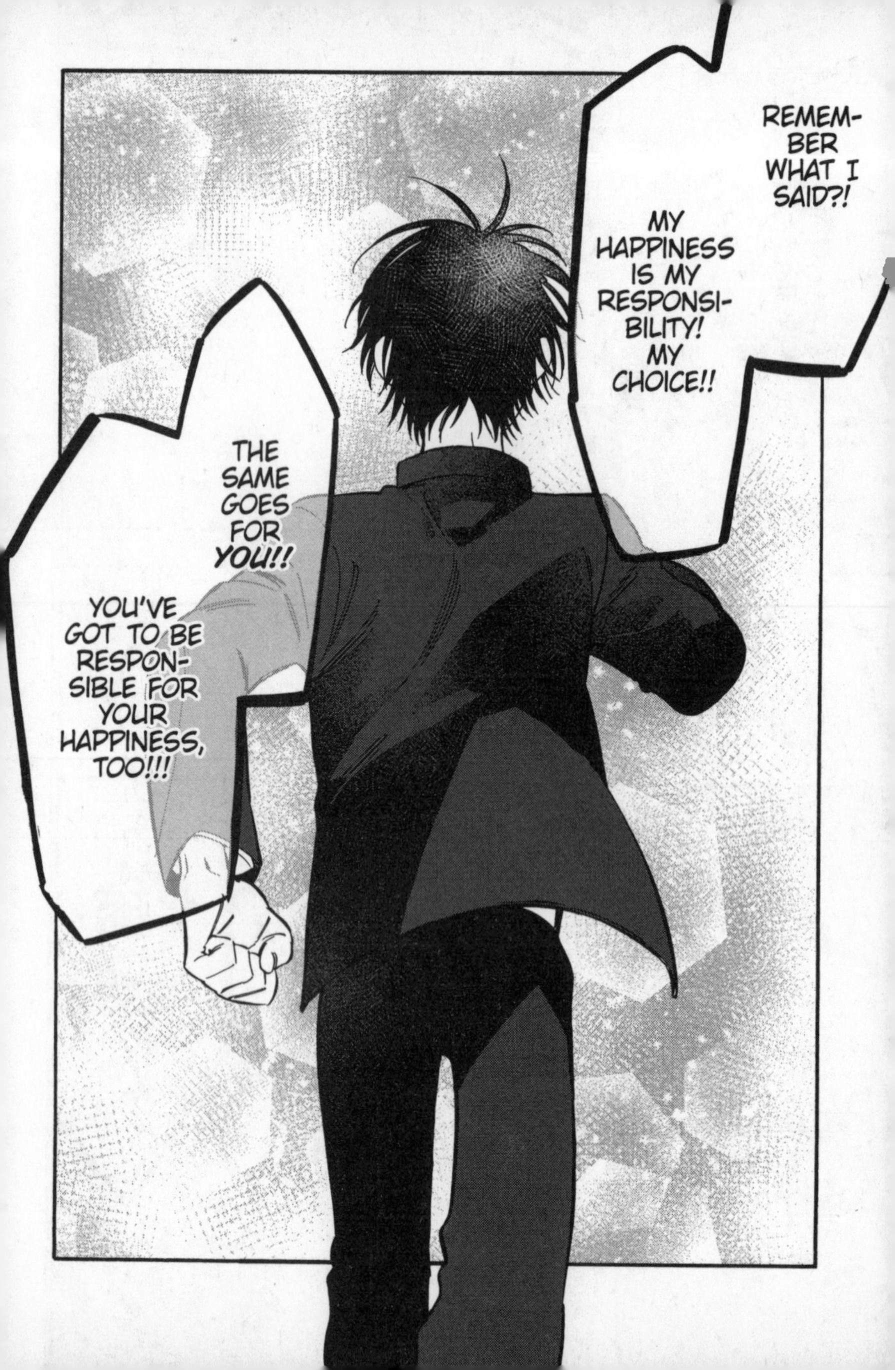
REMEMBER WHAT I SAID?!
MY HAPPINESS IS MY RESPONSIBILITY! MY CHOICE!!
THE SAME GOES FOR *YOU*!!
YOU'VE GOT TO BE RESPONSIBLE FOR YOUR HAPPINESS, TOO!!!

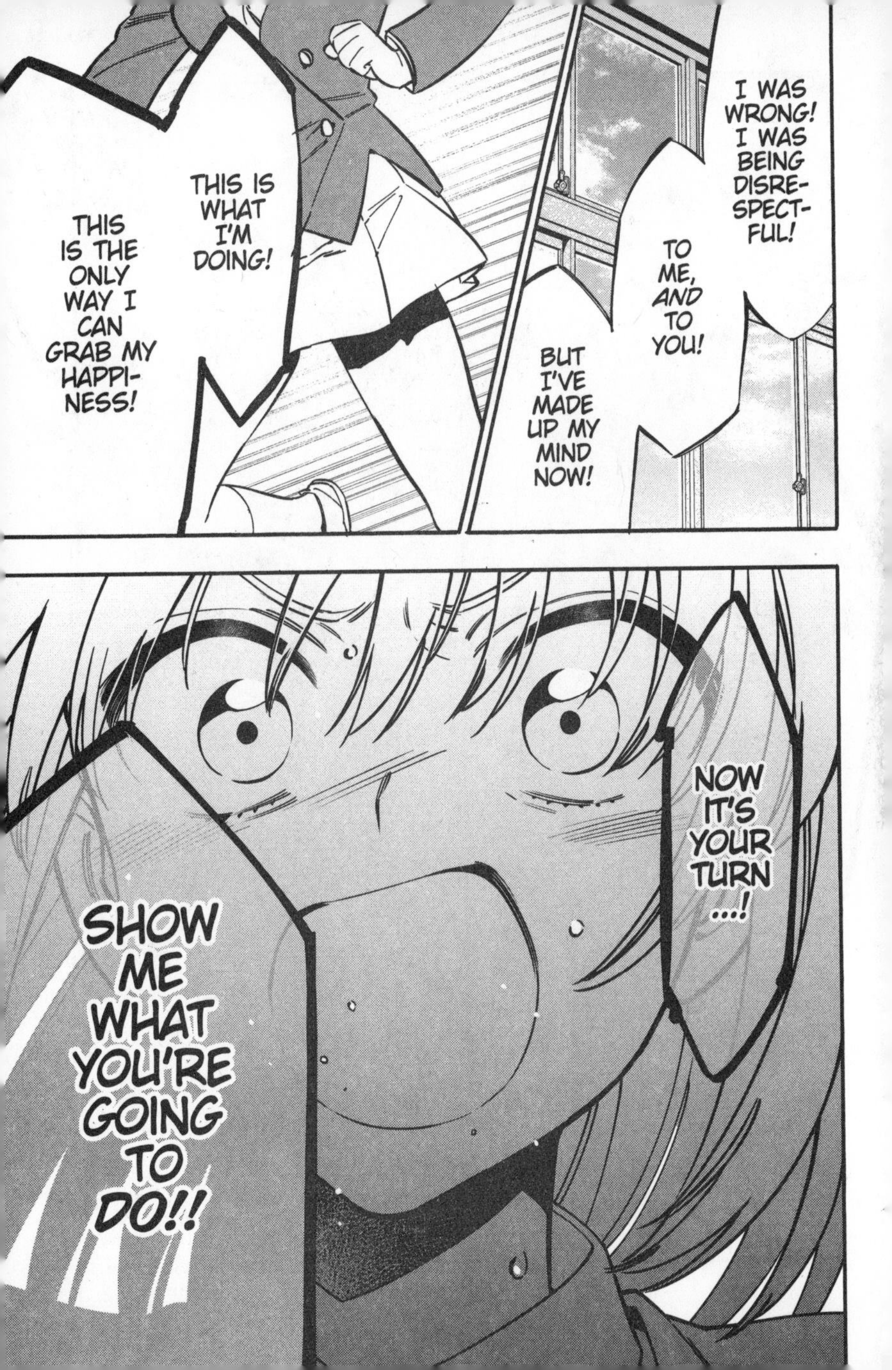
I WAS WRONG! I WAS BEING DISRE-SPECT-FUL!
TO ME, AND TO YOU!
BUT I'VE MADE UP MY MIND NOW!
THIS IS WHAT I'M DOING!
THIS IS THE ONLY WAY I CAN GRAB MY HAPPI-NESS!
NOW IT'S YOUR TURN ...!
SHOW ME WHAT YOU'RE GOING TO DO!!

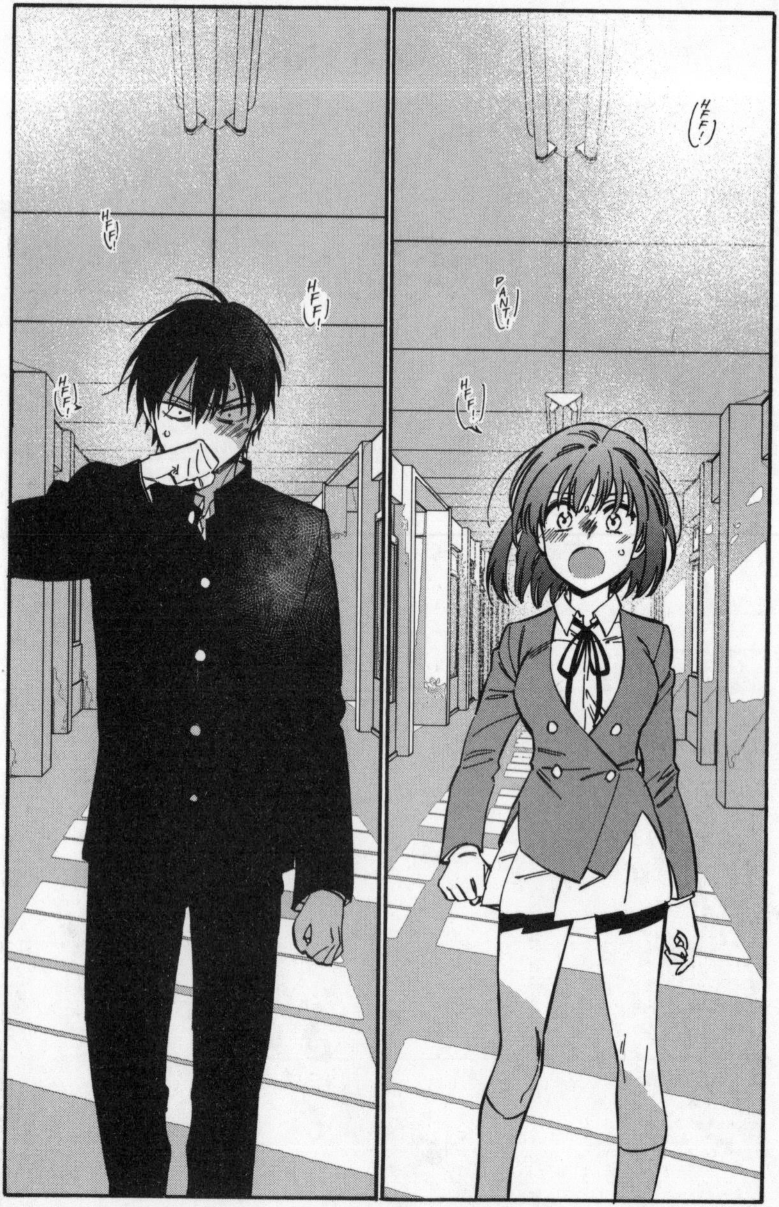
HFF!
PANT!
HFF!
HFF!
HFF!
HFF!

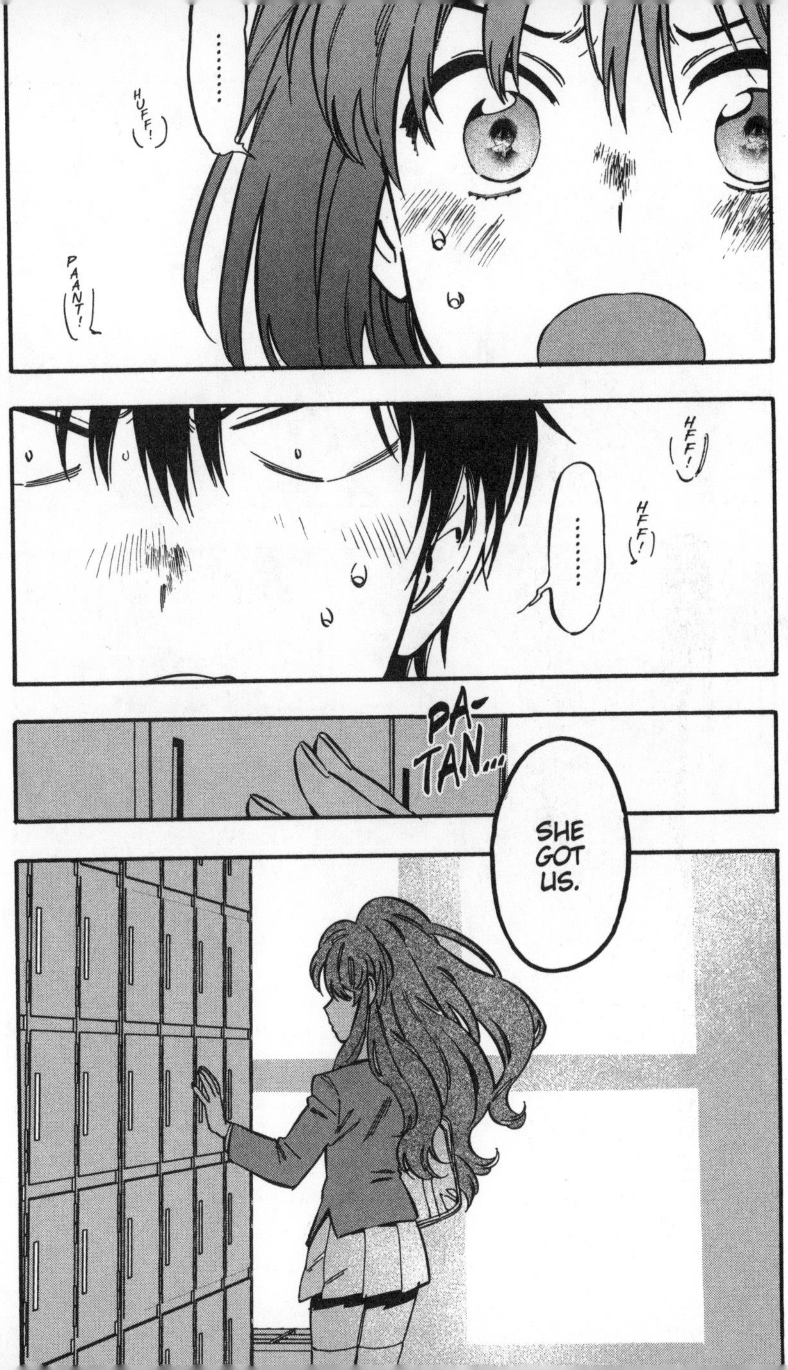
......
HUFF!
PAANT!
HFF!
HFF!
......
PA-TAN...
SHE GOT US.

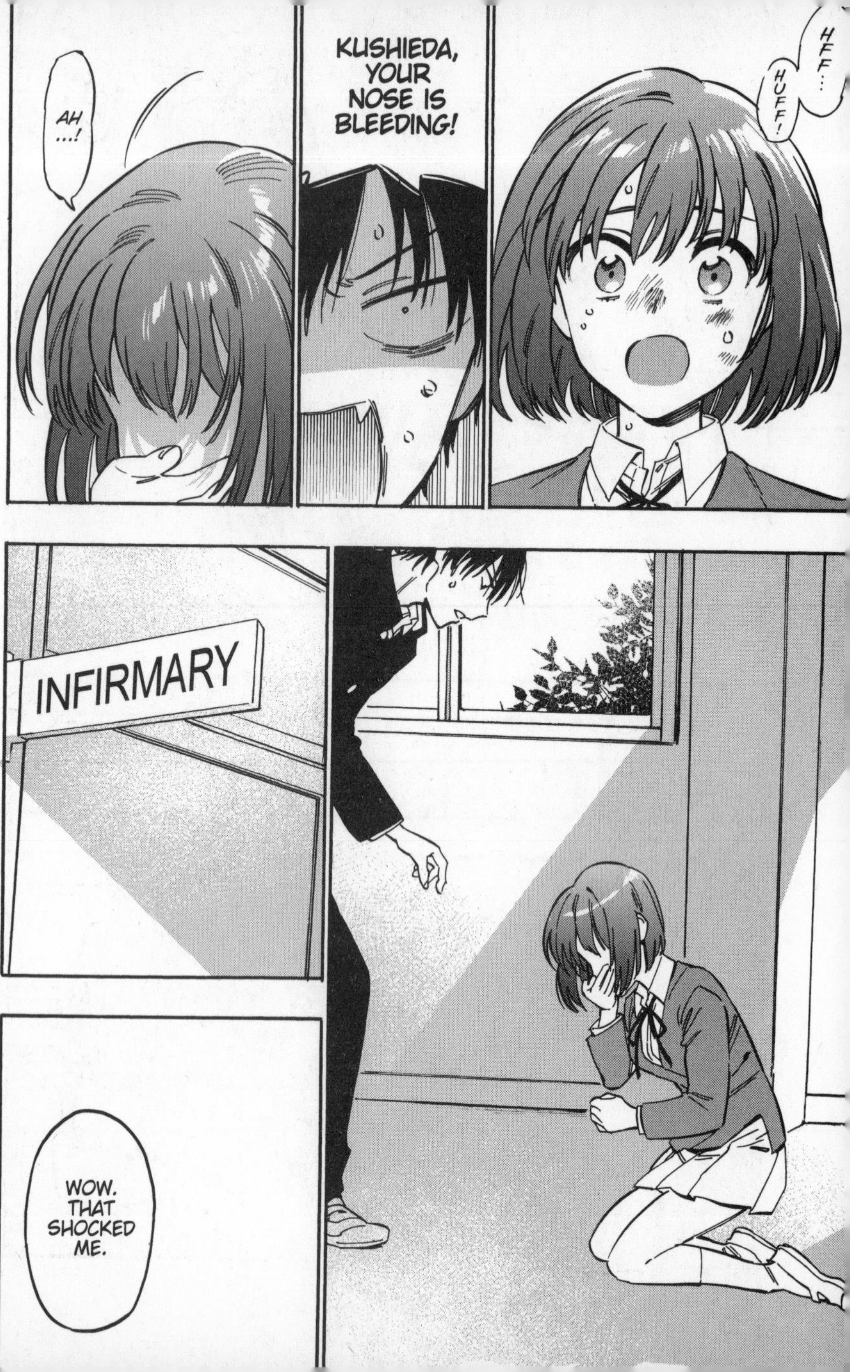
HFF... HUFF!
KUSHIEDA, YOUR NOSE IS BLEEDING!
AH ...!
INFIRMARY
WOW. THAT SHOCKED ME.

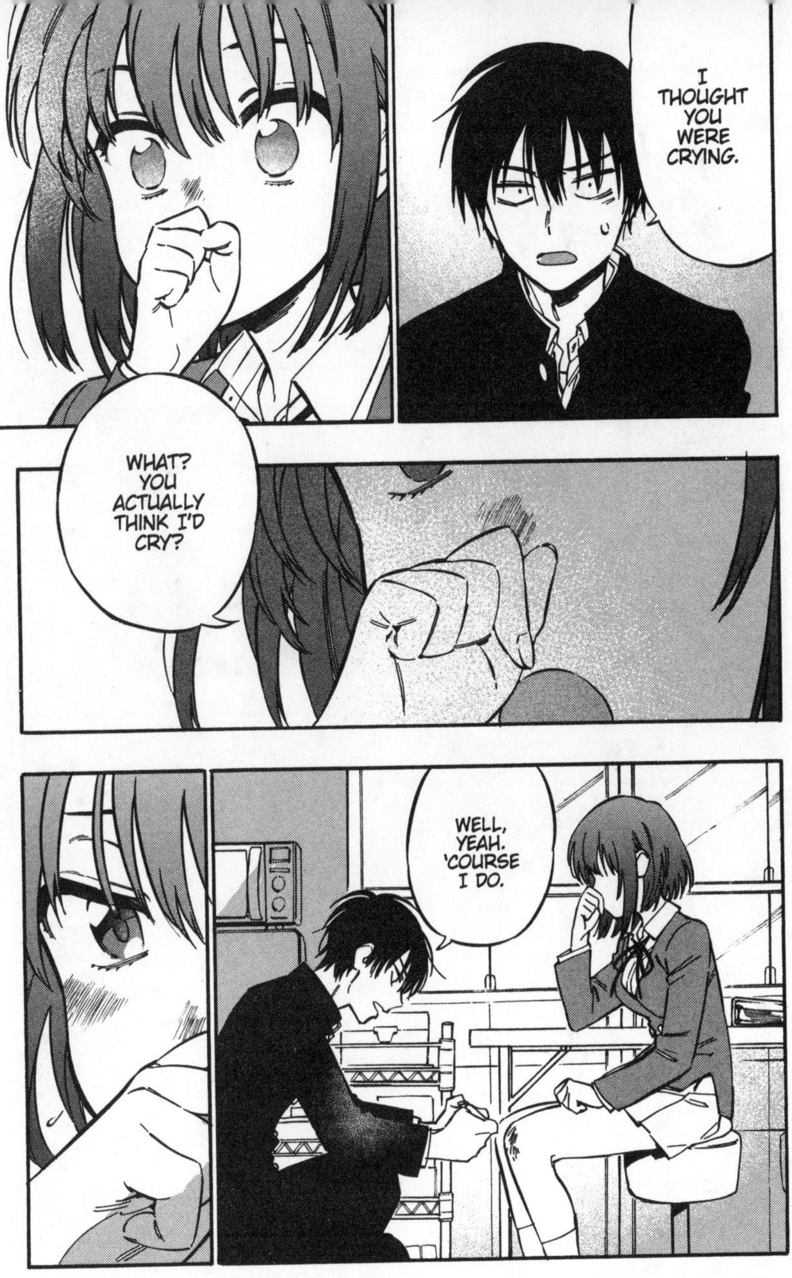
I THOUGHT YOU WERE CRYING.
WHAT? YOU ACTUALLY THINK I'D CRY?
WELL, YEAH. 'COURSE I DO.

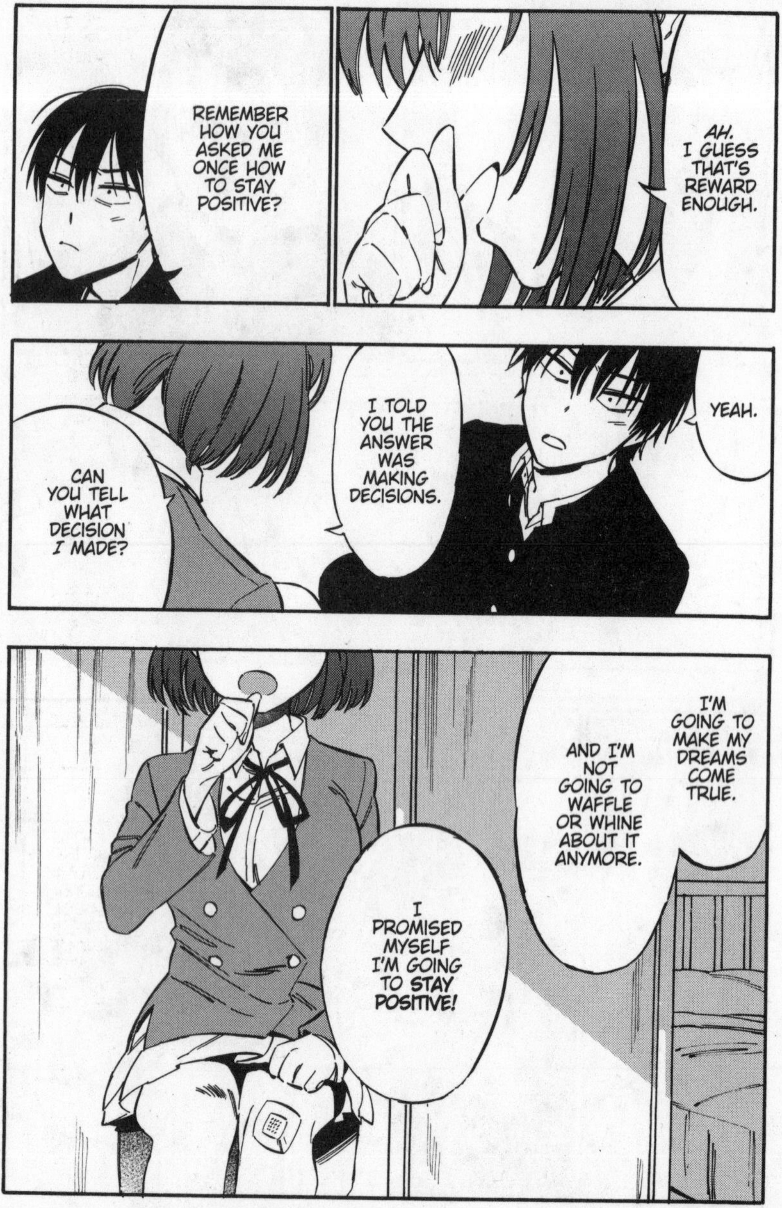
AH. I GUESS THAT'S REWARD ENOUGH.
REMEMBER HOW YOU ASKED ME ONCE HOW TO STAY POSITIVE?
YEAH.
I TOLD YOU THE ANSWER WAS MAKING DECISIONS.
CAN YOU TELL WHAT DECISION I MADE?
I'M GOING TO MAKE MY DREAMS COME TRUE.
AND I'M NOT GOING TO WAFFLE OR WHINE ABOUT IT ANYMORE.
I PROMISED MYSELF I'M GOING TO STAY POSITIVE!

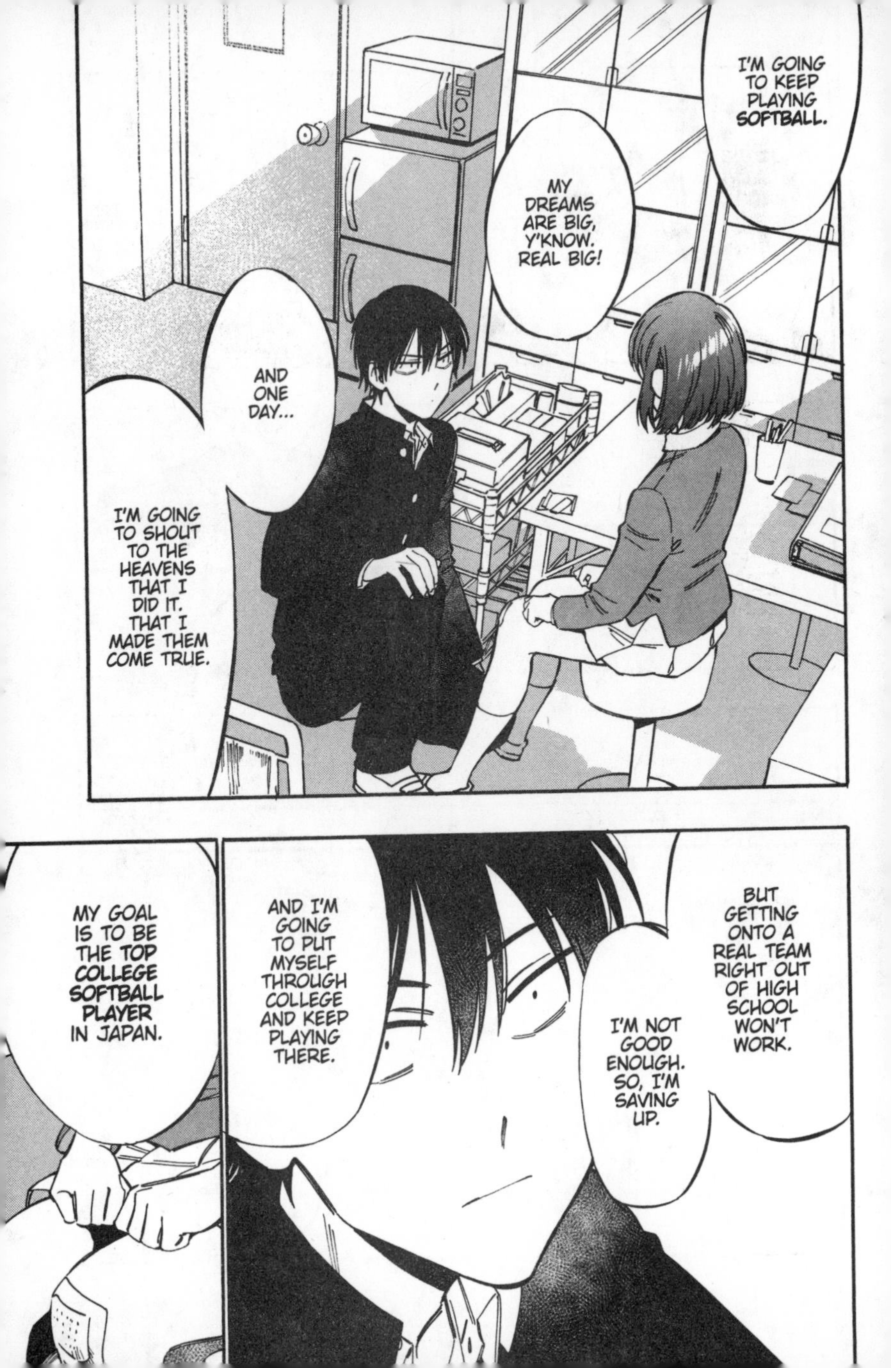

I'M GOING TO KEEP PLAYING SOFTBALL.
MY DREAMS ARE BIG, Y'KNOW. REAL BIG!
AND ONE DAY...
I'M GOING TO SHOUT TO THE HEAVENS THAT I DID IT. THAT I MADE THEM COME TRUE.
BUT GETTING ONTO A REAL TEAM RIGHT OUT OF HIGH SCHOOL WON'T WORK.
I'M NOT GOOD ENOUGH. SO, I'M SAVING UP.
AND I'M GOING TO PUT MYSELF THROUGH COLLEGE AND KEEP PLAYING THERE.
MY GOAL IS TO BE THE TOP COLLEGE SOFTBALL PLAYER IN JAPAN.

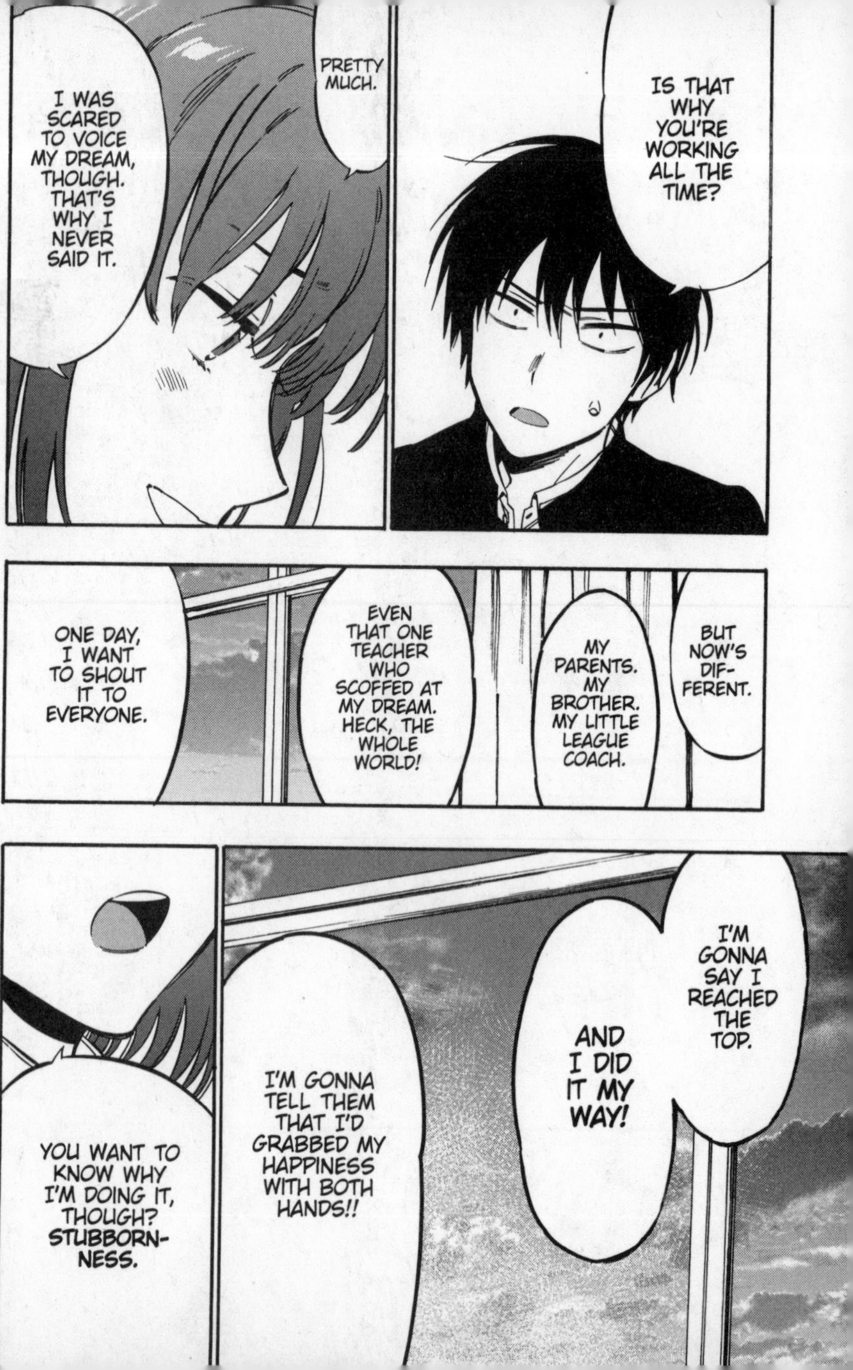
IS THAT WHY YOU'RE WORKING ALL THE TIME?
PRETTY MUCH.
I WAS SCARED TO VOICE MY DREAM, THOUGH. THAT'S WHY I NEVER SAID IT.
BUT NOW'S DIF-FERENT.
MY PARENTS. MY BROTHER. MY LITTLE LEAGUE COACH.
EVEN THAT ONE TEACHER WHO SCOFFED AT MY DREAM. HECK, THE WHOLE WORLD!
ONE DAY, I WANT TO SHOUT IT TO EVERYONE.
I'M GONNA SAY I REACHED THE TOP.
AND I DID IT MY WAY!
I'M GONNA TELL THEM THAT I'D GRABBED MY HAPPINESS WITH BOTH HANDS!!
YOU WANT TO KNOW WHY I'M DOING IT, THOUGH? STUBBORN-NESS.

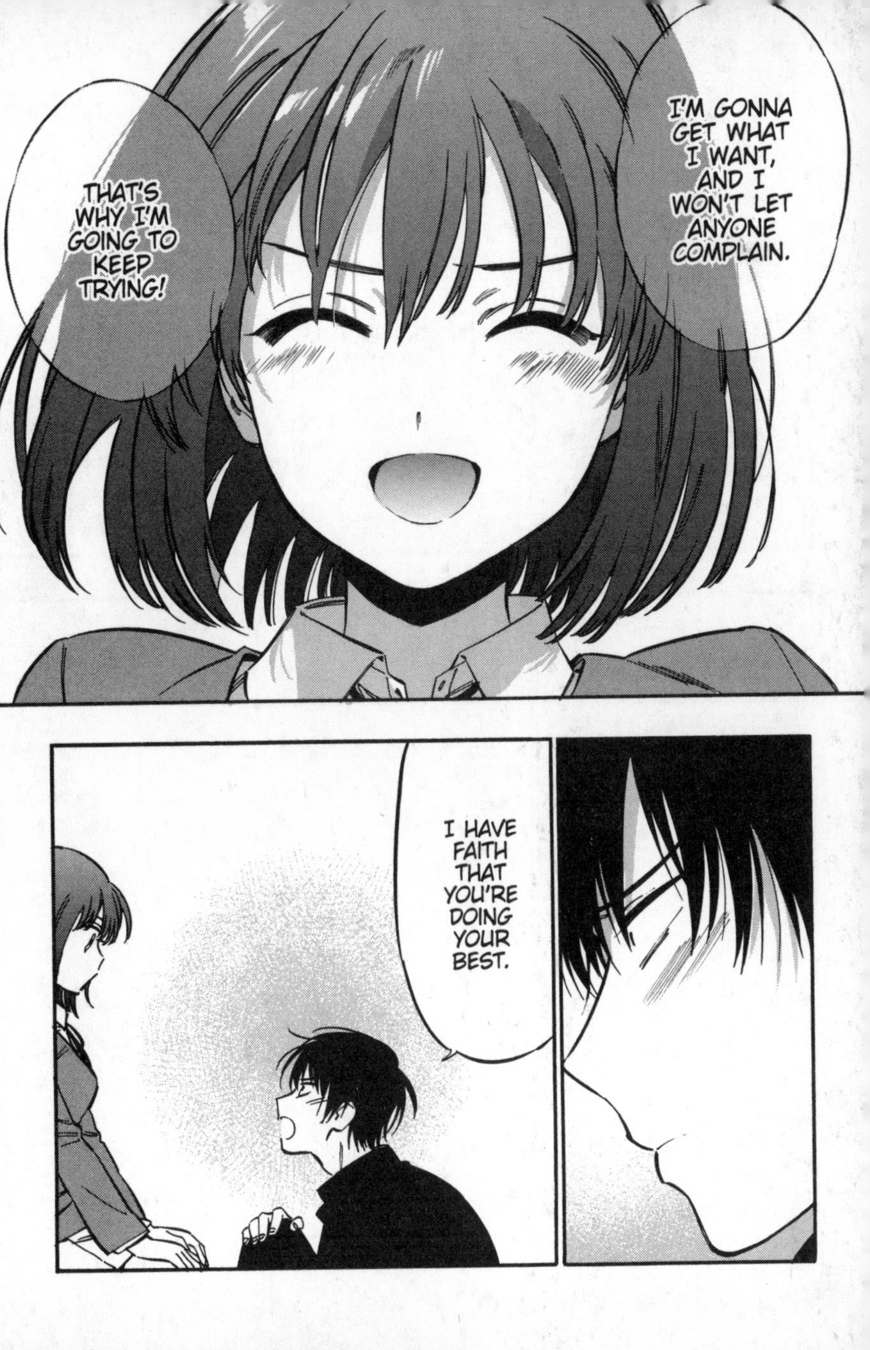
I'M GONNA GET WHAT I WANT, AND I WON'T LET ANYONE COMPLAIN.
THAT'S WHY I'M GOING TO KEEP TRYING!
I HAVE FAITH THAT YOU'RE DOING YOUR BEST.

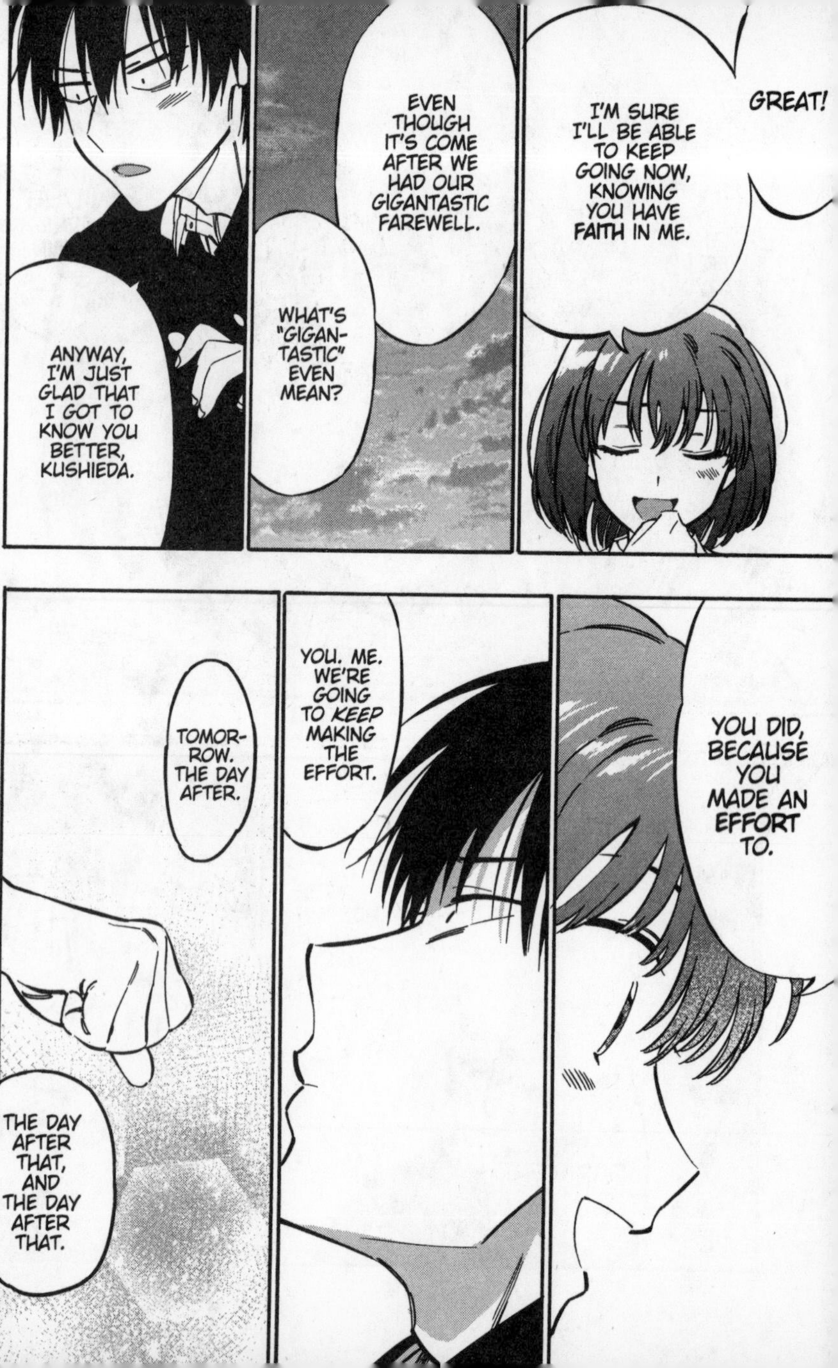
GREAT!
I'M SURE I'LL BE ABLE TO KEEP GOING NOW, KNOWING YOU HAVE FAITH IN ME.
EVEN THOUGH IT'S COME AFTER WE HAD OUR GIGANTASTIC FAREWELL.
WHAT'S "GIGAN-TASTIC" EVEN MEAN?
ANYWAY, I'M JUST GLAD THAT I GOT TO KNOW YOU BETTER, KUSHIEDA.
YOU DID, BECAUSE YOU MADE AN EFFORT TO.
YOU. ME. WE'RE GOING TO *KEEP* MAKING THE EFFORT.
TOMOR-ROW. THE DAY AFTER.
THE DAY AFTER THAT, AND THE DAY AFTER THAT.

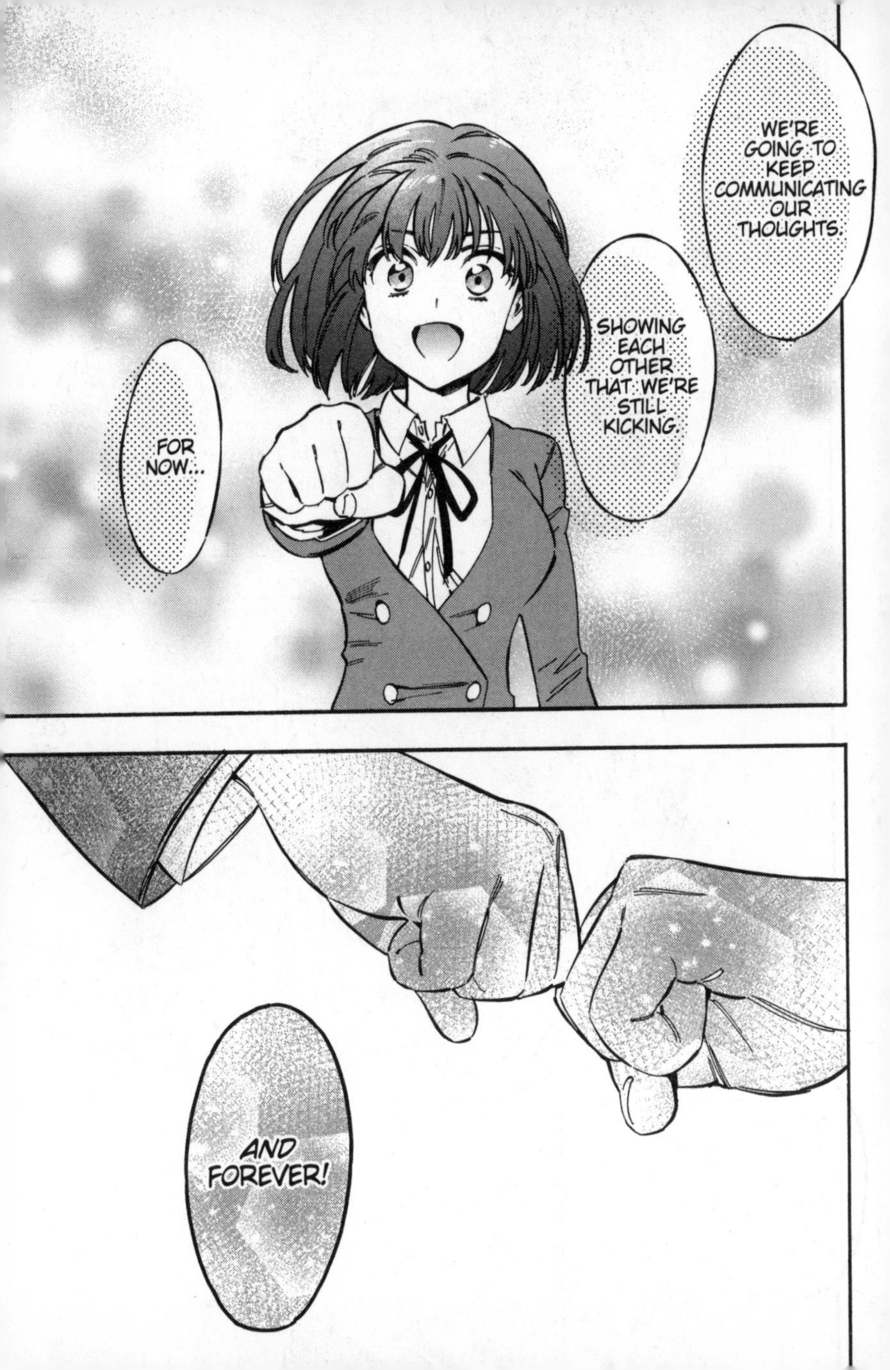
WE'RE GOING TO KEEP COMMUNICATING OUR THOUGHTS.
SHOWING EACH OTHER THAT WE'RE STILL KICKING.
FOR NOW...
AND FOREVER!

# Chapter 96
# Time's Up

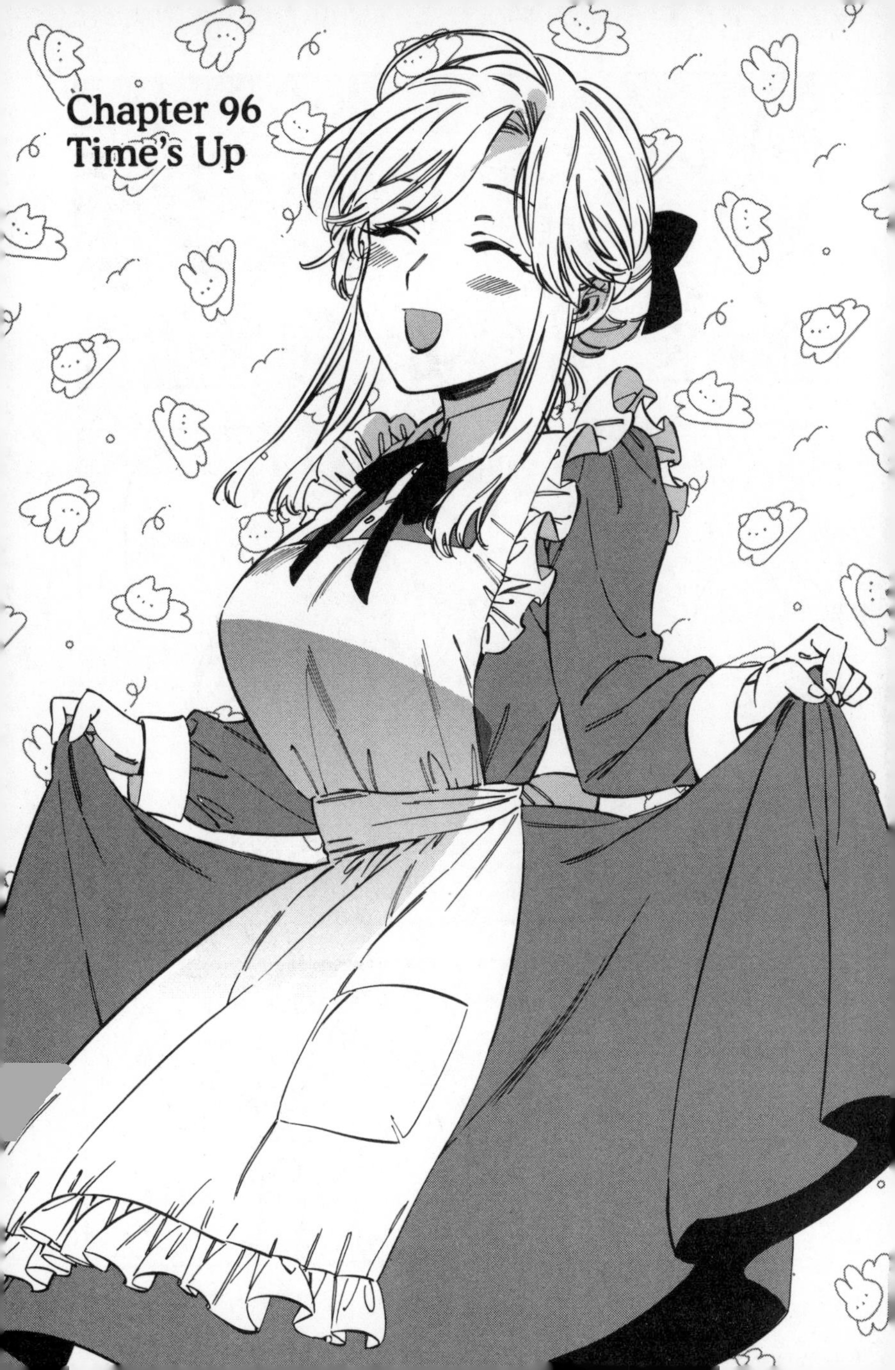

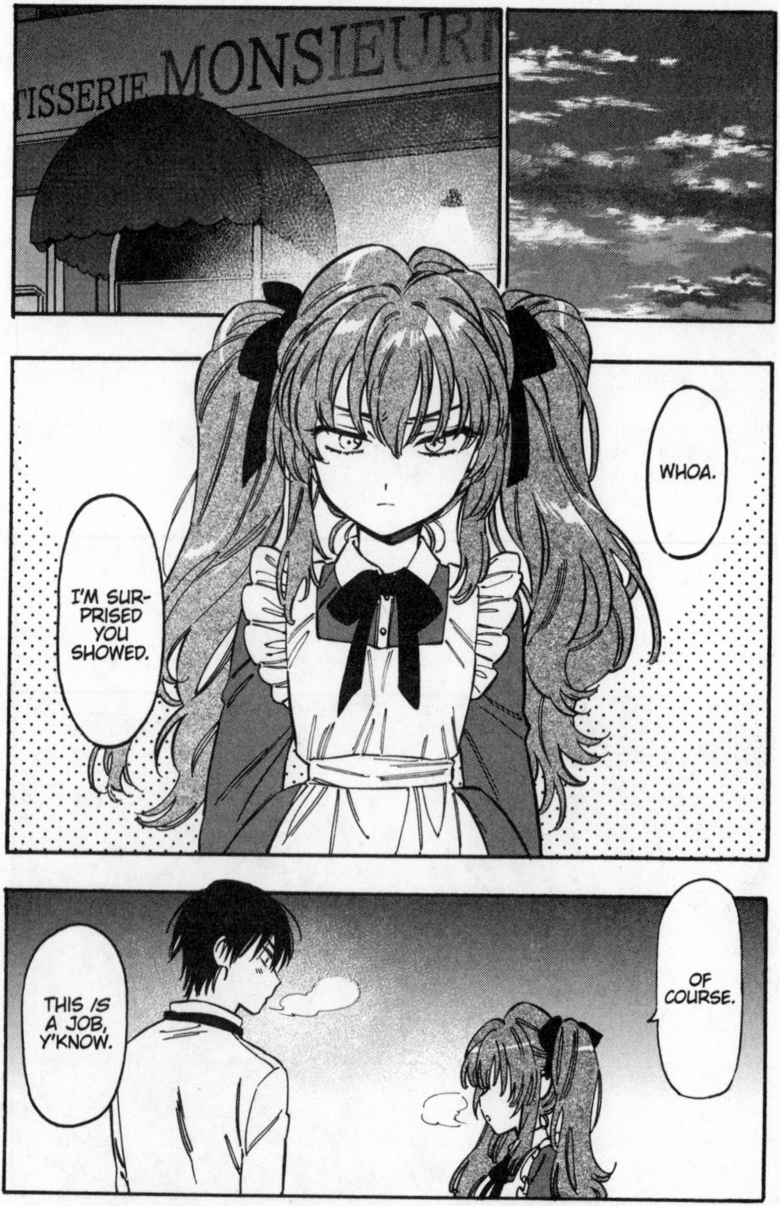
TISSERIE MONSIEUR
WHOA.
I'M SURPRISED YOU SHOWED.
OF COURSE.
THIS IS A JOB, Y'KNOW.

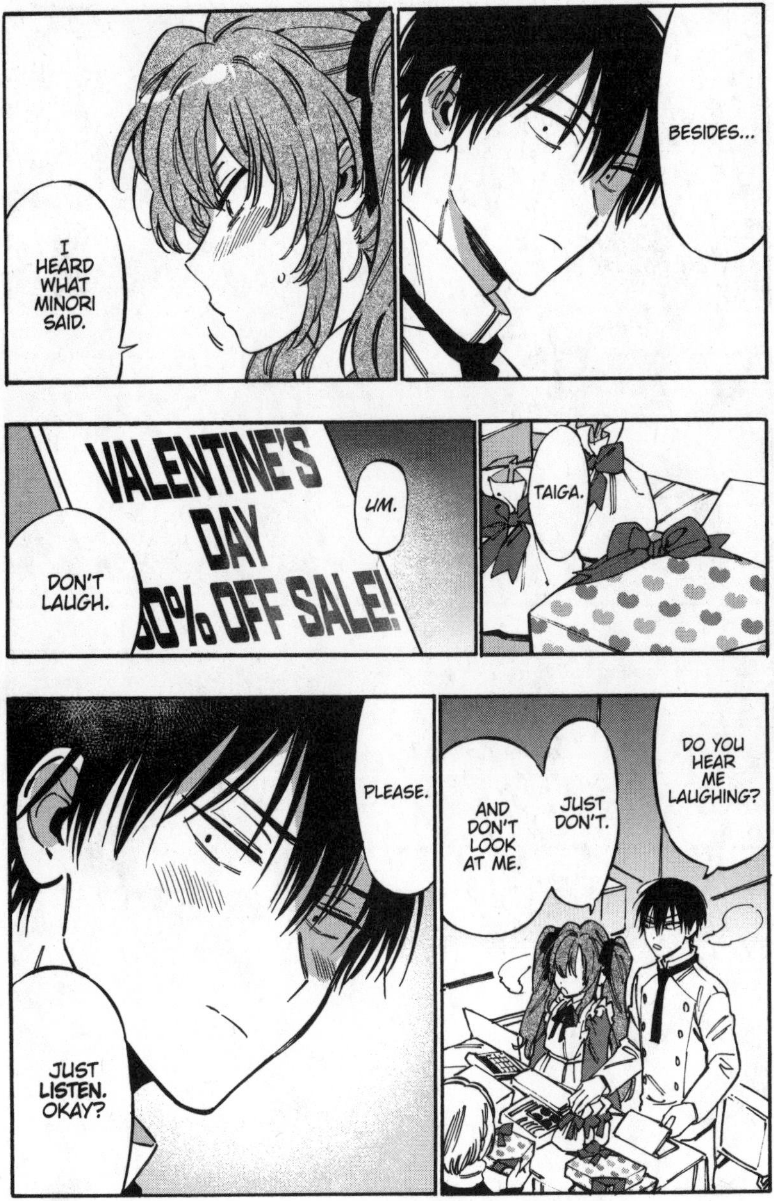
BESIDES...
I HEARD WHAT MINORI SAID.
TAIGA.
UM.
VALENTINE'S DAY
0% OFF SALE!
DON'T LAUGH.
DO YOU HEAR ME LAUGHING?
JUST DON'T.
AND DON'T LOOK AT ME.
PLEASE.
JUST LISTEN. OKAY?

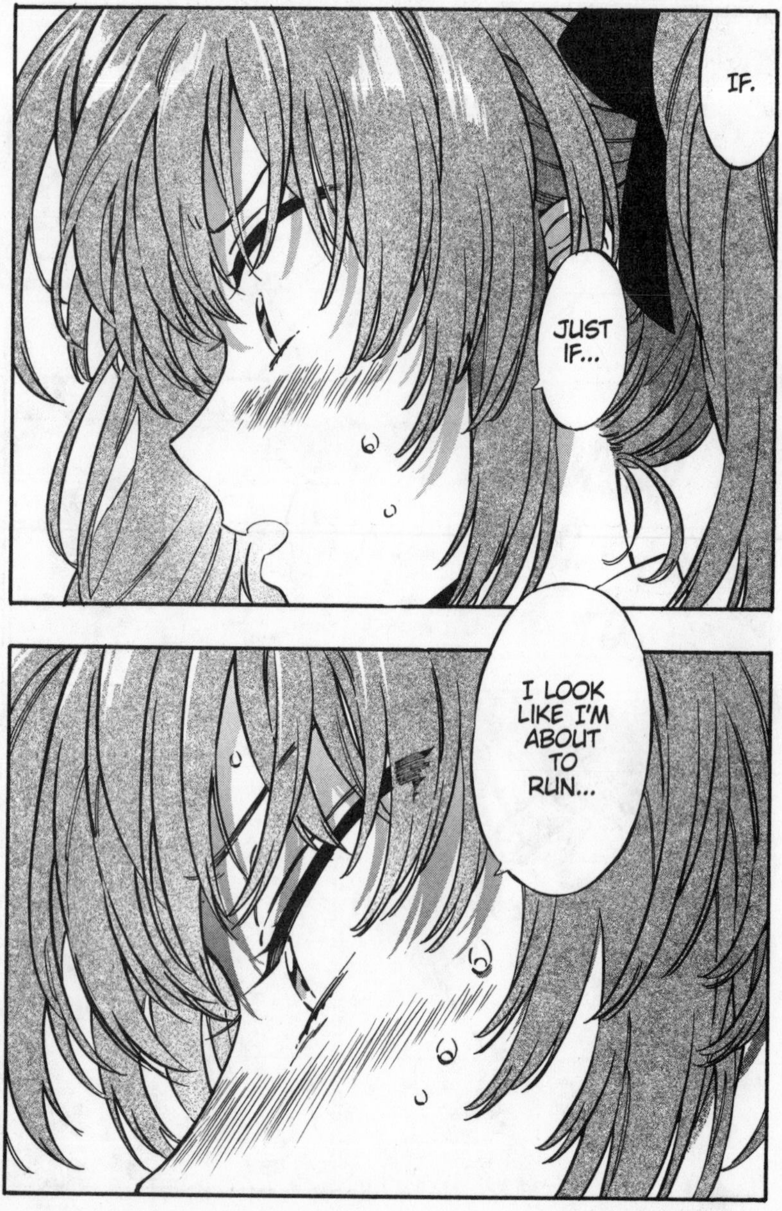
IF.
JUST IF...
I LOOK LIKE I'M ABOUT TO RUN...

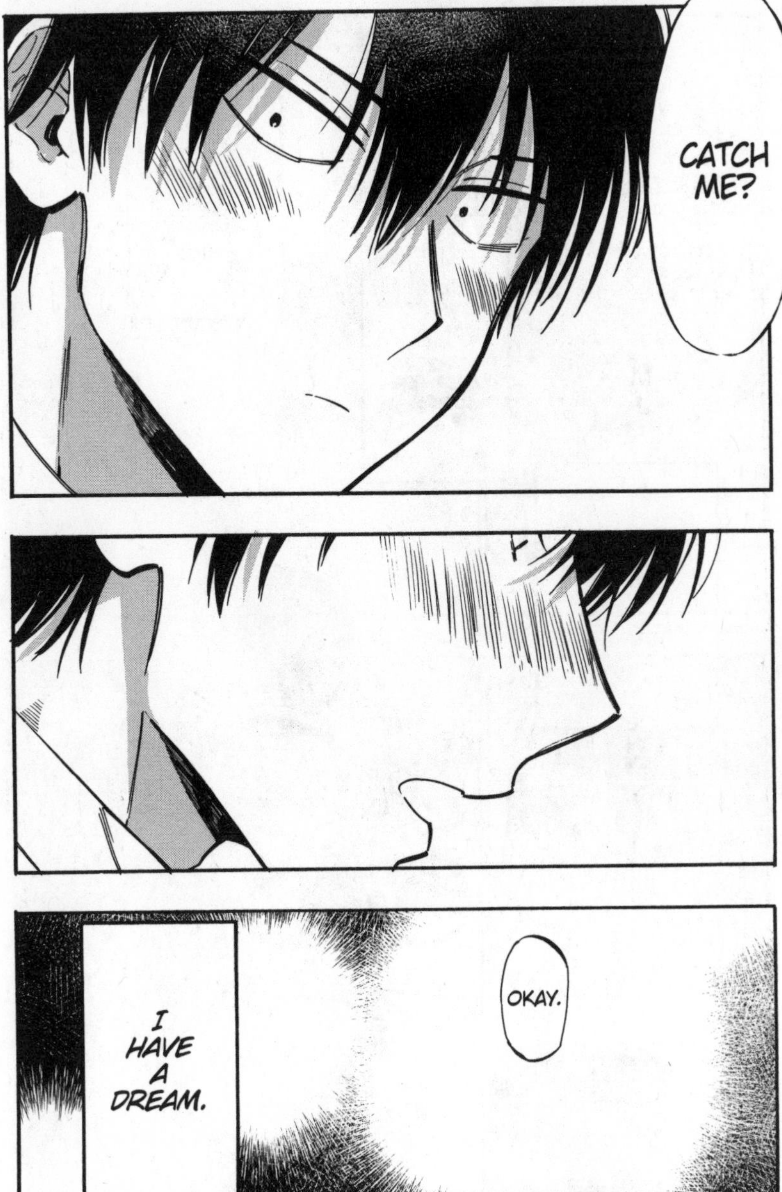
CATCH ME?
OKAY.
I HAVE A DREAM.

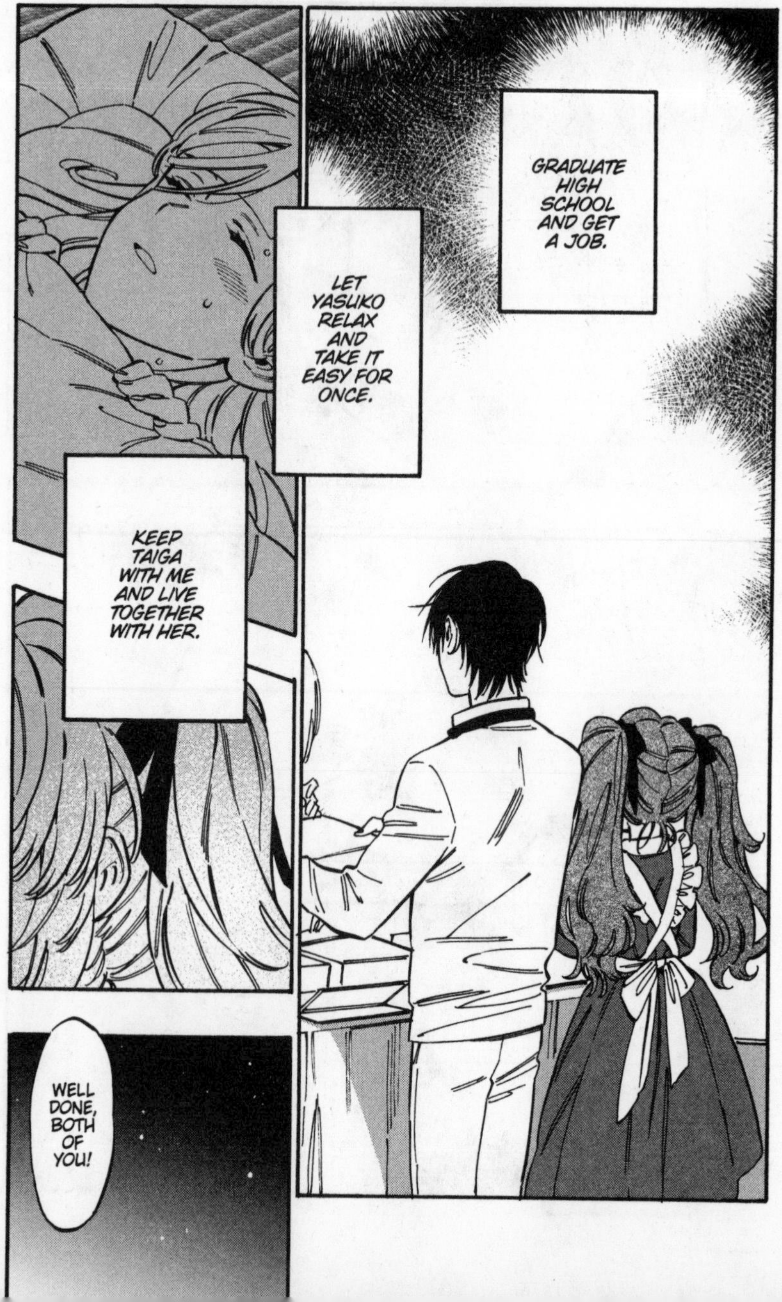
GRADUATE HIGH SCHOOL AND GET A JOB.
LET YASUKO RELAX AND TAKE IT EASY FOR ONCE.
KEEP TAIGA WITH ME AND LIVE TOGETHER WITH HER.
WELL DONE, BOTH OF YOU!

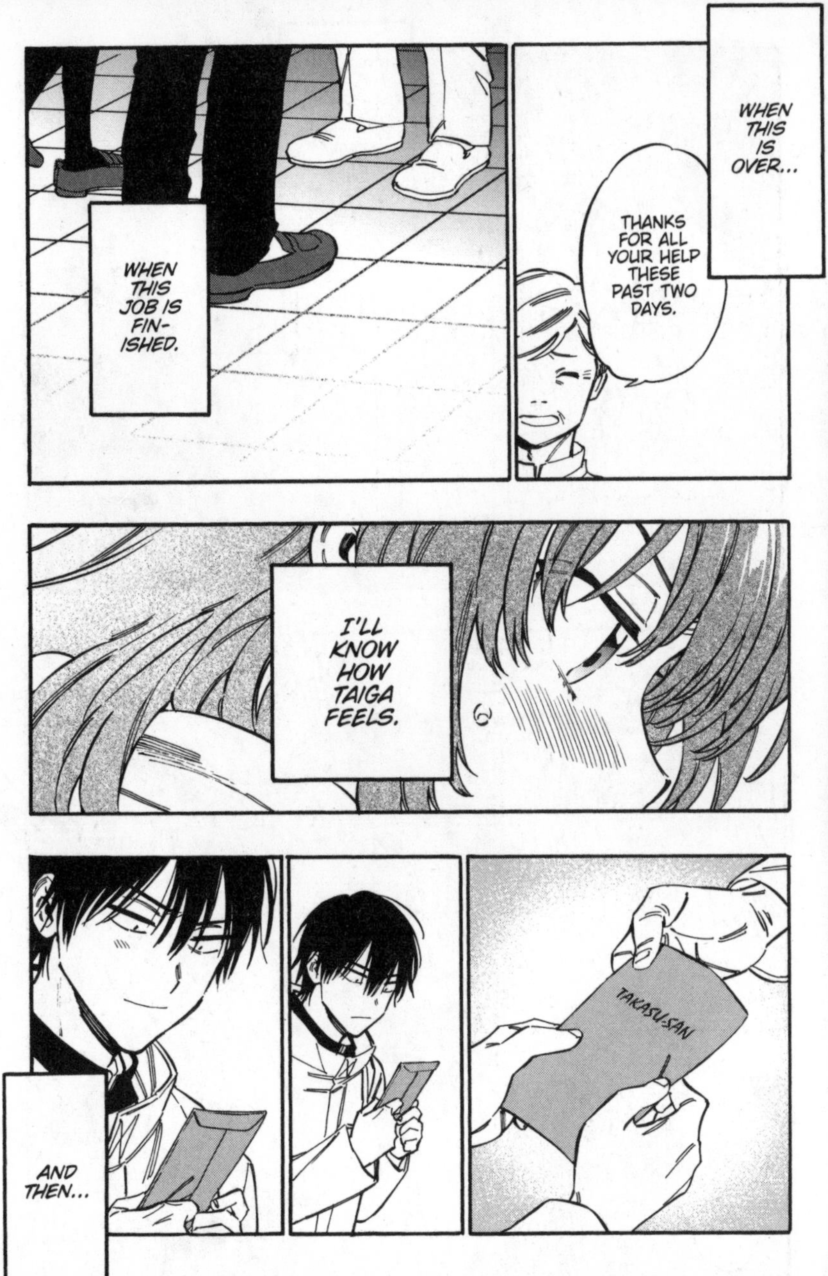
WHEN THIS IS OVER...
THANKS FOR ALL YOUR HELP THESE PAST TWO DAYS.
WHEN THIS JOB IS FIN-ISHED.
I'LL KNOW HOW TAIGA FEELS.
TAKASU-SAN
AND THEN...

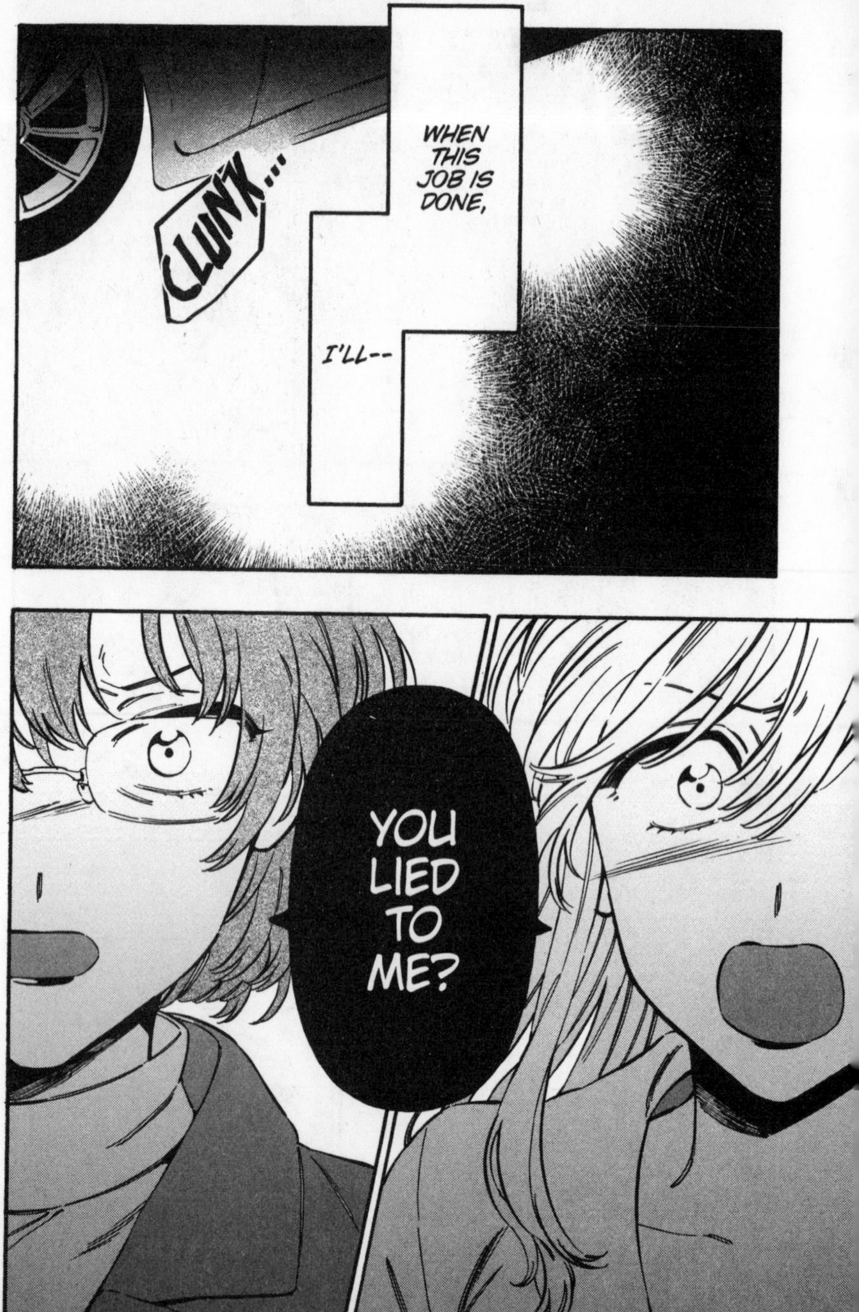
WHEN THIS JOB IS DONE,
I'LL--
CLUNK...
YOU LIED TO ME?
!
!

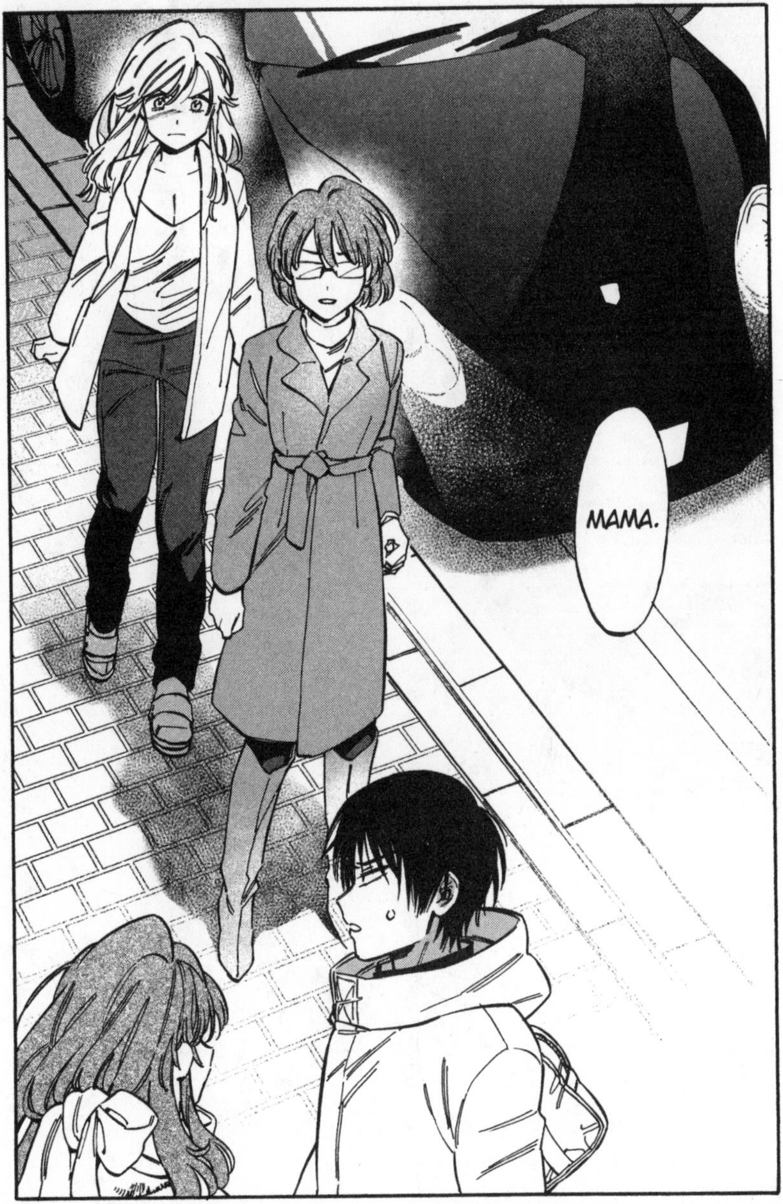
MAMA.

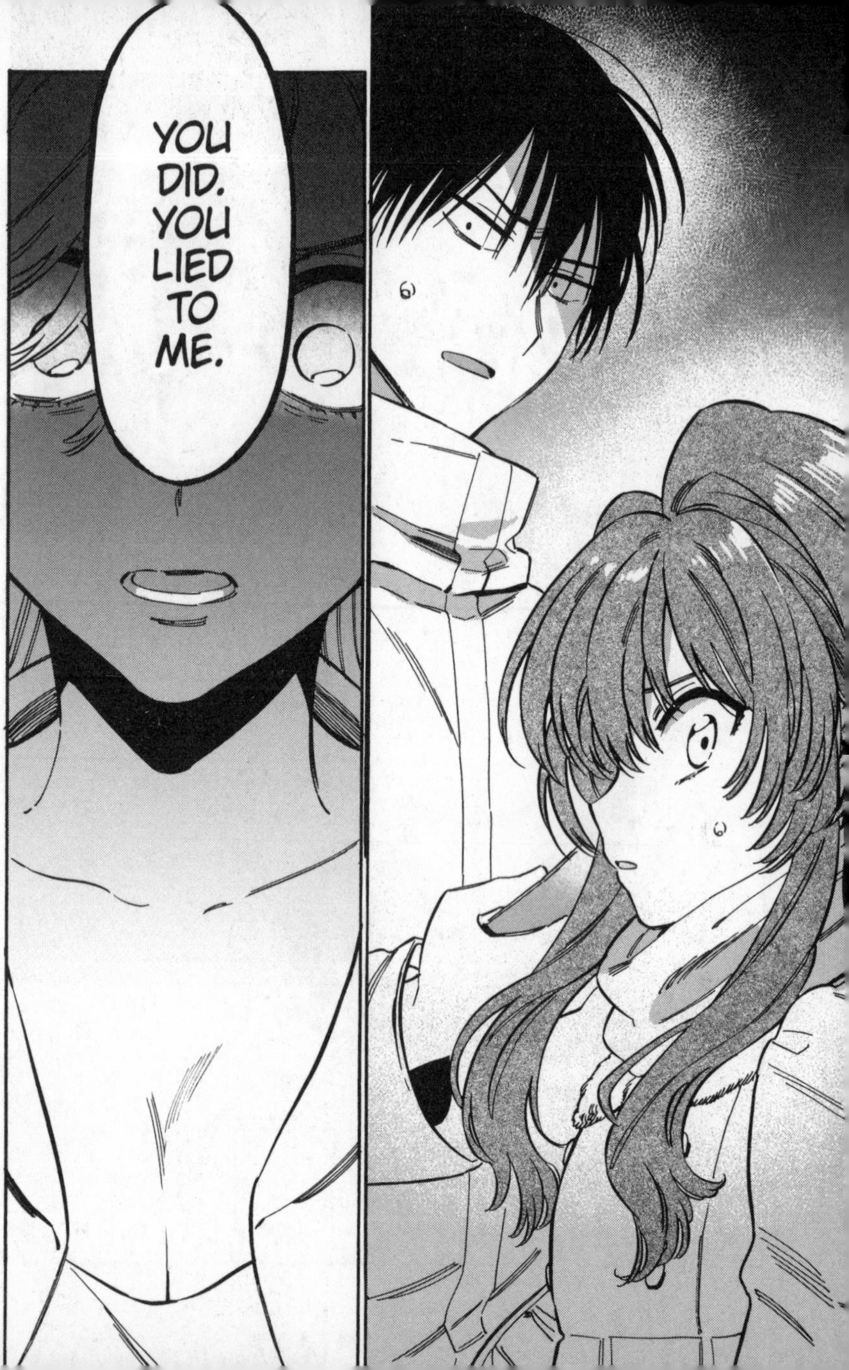
YOU DID. YOU LIED TO ME.

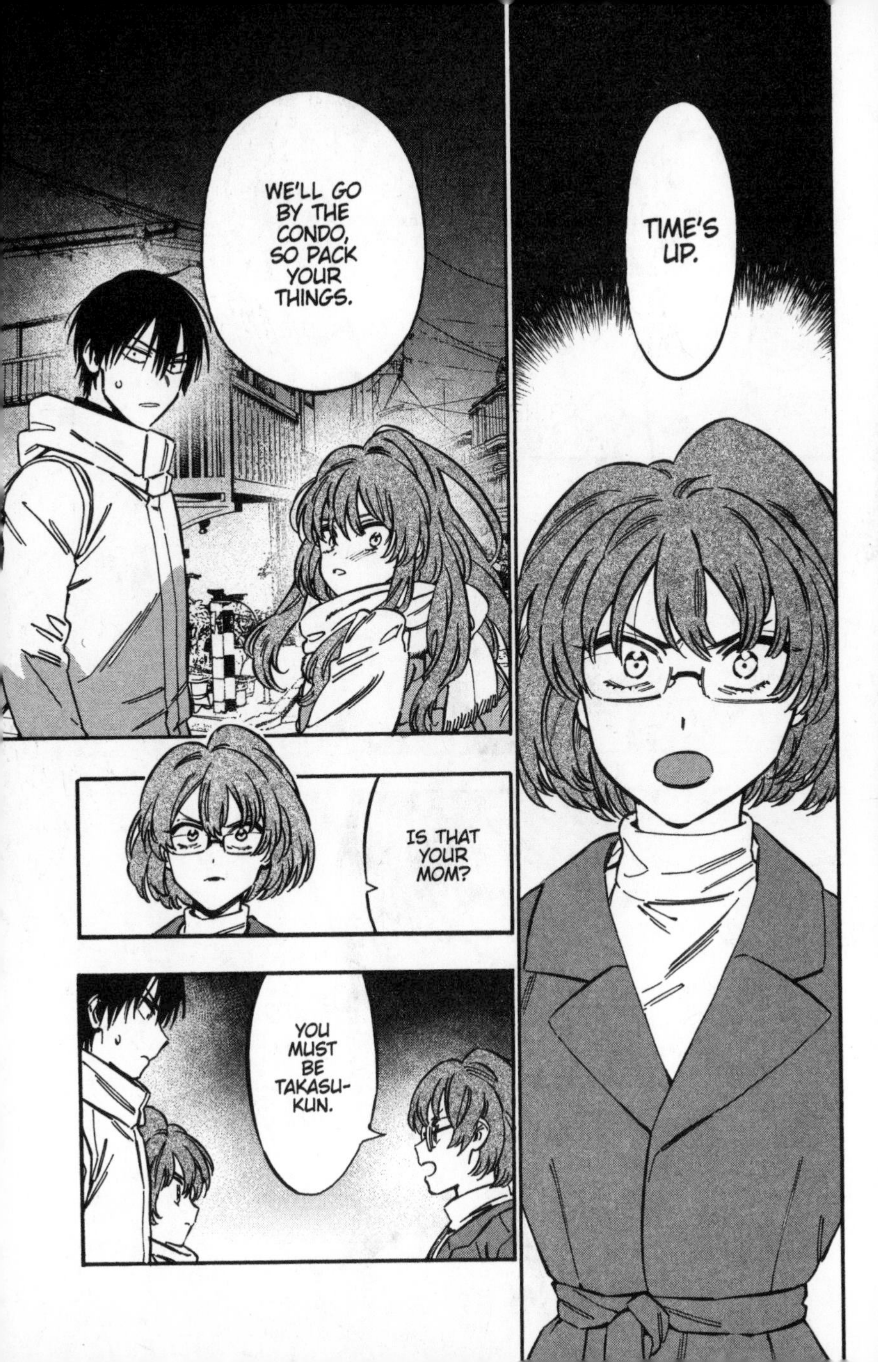
TIME'S UP.
WE'LL GO BY THE CONDO, SO PACK YOUR THINGS.
IS THAT YOUR MOM?
YOU MUST BE TAKASU-KUN.

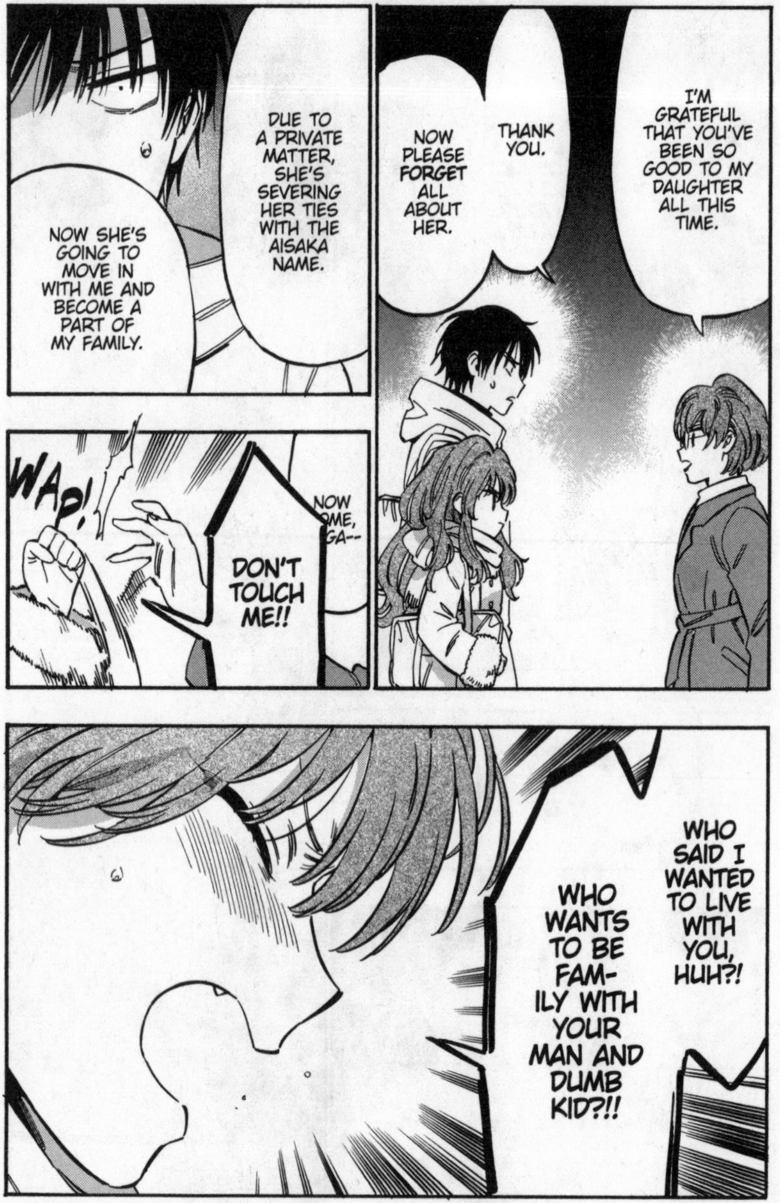
I'M GRATEFUL THAT YOU'VE BEEN SO GOOD TO MY DAUGHTER ALL THIS TIME.
THANK YOU.
NOW PLEASE FORGET ALL ABOUT HER.
DUE TO A PRIVATE MATTER, SHE'S SEVERING HER TIES WITH THE AISAKA NAME.
NOW SHE'S GOING TO MOVE IN WITH ME AND BECOME A PART OF MY FAMILY.
NOW OME, GA--
DON'T TOUCH ME!!
WAP!
WHO SAID I WANTED TO LIVE WITH YOU, HUH?!
WHO WANTS TO BE FAM- ILY WITH YOUR MAN AND DUMB KID?!!

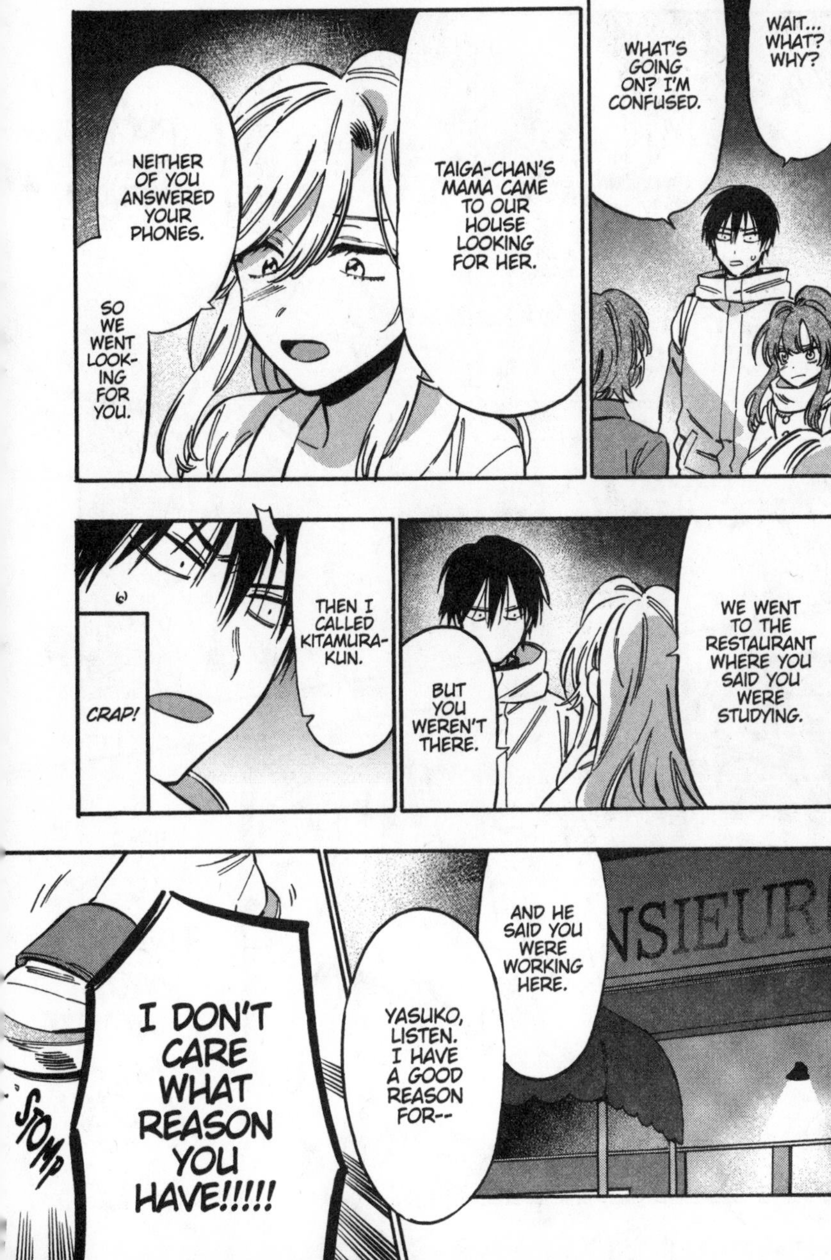
WAIT... WHAT? WHY?
WHAT'S GOING ON? I'M CONFUSED.
TAIGA-CHAN'S MAMA CAME TO OUR HOUSE LOOKING FOR HER.
NEITHER OF YOU ANSWERED YOUR PHONES.
SO WE WENT LOOKING FOR YOU.
WE WENT TO THE RESTAURANT WHERE YOU SAID YOU WERE STUDYING.
BUT YOU WEREN'T THERE.
THEN I CALLED KITAMURA-KUN.
CRAP!
NSIEUR
AND HE SAID YOU WERE WORKING HERE.
YASUKO, LISTEN. I HAVE A GOOD REASON FOR--
I DON'T CARE WHAT REASON YOU HAVE!!!!!
STOMP

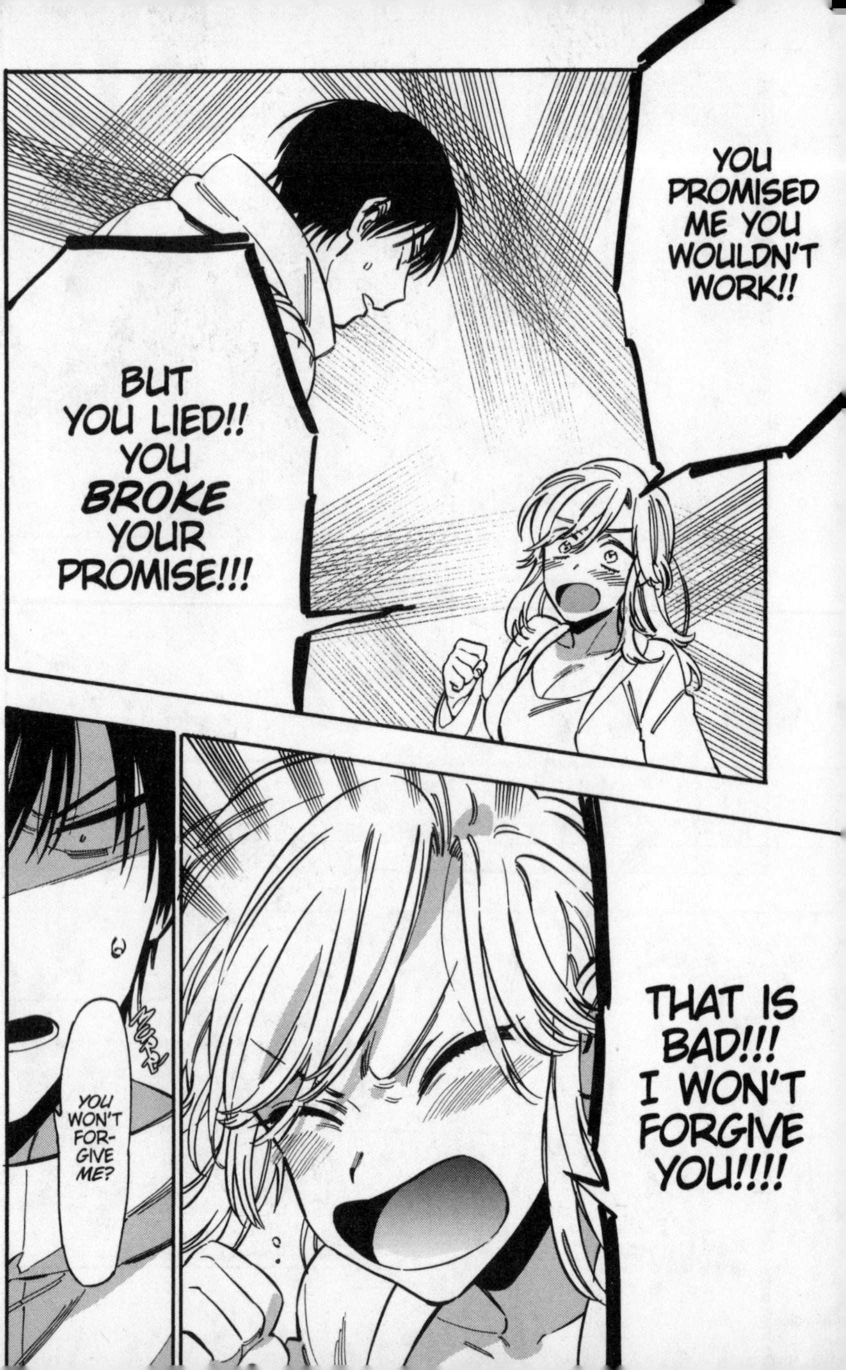
YOU PROMISED ME YOU WOULDN'T WORK!!
BUT YOU LIED!! YOU BROKE YOUR PROMISE!!!
THAT IS BAD!!! I WON'T FORGIVE YOU!!!!
YOU WON'T FOR-GIVE ME?

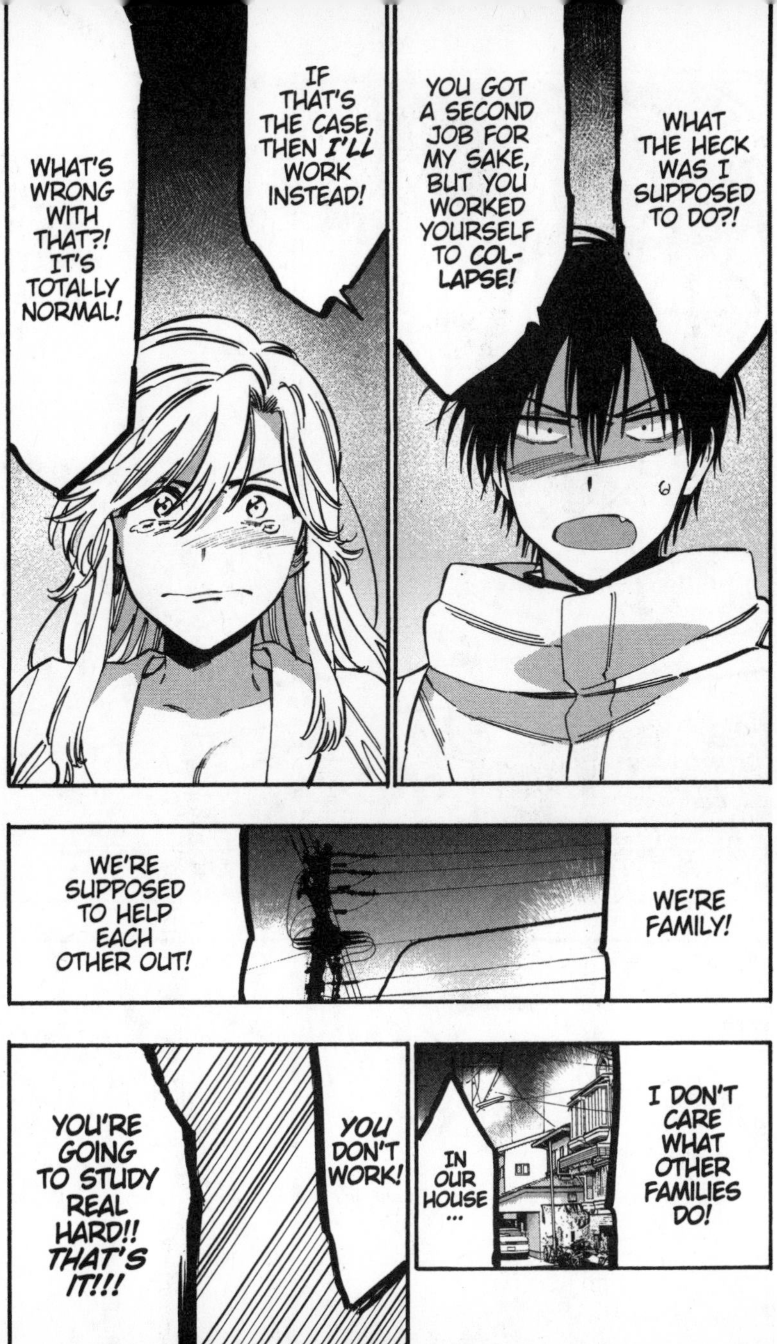
WHAT THE HECK WAS I SUPPOSED TO DO?!
YOU GOT A SECOND JOB FOR MY SAKE, BUT YOU WORKED YOURSELF TO COL-LAPSE!
IF THAT'S THE CASE, THEN *I'LL* WORK INSTEAD!
WHAT'S WRONG WITH THAT?! IT'S TOTALLY NORMAL!
WE'RE FAMILY!
WE'RE SUPPOSED TO HELP EACH OTHER OUT!
I DON'T CARE WHAT OTHER FAMILIES DO!
IN OUR HOUSE...
*YOU* DON'T WORK!
YOU'RE GOING TO STUDY REAL HARD!! *THAT'S IT!!!*

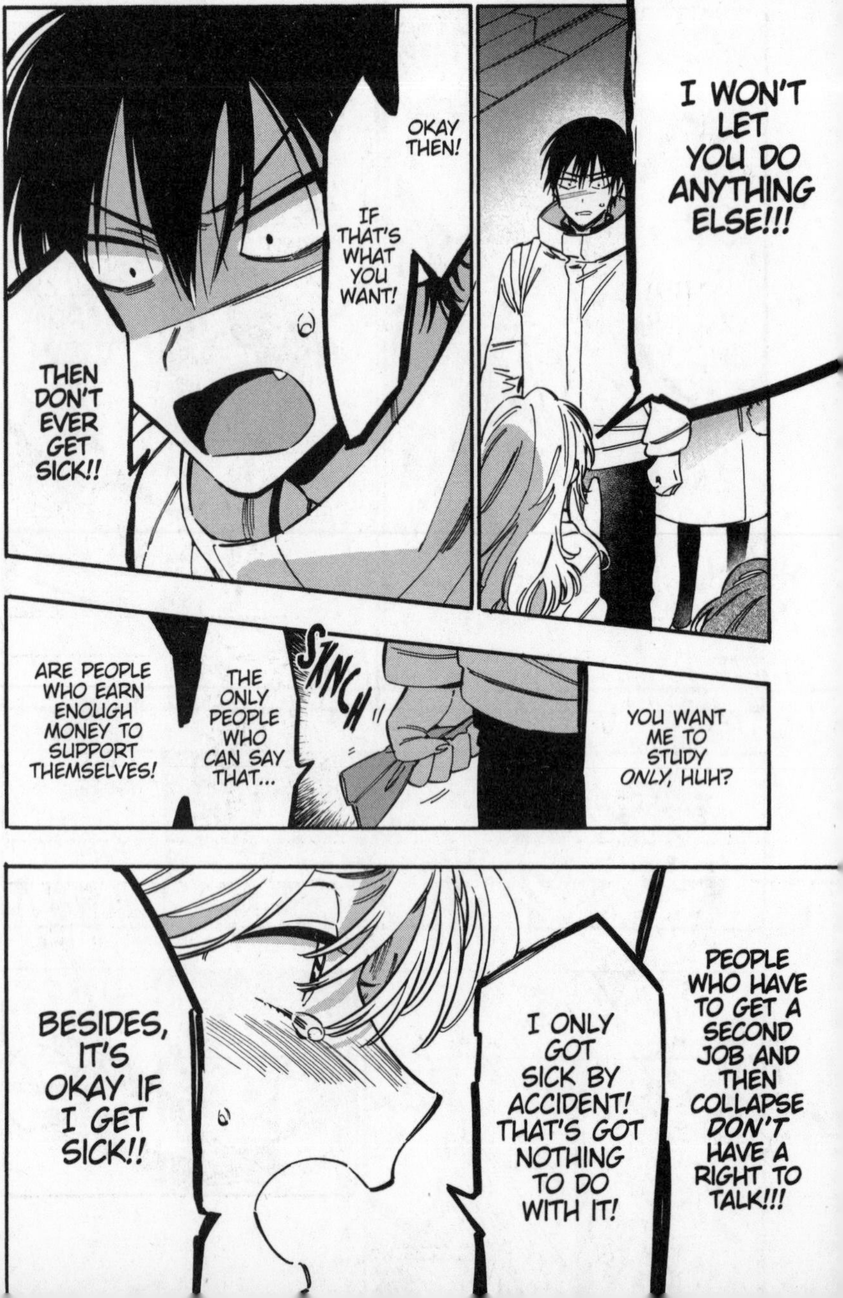
I WON'T LET YOU DO ANYTHING ELSE!!!
OKAY THEN!
IF THAT'S WHAT YOU WANT!
THEN DON'T EVER GET SICK!!
YOU WANT ME TO STUDY *ONLY*, HUH?
SKNCH
THE ONLY PEOPLE WHO CAN SAY THAT...
ARE PEOPLE WHO EARN ENOUGH MONEY TO SUPPORT THEMSELVES!
PEOPLE WHO HAVE TO GET A SECOND JOB AND THEN COLLAPSE *DON'T* HAVE A RIGHT TO TALK!!!
I ONLY GOT SICK BY ACCIDENT! THAT'S GOT NOTHING TO DO WITH IT!
BESIDES, IT'S OKAY IF I GET SICK!!

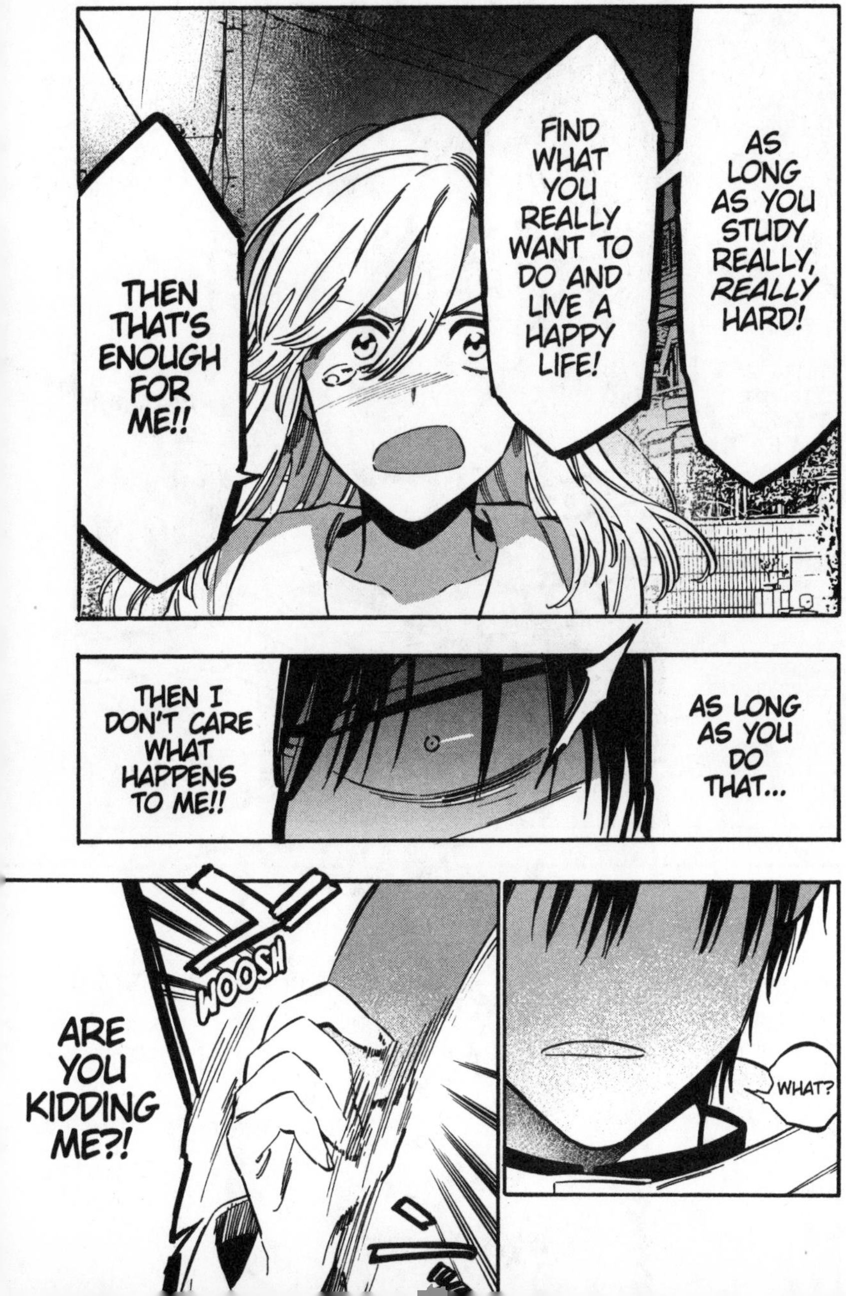
AS LONG AS YOU STUDY REALLY, *REALLY* HARD!
FIND WHAT YOU REALLY WANT TO DO AND LIVE A HAPPY LIFE!
THEN THAT'S ENOUGH FOR ME!!
AS LONG AS YOU DO THAT...
THEN I DON'T CARE WHAT HAPPENS TO ME!!
WHAT?
WOOSH
ARE YOU KIDDING ME?!

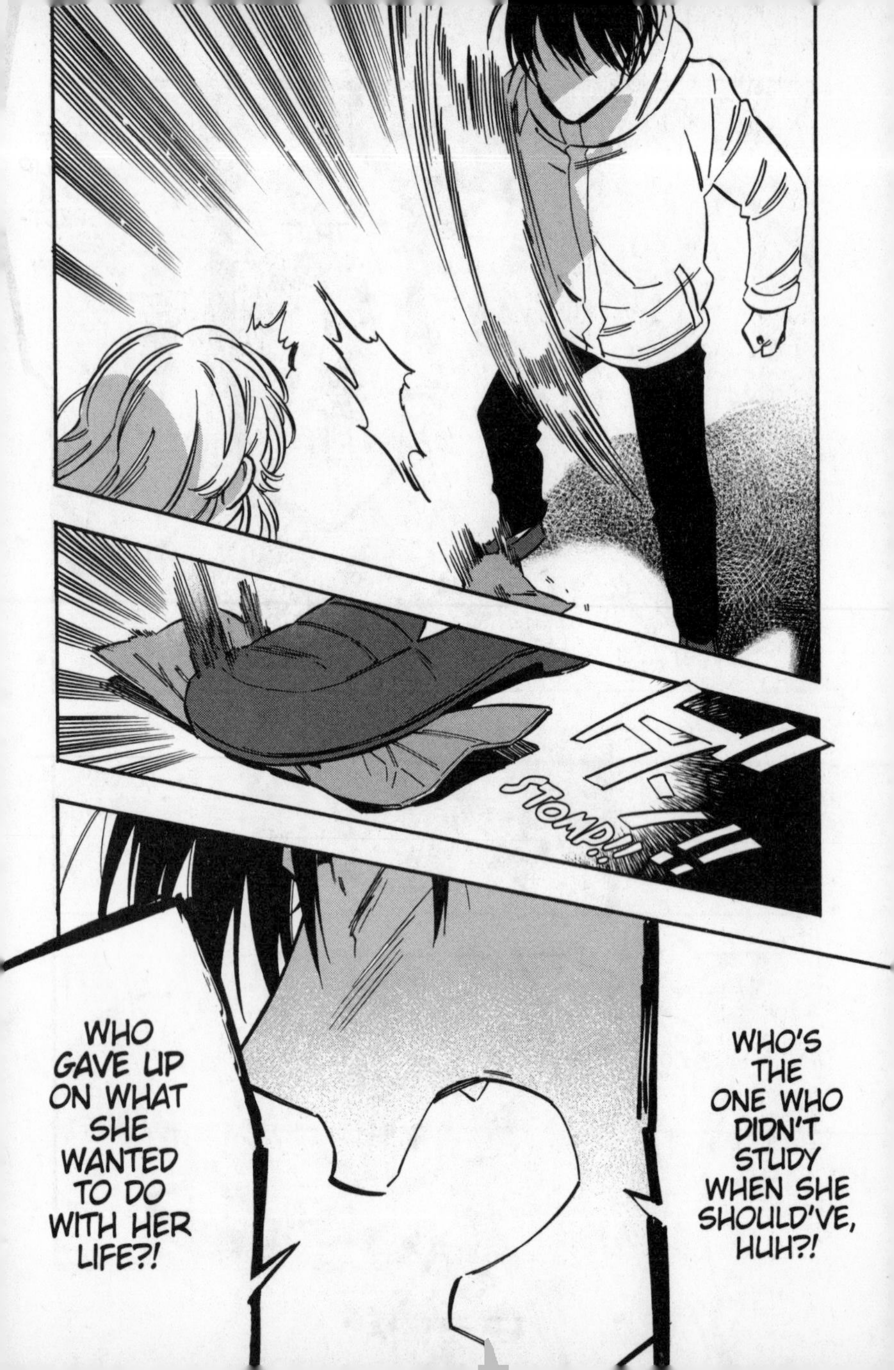

STOMP!!
WHO'S THE ONE WHO DIDN'T STUDY WHEN SHE SHOULD'VE, HUH?!
WHO GAVE UP ON WHAT SHE WANTED TO DO WITH HER LIFE?!

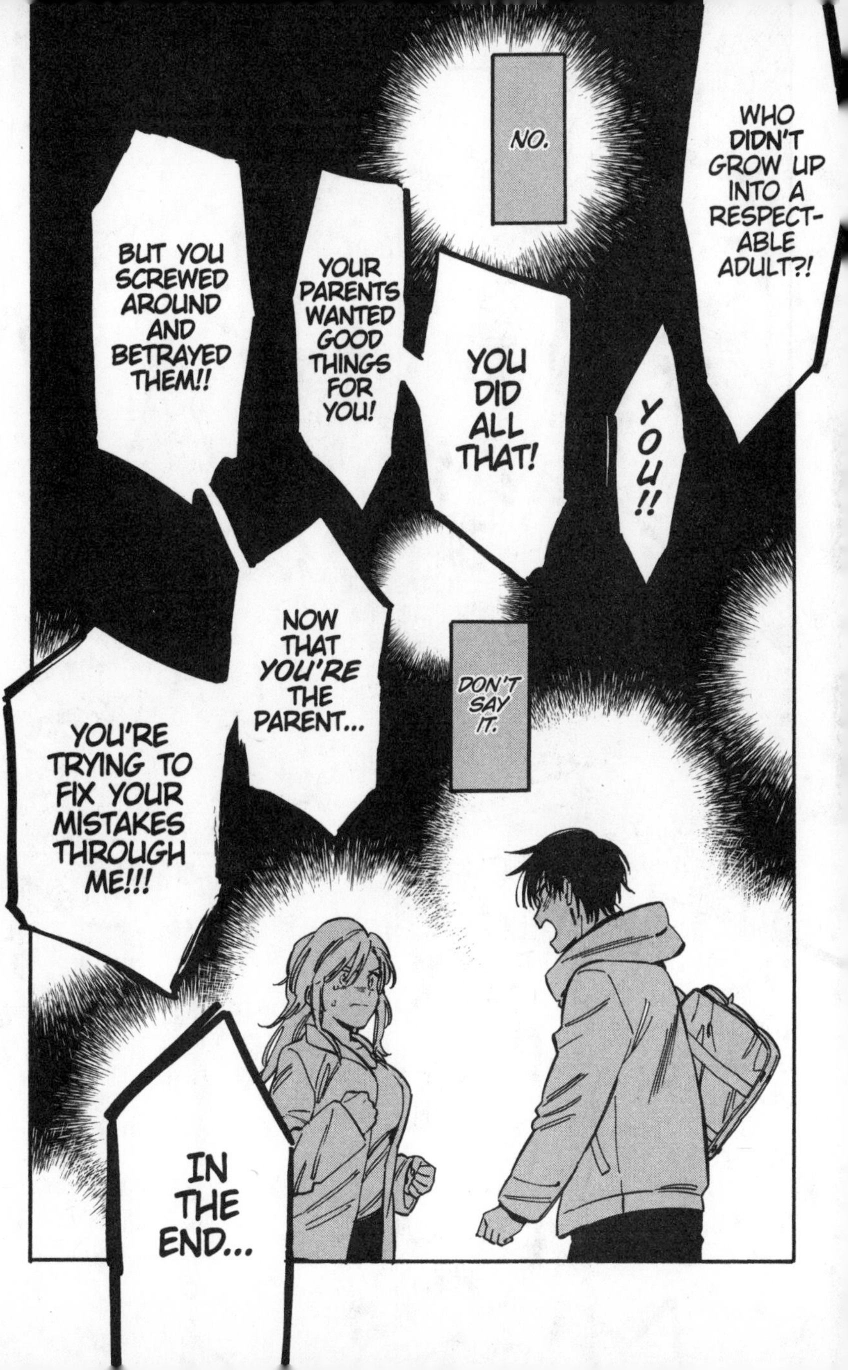
WHO DIDN'T GROW UP INTO A RESPECT-ABLE ADULT?!
NO.
YOU!!
YOU DID ALL THAT!
YOUR PARENTS WANTED GOOD THINGS FOR YOU!
BUT YOU SCREWED AROUND AND BETRAYED THEM!!
DON'T SAY IT.
NOW THAT *YOU'RE* THE PARENT...
YOU'RE TRYING TO FIX YOUR MISTAKES THROUGH ME!!!
IN THE END...

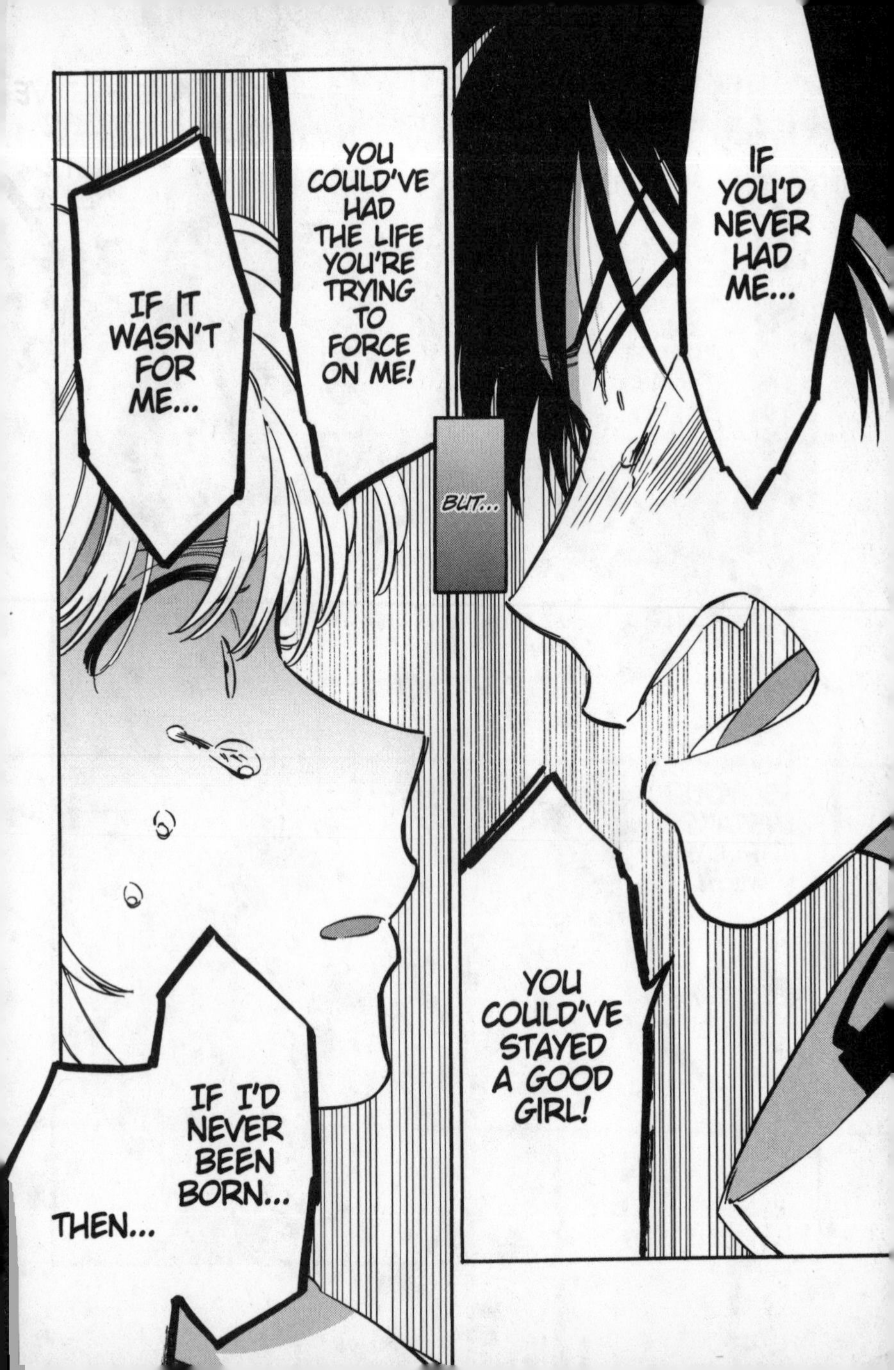
IF YOU'D NEVER HAD ME...
YOU COULD'VE STAYED A GOOD GIRL!
BUT...
IF IT WASN'T FOR ME...
YOU COULD'VE HAD THE LIFE YOU'RE TRYING TO FORCE ON ME!
IF I'D NEVER BEEN BORN...
THEN...

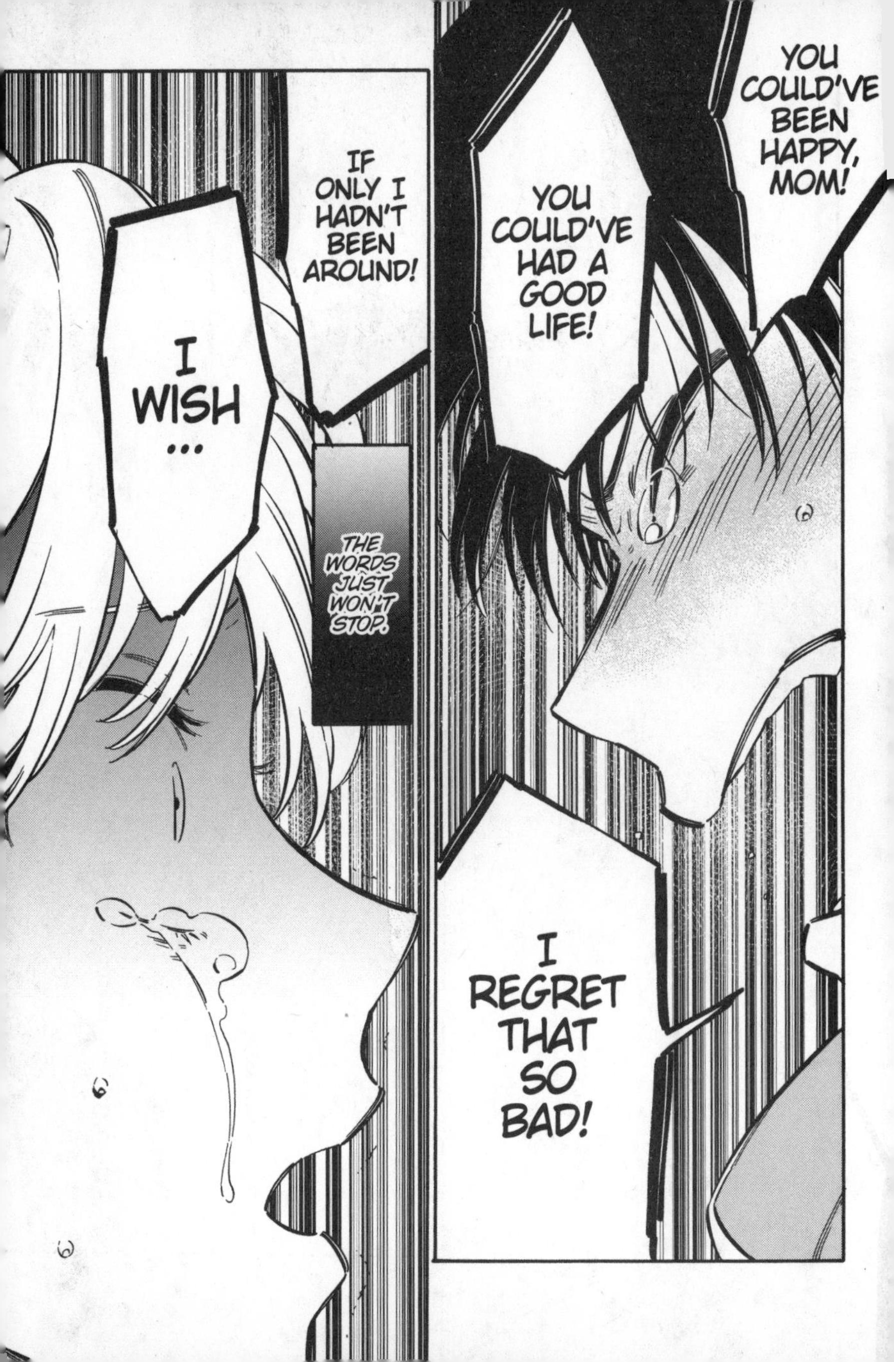
YOU COULD'VE BEEN HAPPY, MOM!
YOU COULD'VE HAD A GOOD LIFE!
I REGRET THAT SO BAD!
IF ONLY I HADN'T BEEN AROUND!
I WISH...
THE WORDS JUST WON'T STOP.

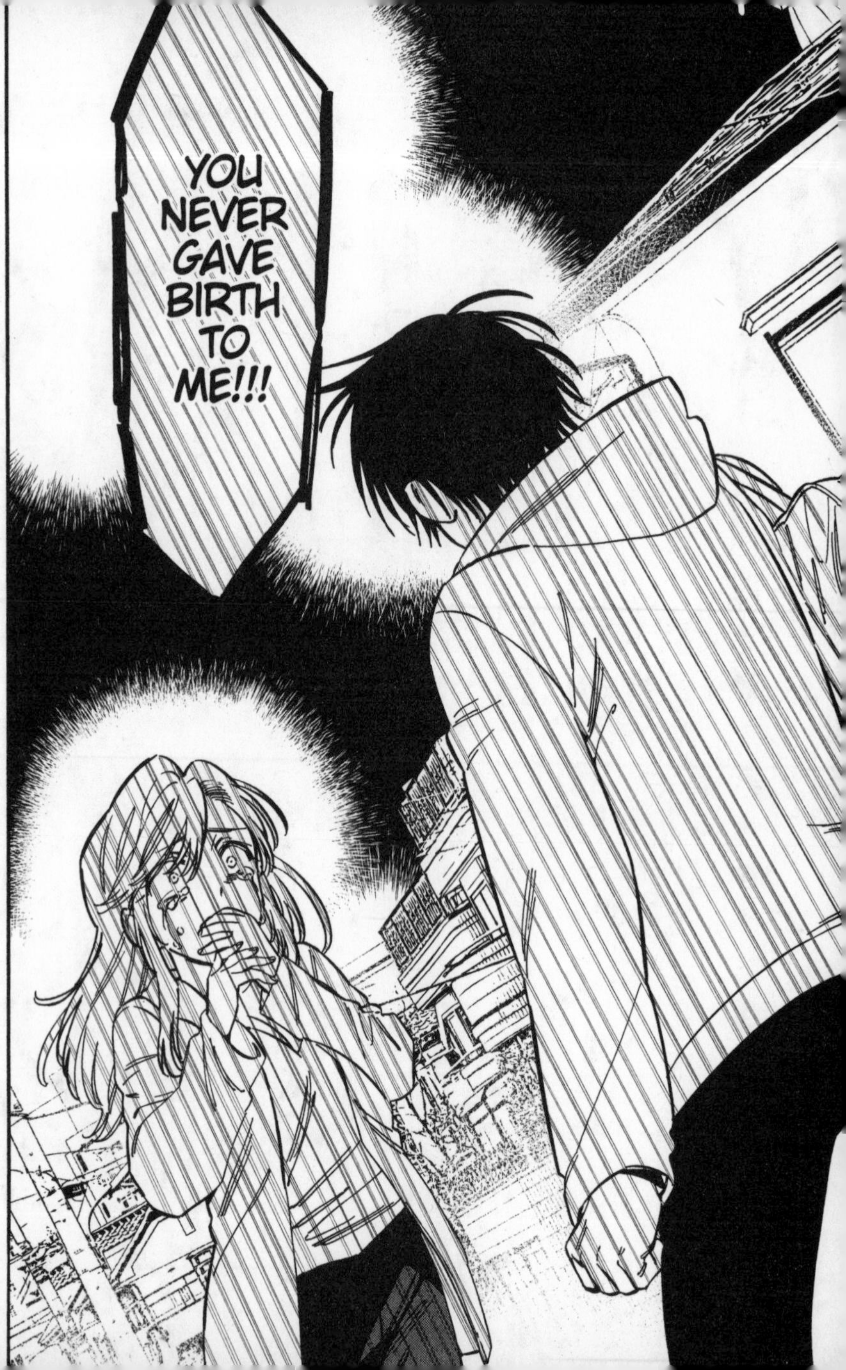
YOU NEVER GAVE BIRTH TO ME!!!

Toradora!

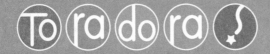

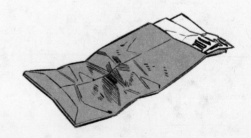

# Chapter 97
# Take My Hand

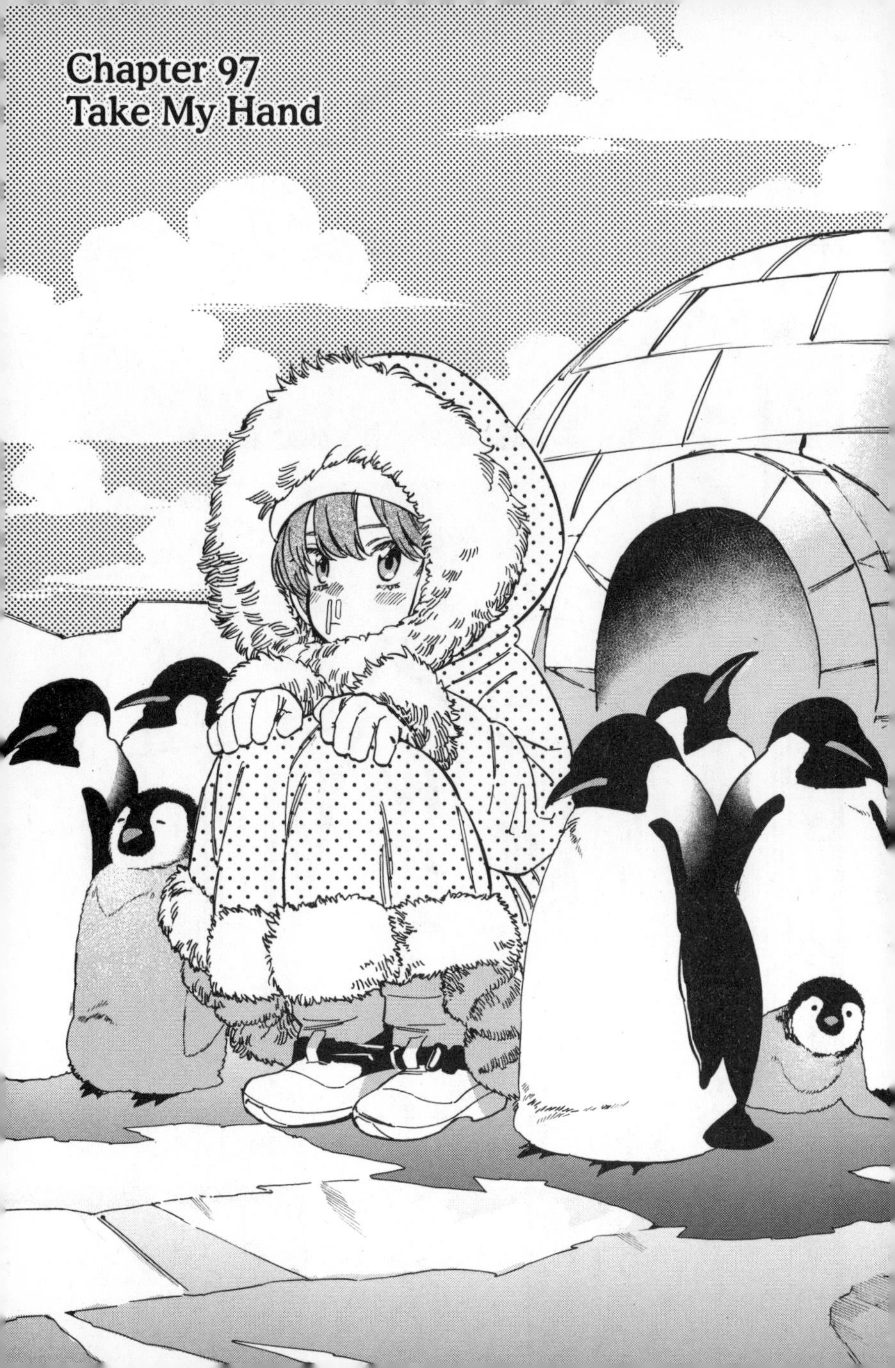

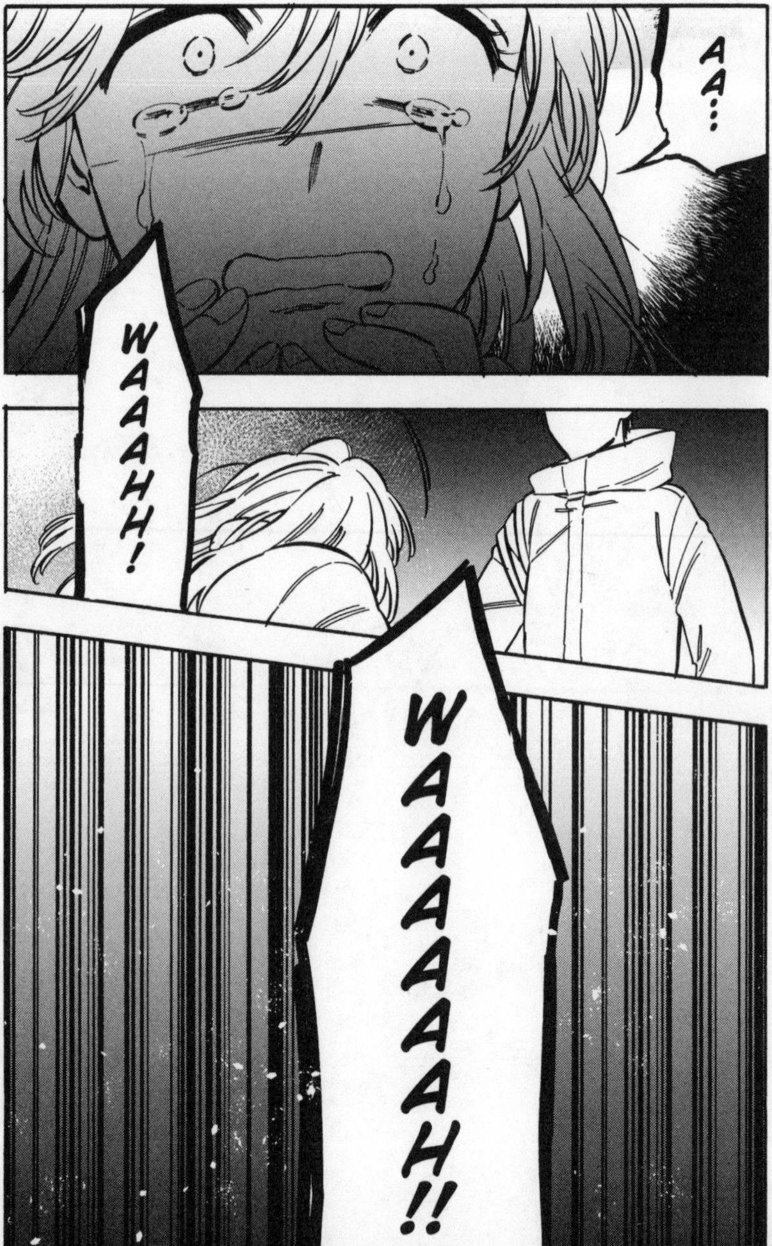
AA..
WAAAAHH!
WAAAAAAAAH!!

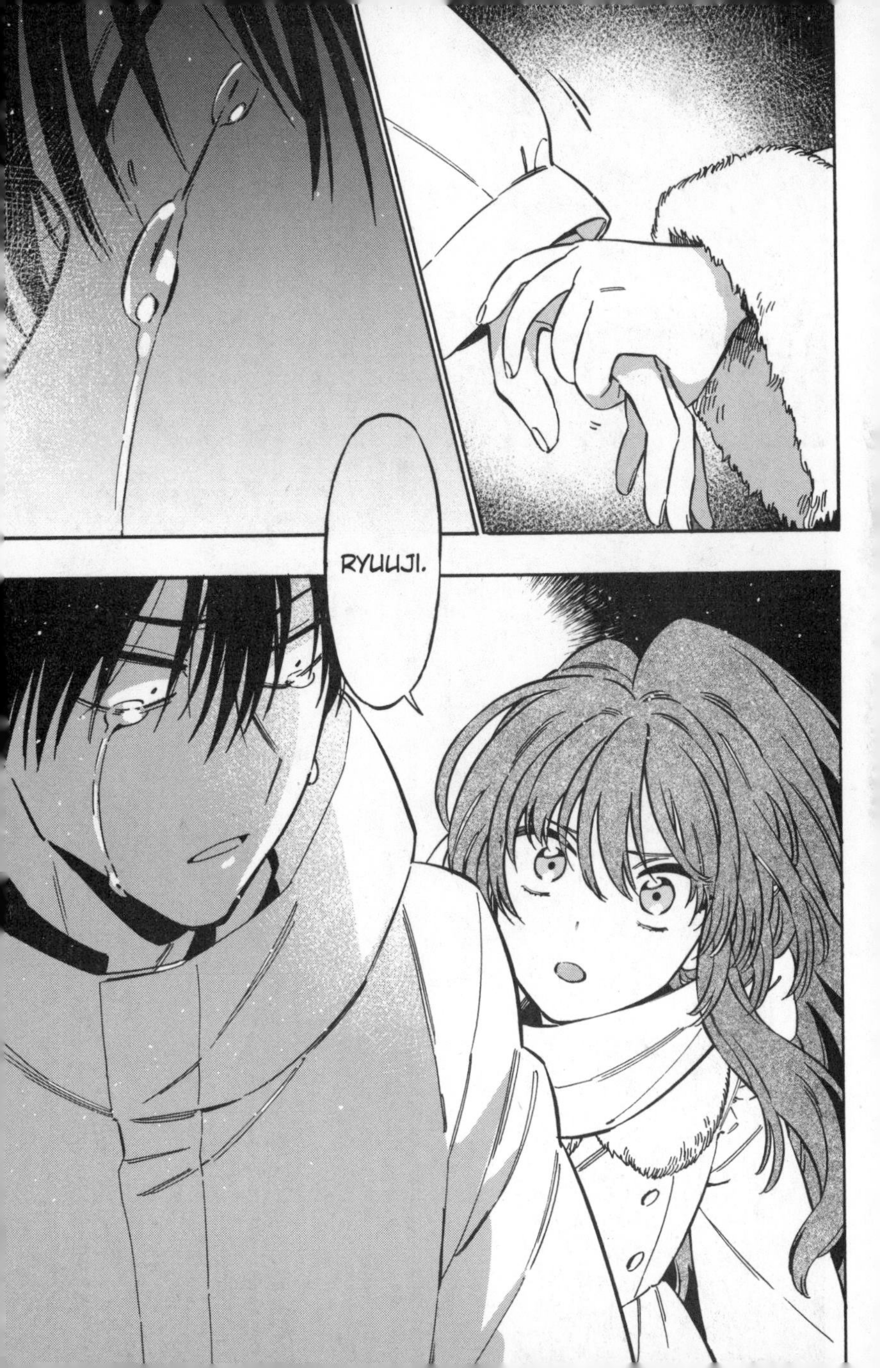
RYUUJI.

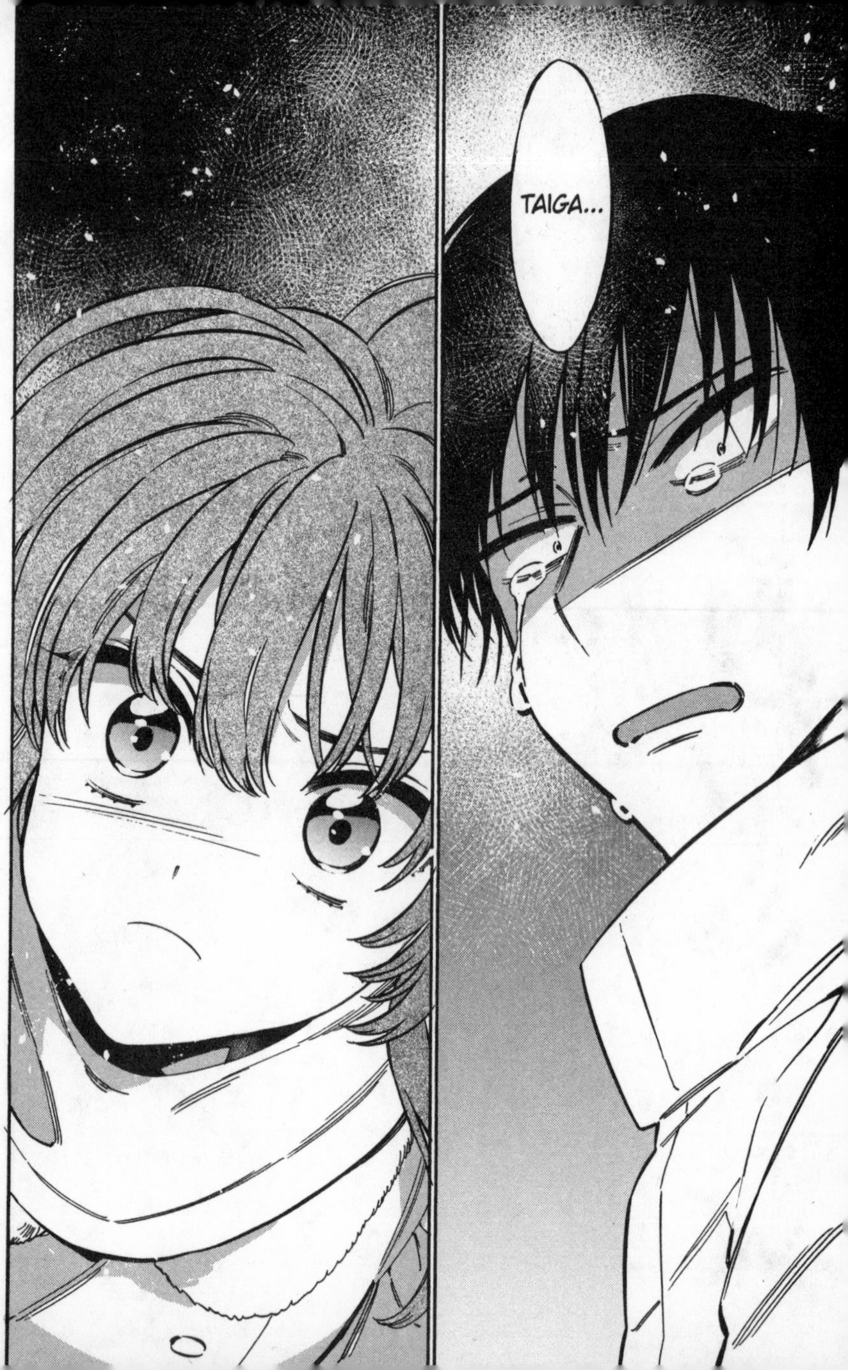
TAIGA...

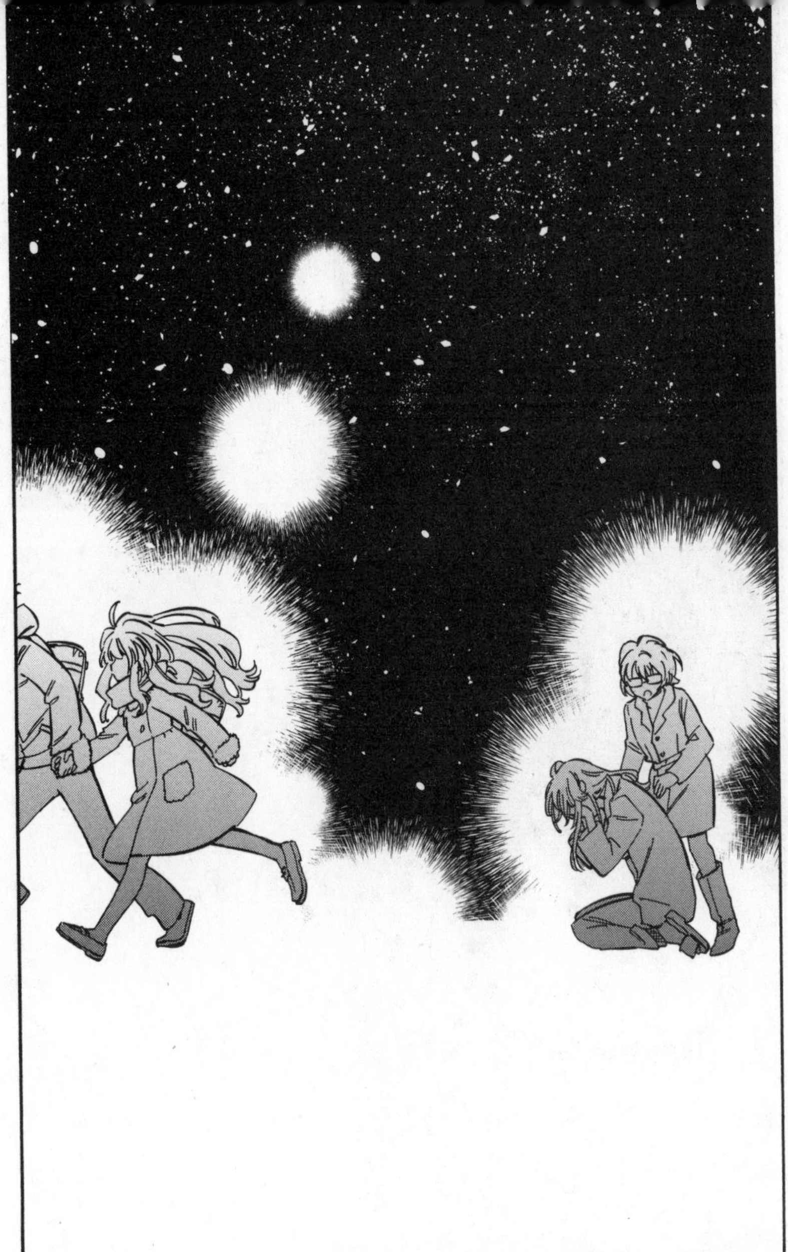

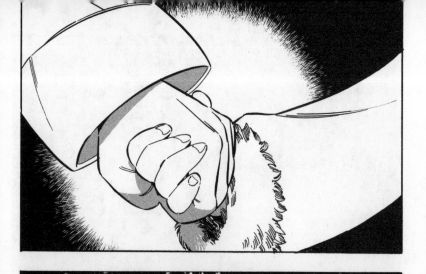

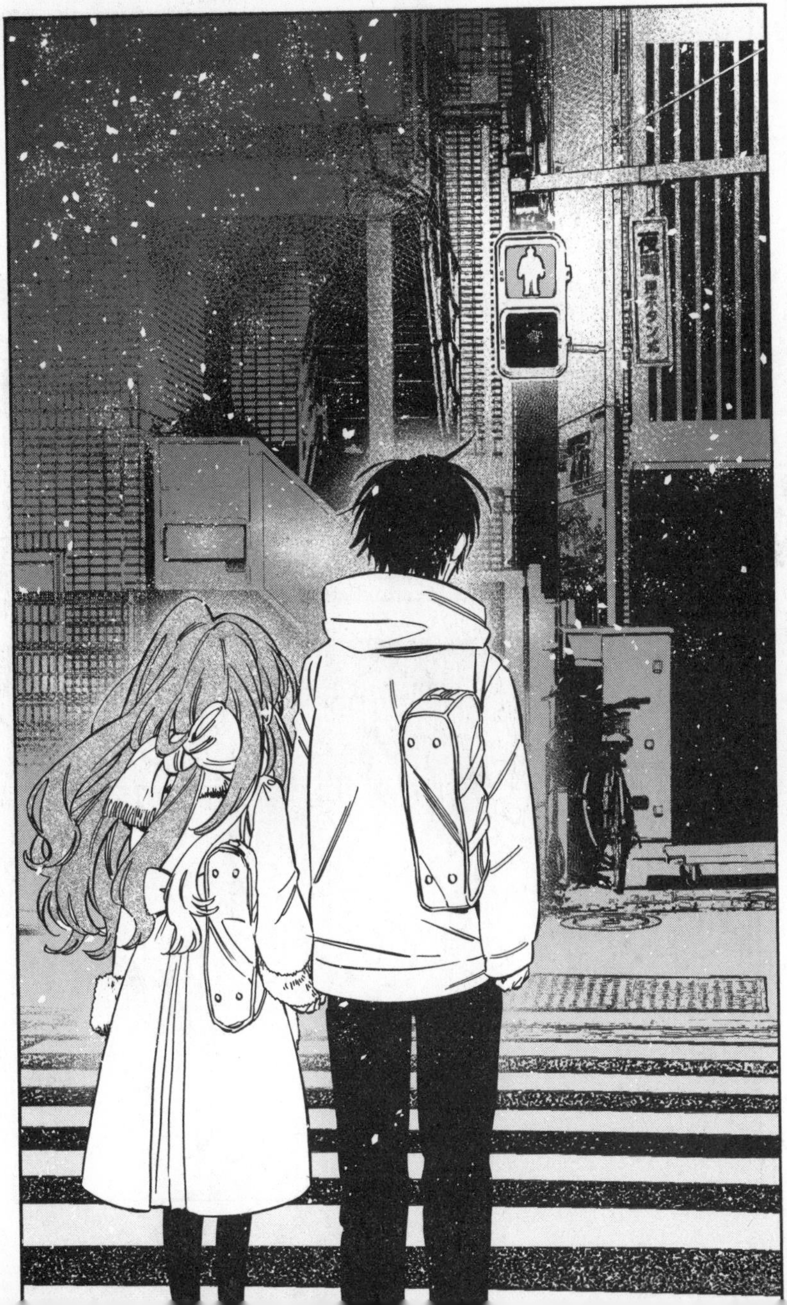

夜間押ボタン式

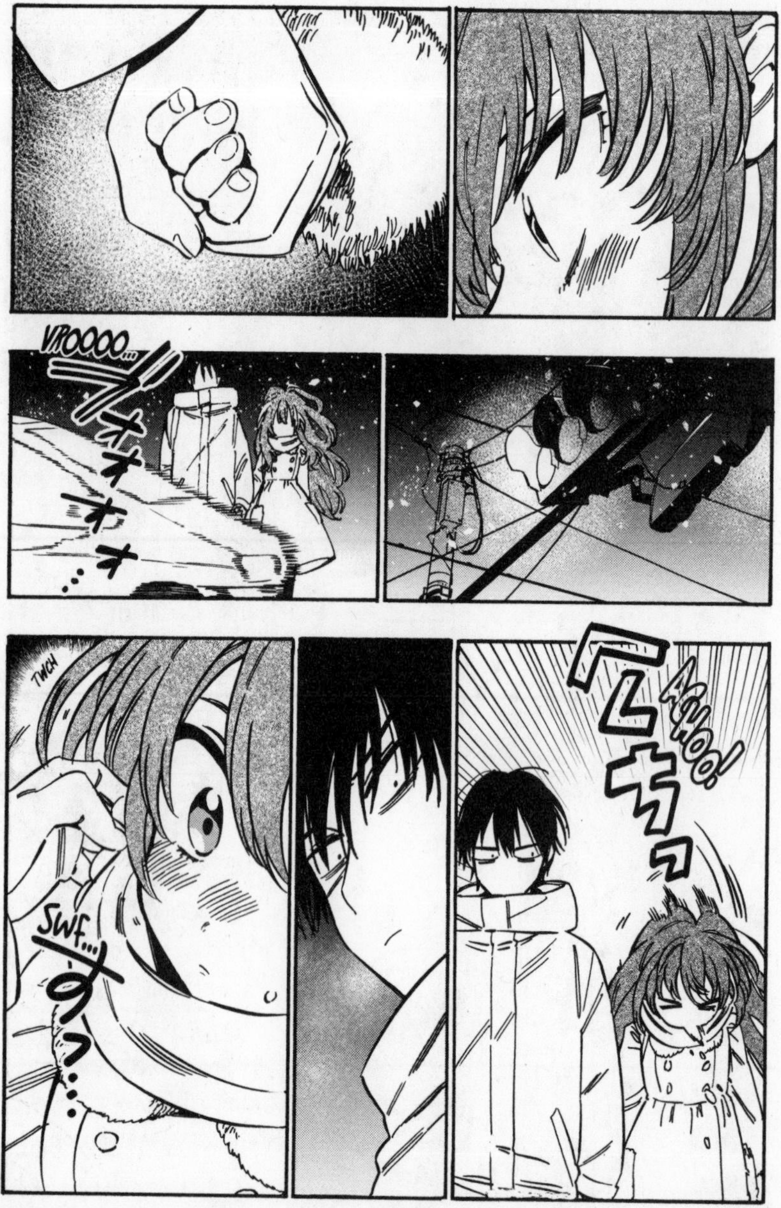
VROOOO...
ブォォォォ…
ACHOO!
へくちっ
TWCH
SWF...
すっ…

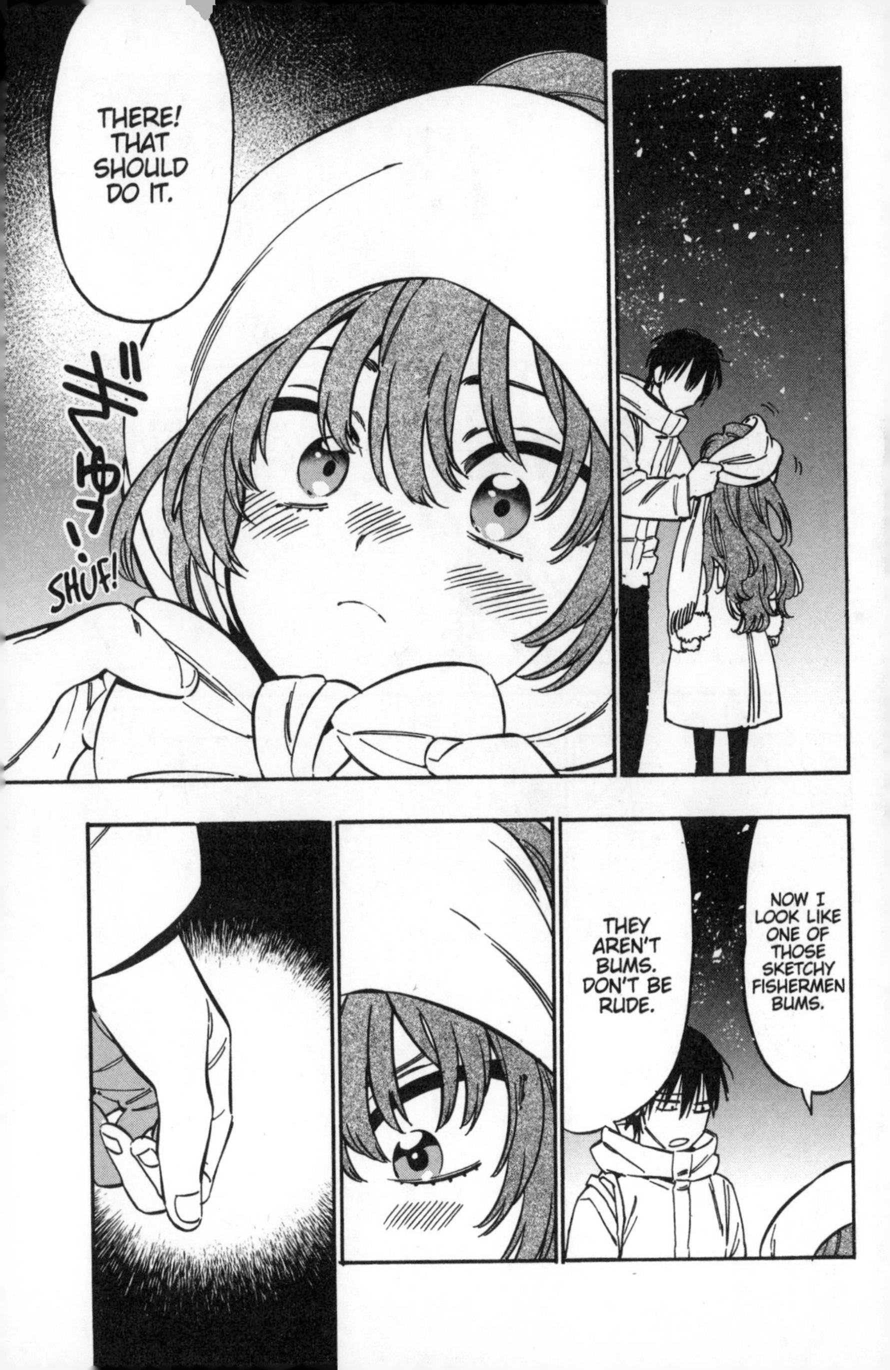
THERE! THAT SHOULD DO IT.
SHUF!
NOW I LOOK LIKE ONE OF THOSE SKETCHY FISHERMEN BUMS.
THEY AREN'T BUMS. DON'T BE RUDE.

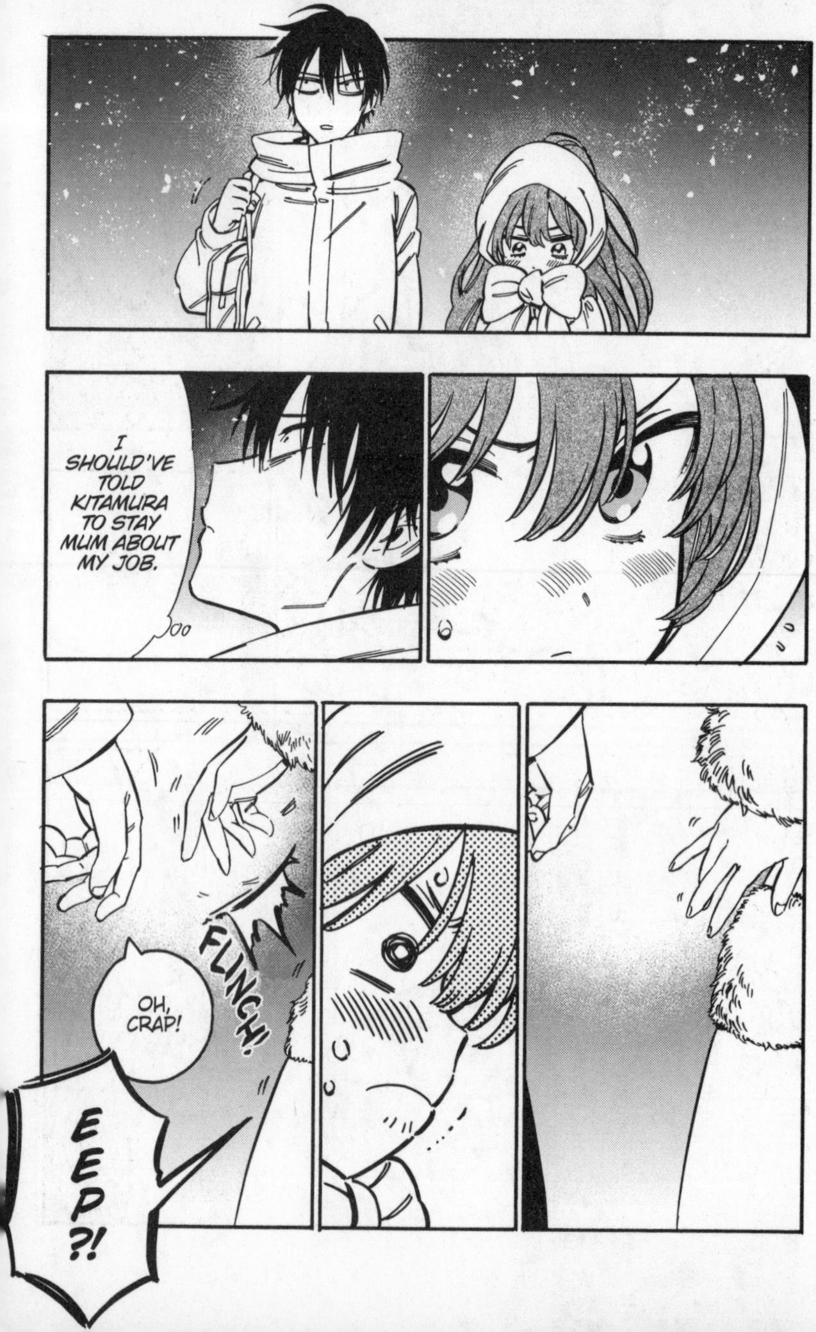
I SHOULD'VE TOLD KITAMURA TO STAY MUM ABOUT MY JOB.
FLINCH!
OH, CRAP!
EEP?!

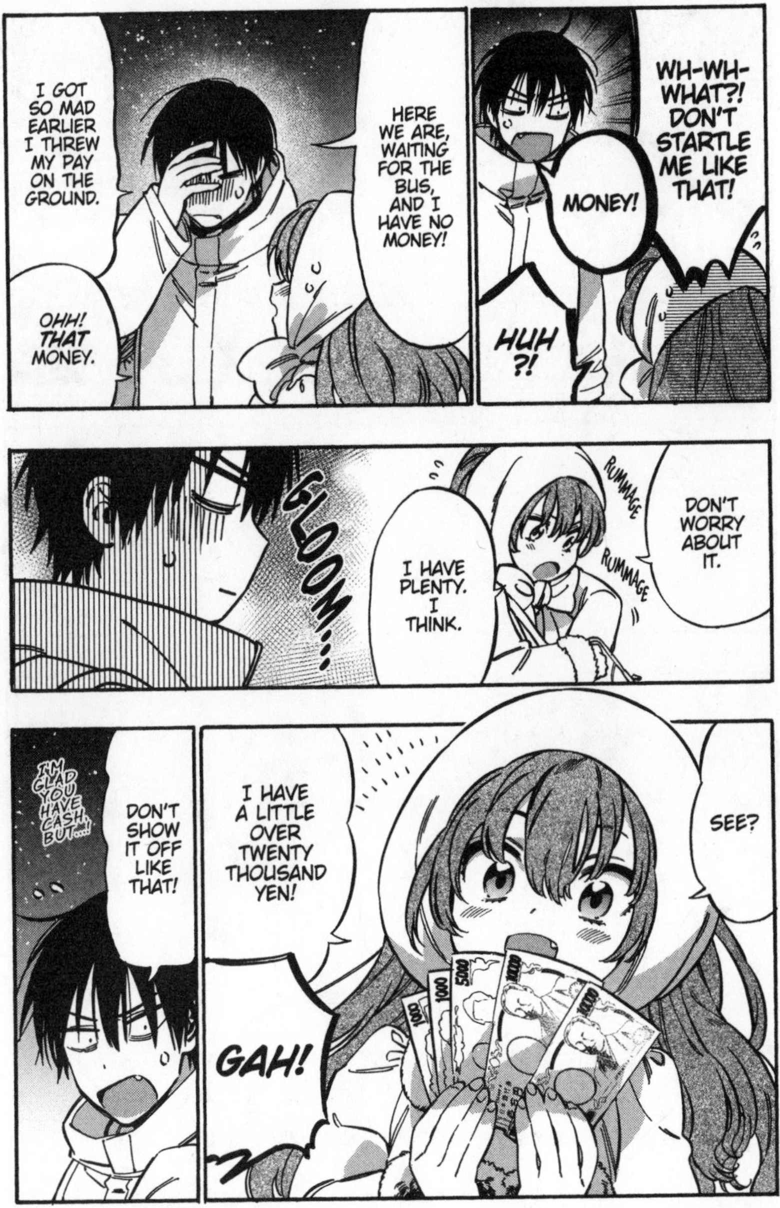
WH-WH-WHAT?! DON'T STARTLE ME LIKE THAT!
MONEY!
HUH ?!
HERE WE ARE, WAITING FOR THE BUS, AND I HAVE NO MONEY!
I GOT SO MAD EARLIER I THREW MY PAY ON THE GROUND.
OHH! THAT MONEY.
DON'T WORRY ABOUT IT.
RUMMAGE
RUMMAGE
I HAVE PLENTY. I THINK.
GLOOM...
SEE?
I HAVE A LITTLE OVER TWENTY THOUSAND YEN!
GAH!
I'M GLAD YOU HAVE CASH, BUT...!
DON'T SHOW IT OFF LIKE THAT!

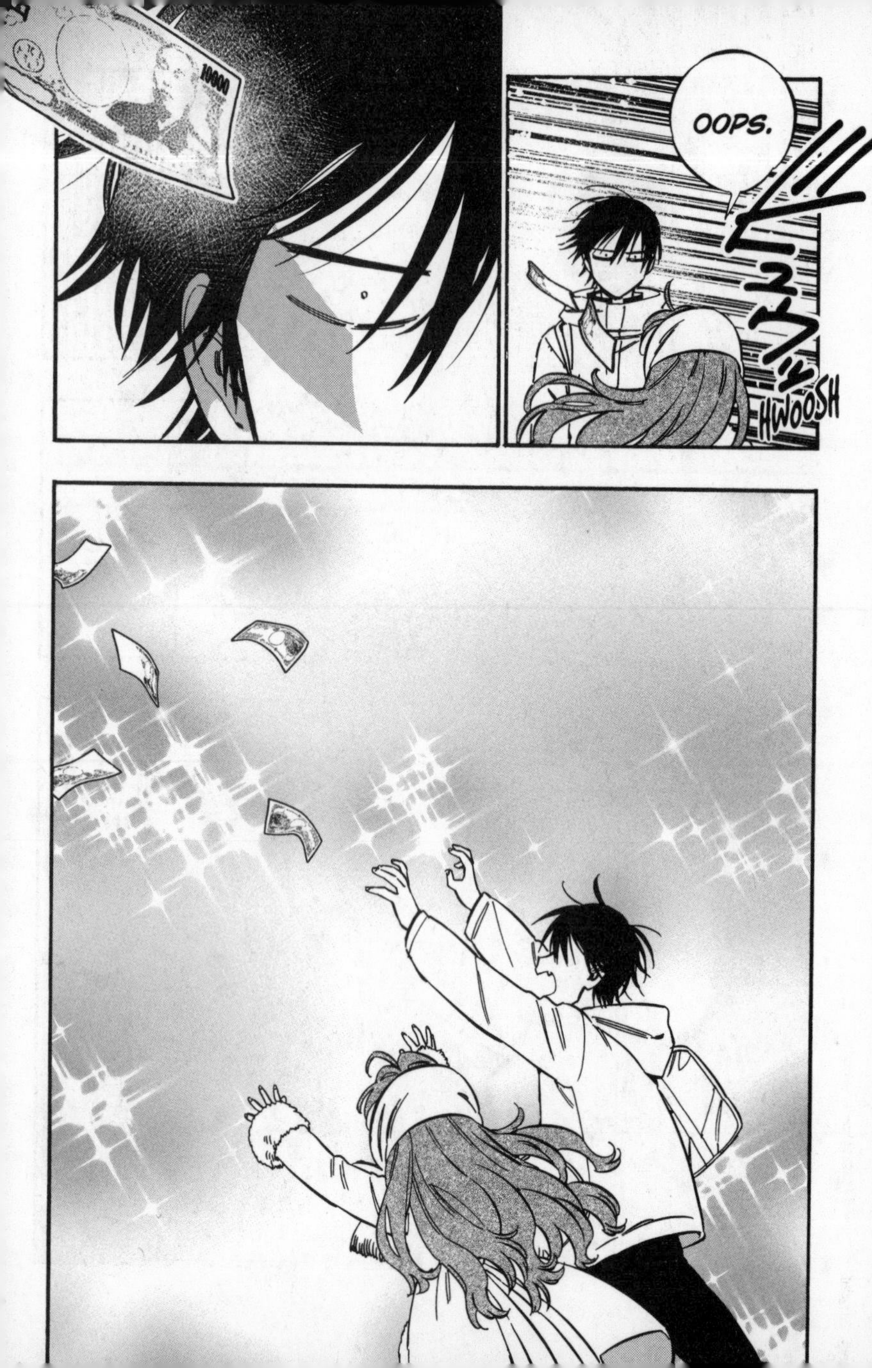
OOPS.
ヒュウッ
HWOOSH

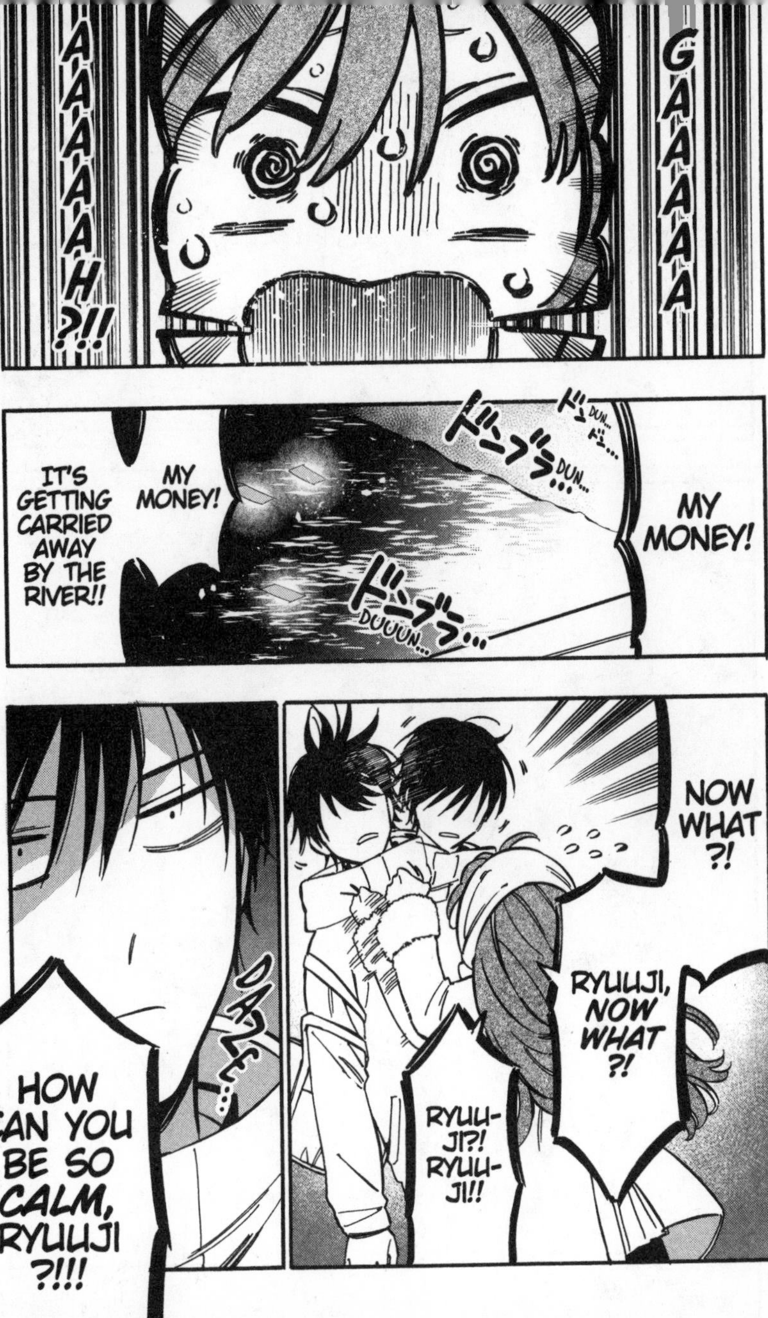
GAAAAAAA
AAAAAAAAH?!!
MY MONEY!
DUN... DUN...
DUN...
DUUUN...
MY MONEY!
IT'S GETTING CARRIED AWAY BY THE RIVER!!
NOW WHAT?!
RYUUJI, NOW WHAT?!
RYUU-JI?! RYUU-JI!!
DAZE...
HOW CAN YOU BE SO CALM, RYUUJI?!!!

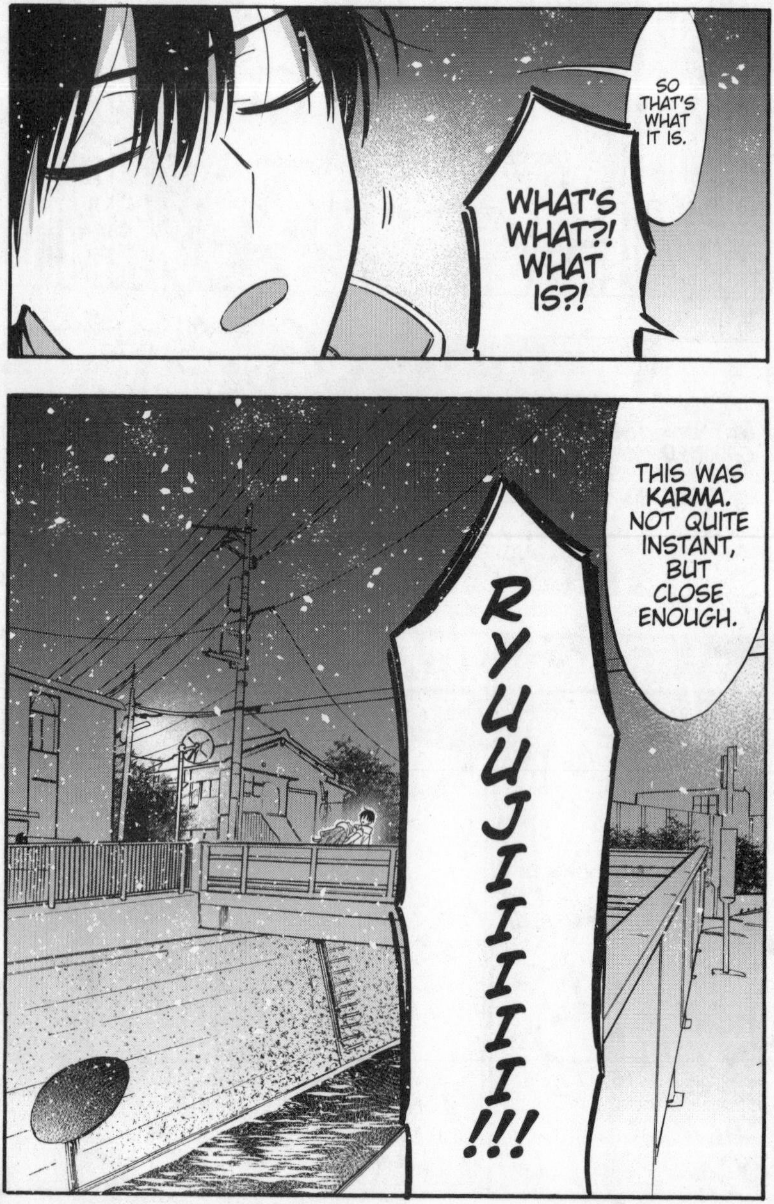
SO THAT'S WHAT IT IS.
WHAT'S WHAT?! WHAT IS?!
THIS WAS KARMA. NOT QUITE INSTANT, BUT CLOSE ENOUGH.
RYUUJIIIII!!!

Toradora!

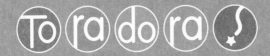

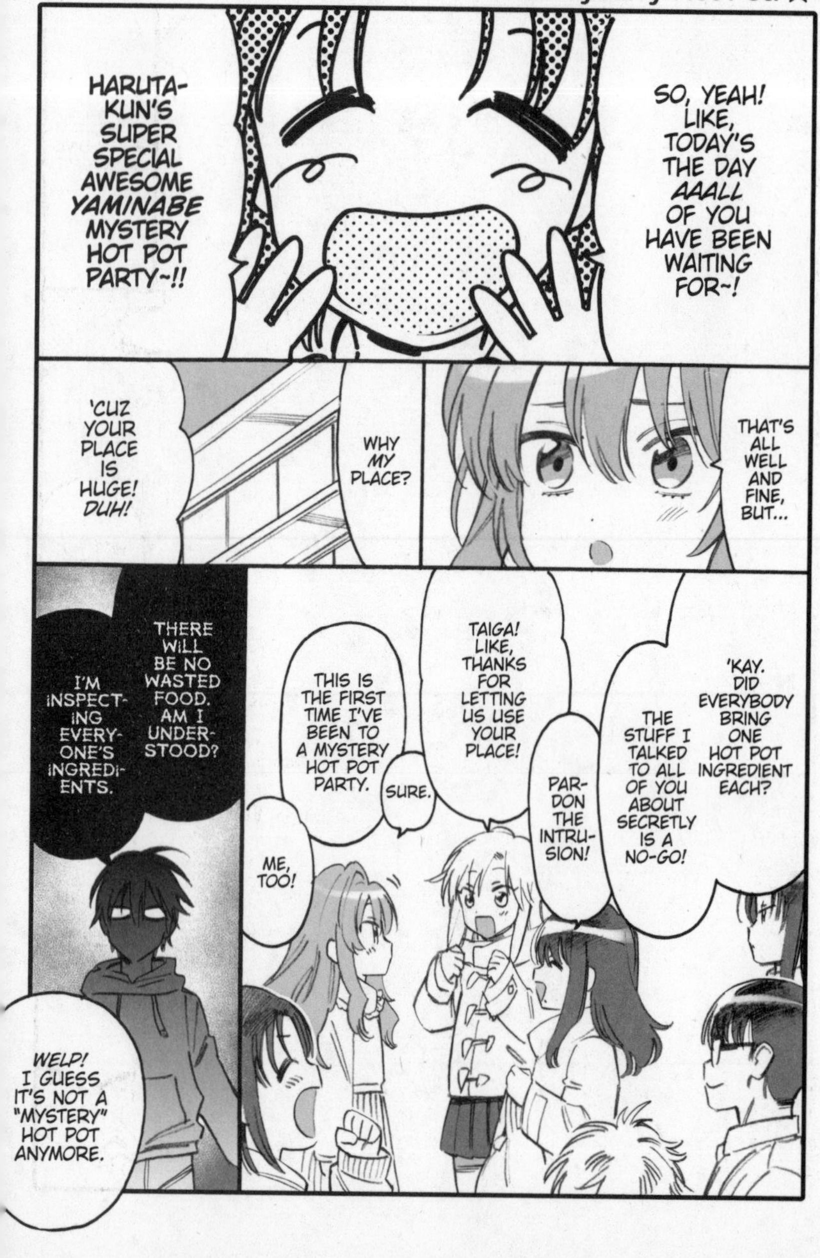
SO, YEAH! LIKE, TODAY'S THE DAY AAALL OF YOU HAVE BEEN WAITING FOR~!
HARUTA-KUN'S SUPER SPECIAL AWESOME YAMINABE MYSTERY HOT POT PARTY~!!
THAT'S ALL WELL AND FINE, BUT...
WHY MY PLACE?
'CUZ YOUR PLACE IS HUGE! DUH!
'KAY. DID EVERYBODY BRING ONE HOT POT INGREDIENT EACH?
THE STUFF I TALKED TO ALL OF YOU ABOUT SECRETLY IS A NO-GO!
TAIGA! LIKE, THANKS FOR LETTING US USE YOUR PLACE!
PARDON THE INTRUSION!
THIS IS THE FIRST TIME I'VE BEEN TO A MYSTERY HOT POT PARTY.
SURE.
ME, TOO!
THERE WILL BE NO WASTED FOOD. AM I UNDERSTOOD?
I'M INSPECTING EVERYONE'S INGREDIENTS.
WELP! I GUESS IT'S NOT A "MYSTERY" HOT POT ANYMORE.

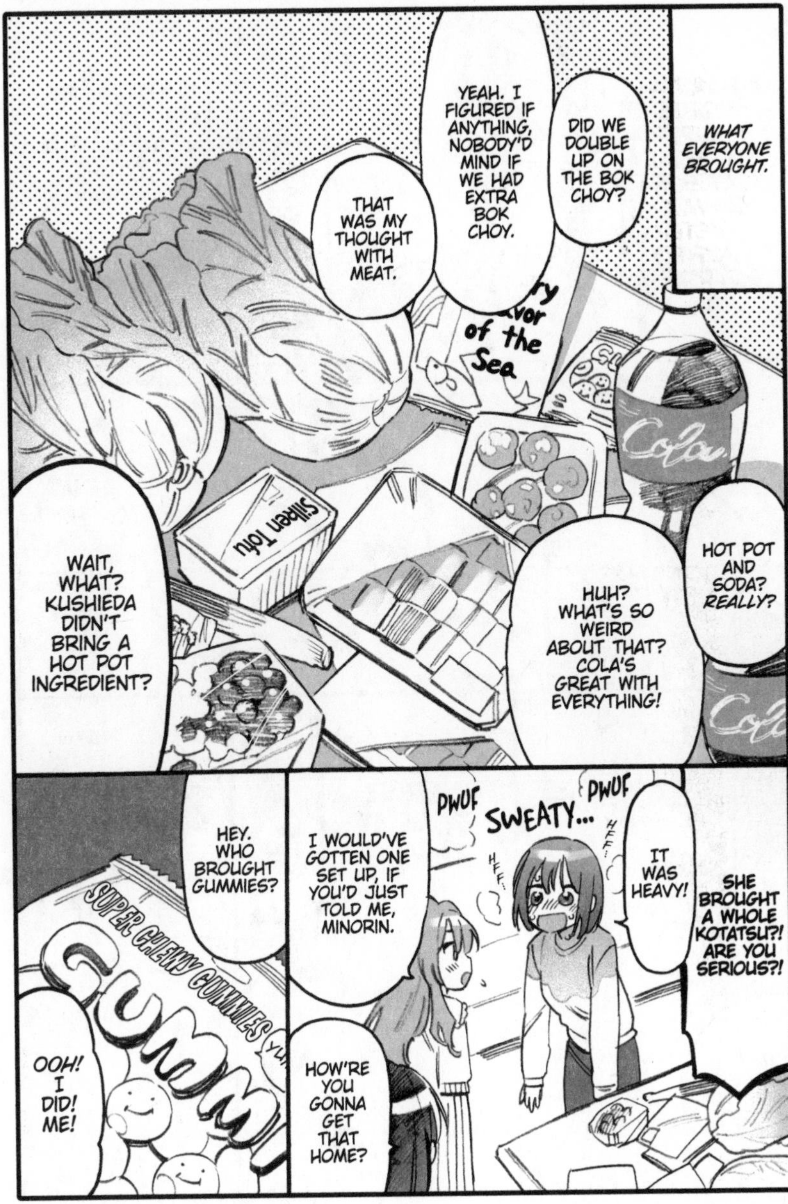
WHAT EVERYONE BROUGHT.
DID WE DOUBLE UP ON THE BOK CHOY?
YEAH. I FIGURED IF ANYTHING, NOBODY'D MIND IF WE HAD EXTRA BOK CHOY.
THAT WAS MY THOUGHT WITH MEAT.
of the Sea
Cola
Silken Tofu
HOT POT AND SODA? REALLY?
HUH? WHAT'S SO WEIRD ABOUT THAT? COLA'S GREAT WITH EVERYTHING!
WAIT, WHAT? KUSHIEDA DIDN'T BRING A HOT POT INGREDIENT?
Cola
SHE BROUGHT A WHOLE KOTATSU?! ARE YOU SERIOUS?!
IT WAS HEAVY!
PWUF
HFF
SWEATY...
PWUF
HFF
I WOULD'VE GOTTEN ONE SET UP, IF YOU'D JUST TOLD ME, MINORIN.
HOW'RE YOU GONNA GET THAT HOME?
HEY. WHO BROUGHT GUMMIES?
SUPER CHEWY GUMMIES
GUMMI
OOH! I DID! ME!

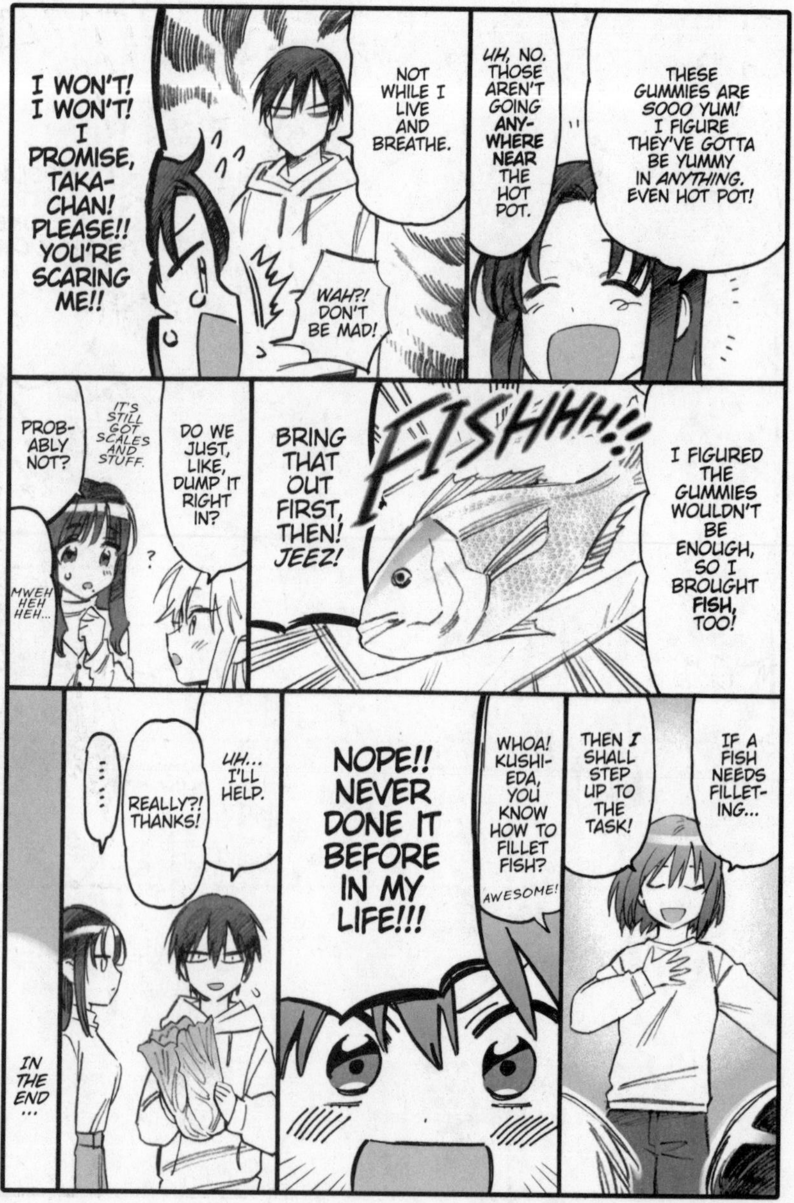
THESE GUMMIES ARE SOOO YUM! I FIGURE THEY'VE GOTTA BE YUMMY IN ANYTHING. EVEN HOT POT!
UH, NO. THOSE AREN'T GOING ANY-WHERE NEAR THE HOT POT.
NOT WHILE I LIVE AND BREATHE.
WAH?! DON'T BE MAD!
I WON'T! I WON'T! I PROMISE, TAKA-CHAN! PLEASE!! YOU'RE SCARING ME!!
I FIGURED THE GUMMIES WOULDN'T BE ENOUGH, SO I BROUGHT FISH, TOO!
FISHHH!!
BRING THAT OUT FIRST, THEN! JEEZ!
DO WE JUST, LIKE, DUMP IT RIGHT IN?
IT'S STILL GOT SCALES AND STUFF.
PROB-ABLY NOT?
?
MWEH HEH HEH...
IF A FISH NEEDS FILLET-ING...
THEN I SHALL STEP UP TO THE TASK!
WHOA! KUSHI-EDA, YOU KNOW HOW TO FILLET FISH?
AWESOME!
NOPE!! NEVER DONE IT BEFORE IN MY LIFE!!!
UH... I'LL HELP.
REALLY?! THANKS!
......
IN THE END...